名师名校名校长

凝聚名师共识
回应名师关怀
打造名师品牌
培育名师群体

基于学科核心素养的
高中英语过程性写作教学设计

胡翠娥　主编

浙江工商大学 出版社

ZHEJIANG GONGSHANG UNIVERSITY PRESS

·杭州·

图书在版编目（CIP）数据

基于学科核心素养的高中英语过程性写作教学设计 /
胡翠娥主编. -- 杭州：浙江工商大学出版社，2024.6.
ISBN 978-7-5178-6088-4

Ⅰ. G633.412

中国国家版本馆CIP数据核字第20243SN254号

基于学科核心素养的高中英语过程性写作教学设计
JIYU XUEKE HEXIN SUYANG DE GAOZHONG YINGYU
GUOCHENGXING XIEZUO JIAOXUE SHEJI

胡翠娥　主编

策划编辑	周敏燕
责任编辑	童江霞
责任校对	林莉燕
封面设计	言之凿
责任印制	包建辉
出版发行	浙江工商大学出版社
	（杭州市教工路198号　邮政编码310012）
	（E-mail：zjgsupress@163.com）
	（网址：http://www.zjgsupress.com）
	电话：0571-88904980，88831806（传真）
排　　版	李　娜
印　　刷	北京政采印刷服务有限公司
开　　本	710mm×1000mm　1/16
印　　张	16
字　　数	307千
版 印 次	2025年3月第1版　2025年3月第1次印刷
书　　号	ISBN 978-7-5178-6088-4
定　　价	58.00元

编 委 会

前 言
FOREWORD

　　《普通高中英语课程标准（2017年版2020年修订）》（以下简称《高中英语课标》）指出：普通高中英语课程的总目标是全面贯彻党的教育方针，培育和践行社会主义核心价值观，落实立德树人根本任务，在义务教育的基础上，进一步促进学生英语学科核心素养的发展，培养具有中国情怀、国际视野和跨文化沟通能力的社会主义建设者和接班人。基于课程的总目标，普通高中英语课程的具体目标是培养和发展学生在接受高中英语教育后应具备的语言能力、文化意识、思维品质、学习能力等学科核心素养。当下的高中英语教学，必须始终把培养学生的英语学科核心素养放在首位。课堂教学是培养与发展学生学科核心素养的主要渠道。

　　高中英语写作在听、说、读、看、写各项技能中是相对较难的，能够比较客观地反映学生综合运用语言的能力。培养学生的写作能力是高中英语教学目标之一。高中阶段写作的目标要求是：能写出连贯且结构完整的短文来叙述事情或表达观点和态度；能根据课文写摘要；能在写作中做到文体规范、语句通顺；能根据文字或图表提供的信息写短文或报告。课程要从学生的学习兴趣、生活经验和认知水平出发，发展学生的综合语言运用能力。现行的高中英语教材不仅内容丰富，而且注重培养阅读能力，强化写作技能训练。教材话题多元，涉及友谊、旅游、天文、地理、科学、体育、健康、生活等。

　　目前，有相当一部分高中生英语写作能力较弱，主要表现在用汉语思维表达英语句子、不善于谋篇布局与衔接过渡、词汇匮乏、单词拼写和语法错误多等方面。他们一看到或听到写作任务就产生恐惧甚至抵触心理。这就要求教师在设计英语写作任务时，遵循循序渐进的原则和以学生为本的原则，运用教材单元话题中的语言条件和语境，创设贴近学生生活的真实情境，选择学生熟悉的话题，让学生从教材单元话题中汲取完成任务所需的语言知识，引导学生掌握并运用各主题语境下的话题词汇及相关的语言知识。

2019年，我们的课题"基于教材主题与话题的高中英语写作教学模式探究"（广东省教育科学"十三五"规划中小学教师教育科研能力提升计划项目）成功立项。课题主持人胡翠娥带领课题组成员叶青容、郭秀云、陈艳丽、陈锦春、赖丽萍、黄茗旎、张伟娟、张美仪、廖敏、何玉琼、吴碧华等，基于过程性写作教学理论，积极探索适合区域内高中师生的英语写作教学模式。具体实施过程如下：

一是通过问卷调查了解区域内高中英语的写作教学现状和师生的需求，以便有针对性地设定研究目标和采取研究策略。

二是组织阅读相关文献资料并撰写读书笔记和读书心得。我们课题组学习了国内外有关高中英语写作教学理论与实践的一些专著，包括《高中英语写作教学设计》《现代高中英语教学案例》《英语教材分析与设计》《英语教学方法与策略》《英语写作教学与研究》《落实学科核心素养在课堂·高中英语写作教学》《英语写作教学》《大学英语写作教学理论与实践》等。

三是积极开展课堂教学实践研究。我们课题组每个成员至少承担一次课例展示，在区域内10余所学校和一线教师一起研课、磨课。每个参与课题研究的成员基于课堂观察进行现场评价，包括亮点和不足，并在研课、磨课活动后形成书面的评价意见。

四是聘请高校教授做理论指导。我们聘请了华南师范大学外国语言文化学院的刘晓斌教授作为课题的顾问，为课题的论证和写作教学模式的提炼提供指导意见；还聘请了华南师范大学外国语言文化学院的黄丽燕教授为课题组及区域一线教师做专题讲座。两位教授的指导提升了课题组成员英语写作教学的理论素养和实践水平。

五是组织撰写总结反思。每次活动后，课题组成员及时撰写教学反思、基于教学案例的论文和活动总结，并进行交流分享。

六是推广研究成果。项目组先后在内蒙古、宁夏、湖北、广东等地的多所学校进行基于高中英语写作教学的研讨交流：主持人胡翠娥做课题组研究的

"高中英语写作教学模式"相关的讲座和成果分享；成员进行课例展示和实践心得分享，与全国各地的同行进行思维碰撞。

经过三年的认真研究、探索与实践，课题组在各级专家的指导下取得丰硕的成果，课题组成员的学科素养得到极大提升。我们真正做到了将教育科研用到教学第一线，真正使教育科研在提高教学质量上发挥作用，并已形成3T-3W高中英语过程性写作教学模式。3T——Textbook、Theme、Topic；3W——Pre-writing、While-writing、Post-writing（三阶）和First writing、Second writing、Third writing（三稿）。现将我们的研究成果《基于学科核心素养的高中英语过程性写作教学设计》一书献给同行，敬请批评指正！

胡翠娥

2023年11月

目　录
CONTENTS

第三章　教学资源

第一章

理论研究

第一节　研究论证

一、课题研究的意义

作为英语学科听、说、读、看、写基本技能之一，写作不论是在学生当前的学习中，还是在接下来大学的学习或将来的社会工作中，都起着重要的作用。根据普通高中英语课程性质和基本理念，培养学生的英语学科核心素养，提高学生的英语表达能力，可以为学生当前应对高考及拓宽视野、扩大知识面、发展个性、提高人文素养打基础，也有利于满足学生今后在学习、工作、生活等方面的需求。高中英语教学的重点是使学生通过学习英语基础知识，培养运用英语表达基本观点的综合能力，最终目的是使学生掌握运用英语获取其他知识的技能，为进入大学学习和进入社会工作奠定基础。英语写作是英语学习的重中之重。在我国传统的教育背景下，大多数高中英语教师为提高学生的英语应试能力而教，大多数学生为应对高考而学。在高考指挥棒的引导下，英语教学陷入了重语用、轻思维的怪圈。教师只重视分数，而忽略了对学生文化素养和国际视野的培养，使英语变成了"聋子英语""哑巴英语"。核心素养的提出和新的课程标准的出台，对于英语教师来说是一个非常好的契机。从一线教学实际出发，扭转这样的英语教学现状，还原英语学习的本质，对于更新目前英语写作教学观念和方法，改革当前的英语写作教学具有重要意义。

本研究结合培养学生核心素养的教育趋势和语言跨文化交际的属性，改变传统高中英语写作教学中重结果轻过程、过度重视语言规则和词汇讲解的普遍做法，强调教师在传授语言知识的同时，引导学生关注、探索、感受、总结英语和汉语在思维和逻辑方面的差异，使学生能够学到真正的英语知识及英语思维，从而体现出基于英语学科核心素养和英汉思维差异的高中英语写作模式的优越性和独特性。

二、课题研究的总体框架、基本内容和目标

（一）课题研究的总体框架

（1）前期问卷调查，了解高中英语写作教学中师生的现状、困惑和需求。

（2）理论学习（听讲座和阅读专著），用专家和同行的先进理念作行动支撑。

（3）课堂教学实践研究。

（4）教学反思研究。

（5）与外校、外地专家以及同行探讨交流。

（6）成果推广。

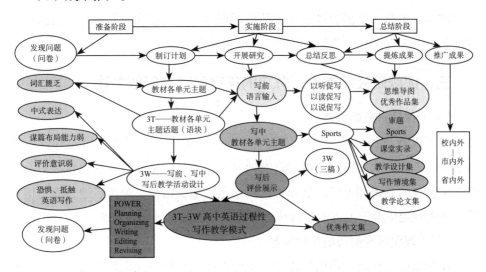

（二）课题研究的基本内容

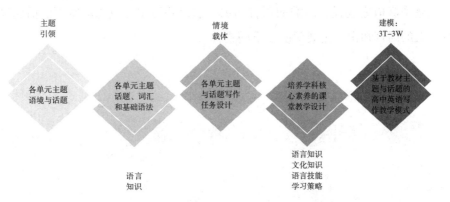

（三）课题研究的目标

1. 理论目标

通过有效的研究与实践，课题组成员了解并掌握高中英语写作教学的基本理论，创新英语写作教学思路和方法，以及英语写作教学结构和模式，提高教师英语写作教学的质量，促进教师的专业成长。同时，探索出高中英语写作的课堂教学模式。

2. 教学实践目标

本课题以培养学生英语学科核心素养为目标，借鉴过程性写作理论，基于已有的相关课题研究，探索构建适合区域高中学生的英语写作教学模式，挖掘影响高中学生写作兴趣和质量的因素，提出面向区域高中学生的提高英语写作水平的相应策略，全面提高学生的英语写作水平，实现在过程性写作实践中使学生获得快乐写作的体验和良好的英语学科核心素养。

三、课题研究的重点、解决的关键问题及创新之处

（一）课题研究的重点

如何设计与各单元主题与话题相关的高中英语写作任务，以过程性写作教学为切入点，利用信息技术进行有效导入，开展学生感兴趣的课堂活动，培养学生写作的意识和习惯，从而实现对学生的学法指导、思维启迪、能力培养等，真正实现培养学生英语学科核心素养，是本课题研究的重点。

（二）课题研究解决的关键问题

课题组成员在高中英语写作教学中创设运用教材单元主题中的语言知识的条件和语境，基于学生已知和生活经验创设真实写作情境，引导学生从教材单元主题中汲取完成任务所需的语言知识，掌握并运用各主题语境下的话题词汇及相关的语言知识。主要解决以下问题：

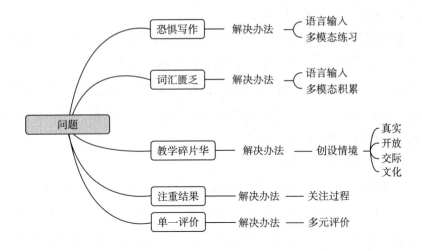

（1）解决学生恐惧英语写作的问题。

（2）解决学生词汇匮乏、用汉语思维方式表达、谋篇布局与衔接过渡能力弱、缺乏语用意识等问题。

（3）解决英语写作教学碎片化、孤立化、片面化，写作情境脱离学生生活实际的问题。

（4）解决英语写作教学注重结果、由教师"主宰"课堂、轻视学生思维过程的问题。

（5）解决英语写作教学单一评价的问题。

（三）课题研究的创新之处

本课题的主要创新之处在于研究的视角新：在新课标提出学科育人的课程目标后不久，本课题基于问题，紧扣"发展英语学科核心素养，落实立德树人根本任务""构建高中英语共同基础，满足学生个性发展需求""实践英语学习活动观，提高学生学用能力""完善英语课程评价体系，促进核心素养形成""重视现代信息技术应用，丰富英语课程学习资源"等基本理念进行高中英语写作教学的探究。

1. 关注学生——理念创新

我们坚持"过程性写作教学"。过程性写作教学着眼于学生在写作实践过程中思维的发展，旨在帮助学生更清楚地认识写作过程，并引导学生反复修改完善习作，强调在写作过程中帮助学生提高发现问题、分析问题和解决问题的能力。

2. 关注过程——模式创新

过程性写作教学关注的是学生在写作过程中所经历的内部运作过程，探讨的是学生在写作中要做什么，如审题、打初稿、修改润色等，而不是最终成品的样子，如文章结构、单词拼写、语法等。教师关注的是引导学生进行写前（Pre-writing）语言输入、写中（While-writing）指导和写后（Post-writing）评价及基于主题的拓展延伸。

3. 关注评价——机制创新

在写作教学过程中，我们借助评价工具和量表，开展教师评价、学生自评、生生互评等，关注学生的未来，促进学生的发展。我们既关注学生对语言知识和语言技能的掌握，又通过评价使学生在学习过程中不断体验进步与成功，认识自我，建立自信，调整学习策略，促进学生语用能力的提高。

4. 关注技术——手段创新

在研究与实践过程中，我们充分利用现代信息技术，依托多模态语篇调动学生的多种感官，刺激学生产生联想，创设真实的情境，使学生体验真实的目标语言环境，提高语用能力。

四、课题研究的理论依据

本课题研究与实践的理论依据主要有建构主义学习理论、以听说读看促写理论、过程性写作教学理论，以及《高中英语课标》中的相关理念等。

（一）建构主义学习理论

建构主义学习理论认为，学习活动是学生通过一定的情境，在教师与同学的帮助下，通过协作和会话的方式，达到对知识的意义建构。在这个过程中，学生是认知活动的主体，教师是学生学习的协助者、促进者、引导者。书本知识的掌握和实践活动都是学习，而通过后者建构的知识是无法靠他人传授获得的。"情境""协作""会话""意义建构"是建构主义学习理论的四大要素。教师要想切实提高课堂教学的效率，必须有效地把握教学的各个环节，充分利用信息技术，创设真实情境，使学生逐步构建起对于外部世界的认识，从而使自身认知结构得到发展。

（二）以听说读看促写理论

在进行写作训练时，在写前或导入（Lead-in）环节设计相关话题文本、音频和视频，让学生通过阅读文本（Reading）、收听音频（Listening）或观看视频（Viewing），进行相关话题的陈述（Speaking），从而获取相关话题的写作词汇、短语、句型以及写作技巧，然后开始写作。我们通过科学系统的听说读看写综合训练，实现以听说读看促写，从而提高学生的素养，特别是写作能力。

（三）过程性写作教学理论

过程性写作教学是把英语写作的重点放在写作过程上的一种方法，区别于结果性写作教学，它强调学生在写作过程中的修改和完善，通过互动、改写等过程切实提高学生的写作水平，开发其写作潜能。有别于传统的结果性写作教学，过程性写作教学重视的是在学生写作过程中帮助他们发现、分析和解决问题。本课题实验倡导的就是过程性写作，更加关注学生"怎么写""取得了哪些进步"，重视关联学生自身的写作经历，以此激发学生的写作兴趣，使学生在写作过程中更加积极、主动。同时，这一方式也更加符合真实写作的循序渐进过程，使学生了解和反思自己的写作过程，学会写作，体会写作的乐趣，从而培养和提高学生的英语写作能力。

（四）《高中英语课标》中的相关理念

1. 教材单元主题引领，发展英语学科核心素养

课题组成员在进行教学设计时，注重以教材单元主题来引领，依托单元多模态语篇，以分析问题、解决问题为目的，创设基于学生知识水平的真实情境，通过以听促写、以说促写、以读促写、以看促写等活动促进其语言知识的学习、文化意识的培养、思维品质和学习能力的提升，以实现学科育人的目的。

2. 写前、写中、写后活动，着力提高学生学用能力

在课堂教学实践中，课题组成员在写前、写中、写后各环节设计具有综合性、关联性和实践性的英语学习活动，通过一系列层层递进的融语言、文化、思维为一体的学习理解、应用实践、迁移创新活动，提高学生学习英语、运用英语的能力。

3. 自评、互评、师评结合，促进学科核心素养有效形成

在写后环节，学生利用评价工具，如帮助明晰写作流程的POWER（Planning、Organizing、Writing、Editing、Revising）、帮助审题的SPORTS（Style、Person、Organizing、Reader、Tense、Structure）、帮助检查语言知识的PANTS（Person、Agreement、Number、Tense、Spelling），通过自评和互评

自主修改和完善习作，最后由教师进行点评。学生在评价的过程中，观察、判断、归纳、探究、合作，思维品质和学习能力不断提升。

4. 现代信息技术融合，丰富英语课程学习资源

在教学实践中，课题组成员运用现代信息技术，进行视频、音频、图片等多模态的语言输入和内化，结合主题创设真实的写作情境，提供视频、音频等拓展延伸的学习材料以丰富学习资源，有效促进学生的学习能力和素养提高。

第二节　研究的成果和成效

一、课题研究取得的主要成果

（一）主要结论

经过三年的实践与研究，课题组已顺利完成各阶段的各项研究内容。参与实验的学生写作兴趣大大提高，成绩明显提升。他们养成了良好的英语写作习惯，包括词汇积累、审题、自评、互评等；学会了在老师的引领和指导下描述身边熟悉的事物；会对单元主题与话题语篇进行模仿训练和情境创设训练。参与实验的教师构建了3T–3W高中英语过程性写作教学模式并在市内外10余所学校推广；探索出了SPORTS审题法；创建了课堂和课后评价量表（Checklist）；积累了丰富的英语教学资源。课题组成员自身的专业素养和教学教研能力都得到了大幅度提升。三年的课题研究取得了丰硕的成果，达成了预期目标。

（二）新的论点

在写前语言输入环节，以多模态语篇加强输入量，为学生搭建"脚手架"，向学生介绍属于同一主题和话题的语篇，引导学生模仿这些语篇的结构特征和语言特征，引导学生基于教材单元主题和话题以思维导图的形式进行语块积累。这有助于消除学生的写作恐惧，激发学生的写作兴趣。

基于学生的兴趣和已有知识，创设激发学生兴趣的真实写作情境，可以让学生对英语写作保持兴趣。

在写中环节，让学生联系自己的生活实际进行写作，这样学生才有话可说。

在写后环节，采用教师评价（教师圈出学生自己能修改的错误，让学生注意并修改）、课堂评析（在课堂上由教师或学生评论和解释习作中的错误，包括结构、逻辑和语法等，集体评改）和生生互评（通过示范和指导，让学生明确评价标准和方法，评改同伴习作，互相学习）相结合的评价方式，组织和引导学生完成以评价为导向的多种评价活动，检测教与学的效果，实现以评促教、以评促学。学生通过一稿多磨、多稿（通常是三稿，即3W）写作和反复修改，主动自我反思和自我调控，提升思维品质和英语写作能力。

（三）突破性进展

经过三年的实践与研究，课题组开发了高中英语过程性写作教学系列资源：《高中英语写作现状调查问卷》《基于教材单元主题与话题的词汇及运用案例》《基于教材单元主题与话题的语块思维导图》《基础语法项目思维导图》《基于教材单元主题与话题的写作课堂导学案》《基于教材主题与话题的课堂教学案例集》《基于教材主题与话题的原创写作情境设计集》《基于教材主题与话题的过程性写作评价生生互评学生作品集》《学生优秀作文集》《基于教材主题与话题的高中英语写作教学模式探究论文集》《高中英语过程性写作教学效果调查问卷》。这些资源适用于各个版本的教材。

（四）研究成果的特色

这些教学资源是课题组成员基于过程性写作教学模式，开展课例研讨，进行课例展示、议课、磨课等活动所撰写的教学设计和反思，以及实验班的学生在指导老师的引导下自主学习和探究，形成的系列知识结构图。

过程性写作教学模式强调教学活动以学生为中心，最大限度地调动学生学习的主动性和自觉性，教师自始至终监控与指导学生学习的各个阶段。在该教学模式下，教师最主要的作用是帮助学生理解和内化写作的全部过程，包括收集信息、制订计划、写草稿、同伴评议和同伴编辑等。这种模式把写作视作一个动态过程，以过程指导为核心，而不是以最终的写作成果为核心，符合新课标理念：单元整体教学，英语学习活动观，真实情境，教、学、评一体化。

（五）主要建树

经过三年扎实有效的研究，在专家的指导下，在课题组全体成员的共同努力下，课题组形成了3T-3W高中英语过程性写作教学模式，汇编了《高中英语写作课堂教学设计》《高中英语原创写作情境创设》《优秀学生单元主题与话题思维导图》等，形成了系列高中英语课堂教学课例。这些资源在银川、武汉、珠海、广州和清远等地的十几所学校展示并得以推广，具有较高的参考价值，获得了较高评价。在课题研究的过程中，课题组成员陆续获得了全国名师工作室发展建设成果一等奖、全国中小学英语教师"教学设计、教学研究、教学实施"三项全能培训会教学设计二等奖和三等奖、全国名师工作室联盟优秀课例一等奖、全国名师工作室创新发展成果博览会优秀教学设计一等奖、全国名师工作室创新发展成果博览会优秀课例一等奖、广东省中小学3A课堂教师资源征集活动优秀作品、广东省义务教育英语教学资源征集活动优秀作品等荣誉，并在省级刊物上发表12篇论文，出版1部专著，拟再出版1部专著。

（六）对成果的自我评价

本课题在全体成员的共同努力下，取得了丰硕的成果。课题的实践与研究，使学生在3T-3W高中英语过程性写作教学模式下养成了愿学、乐学、会学、善学的习惯，给我们实验班的英语写作教学带来丰硕的成果和收获。同时，也给我们课题研究组带来了诸多可喜的改变。

1. 探索出了3T-3W过程性写作教学模式

我们主要结合教材〔人教版普通高中课程标准实验教科书（人教新课标版）和人教版普通高中教科书（新人教版）〕单元主题与话题中的词汇、句型和语篇对高中英语写作课堂教学的有效设计、学生英语写作方法的有效指导、学生英语写作兴趣的有效激发等进行了较为深入的研究，形成了3T-3W高中英语过程性写作教学模式。

我们充分认识到3T-3W高中英语过程性写作教学模式的重要性，一致认为该写作教学模式是对学生的一种过程性写作指导，通过搭建语言支架→创设写作情境→进行写作指导→组织多形式评价→展示优秀成稿，层层铺垫，步步推进，非常适用于对高中学生尤其是清远市第二中学学生以及一些英语基础较薄弱的学生的写作指导。

我们运用这种模式营造了一种轻松的写作课堂教学氛围，人人改变了以前的"学生写，教师评"或"教师提示，学生写"的沉闷课堂气氛。学生根据评价量表自评、互评，自主学习、相互学习。利用多模态语篇（音频、视频、图片、表格等）导入，使学生在直观的视觉和听觉刺激下自然完成语言输入；在话题词汇拓展的头脑风暴环节，学生争先恐后展示并在课后形成思维导图；安排相关主题和话题的文本阅读，为学生搭建结构和语言支架提供素材；句型运用环节，学生呈现意想不到的好句子；小组合作进行语篇训练。学生参与度非常高，整个课堂活而不乱，完全不同于以前的写作课，成为"大部分学生的展示课"。

2. 凝练了一批有参考价值的理论成果

为了科学地总结课题研究各阶段的工作，提炼相关研究成果，向同行提供相关教育科研信息，丰富相关教育科研的理论资源，以利于后续学术借鉴和交流，我们撰写了内容翔实、结构合理、具有理论价值和实践价值的结题报告、研究报告、成果公报等。在课题研究的过程中，主持人胡翠娥就课题研究的具体流程、课题研究过程的材料积累和成果提炼、中期检查材料的准备、结题材料的准备以及研究时应注意的问题等多次做指导性讲座，并将讲座课件分享给同行。

3. 汇编了丰富的高中英语写作教学资源

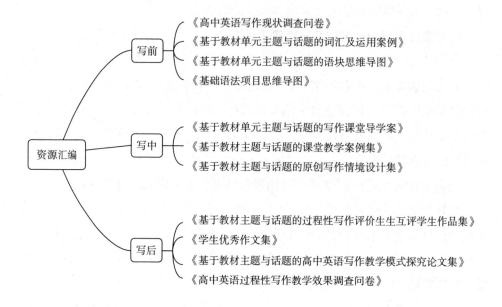

（1）写前阶段

①《高中英语写作现状调查问卷》

在课题准备阶段，设计了了解学生写作现状的调查问卷，以便有针对性地开展研究。

②《基于教材单元主题与话题的词汇及运用》

词是语言的建构材料，也是最小的能够独立运用的语言单位。词汇中的任何词语都是通过一定的句法关系和语义关系与其他词语建立起一定的联系，并在语境中传递信息的。课题组除了引导学生理解和运用课本词汇外，还运用构词法等方式拓展相关词汇，扩大学生的词汇量，同时，创设句子或语篇语境，提高学生运用词汇确切表达意义的能力。为了让学生更有针对性地掌握词汇，课题组还把教材词汇分成写作词汇和阅读词汇。课题组对目前清远地区使用过的三个版本的教材（北师大版、人教新课标版、新人教版）的单元词汇进行了整理。

③《基于教材单元主题与话题的语块思维导图》

徐昉在《英语写作教学与研究》一书中指出，范文分析的重点在于从篇章段落上看文本结构和从字词句上看写作的语言特征。不管是采用体裁教学法、内容教学法还是采用任务教学法，教师都有必要引导学生在写前的语言输入中注意那些与写作话题相关的常用语块。近年来国内外有关写作的语块研究表明，常用高频语块的输入和输出，是提高英语口语流利度的重要方法。学生要使写作语言流利、地道、自然，在写前阶段，重要的是关注与话题相关的常用词汇、词组或者句式，因此，引导学生积累和使用常用语块应该成为写作教学的一个重要部分。课题组在研究的过程中，非常注重在写前环节进行常用语块的积累，不管是新授课还是复习课，都指导学生基于教材单元主题与话题，以思维导图的形式进行相关主题与话题语块的归纳与积累。为了激发学生学习的积极性，课题组对学生的作品进行评比，并将优秀作品结集成册，在校内外进行分享与交流。

④《基础语法项目思维导图》

三维动态语法观，即形式—意义—使用。拉森·弗里曼（Larsen Freeman）认为，应将语法作为一种与听、说、读、看、写并行的动态技能教给学生。写英语作文离不开语法的运用，为了让学生在自己的作文中准确、有意义、得体地运用所学语法知识，课题组在具体的教学实践中引导学生在单元语篇的语境和创设的语境中发现语法现象，自行归纳语法结构，并以思维导图的形式绘成知识结构图，引导学生在学中用、用中学，活学活用。

（2）写中阶段

①《基于教材单元主题与话题的写作课堂导学案》

我们基于教材单元主题与话题相关词汇，根据学生层次、个性特点和课程标准，进行个性情境创设及相关训练的研究。教师教会学生运用单元话题词汇及拓展的相关词汇创设情境进行句型训练、连句成篇的训练和篇章训练。课题组编写了3T-3W高中英语过程性写作教学模式的课堂导学案，并且结集成册，在清远市第二中学推广使用。其他学校的课题组成员也在自己任教学校推广使用。

②《基于教材主题与话题的课堂教学案例集》

课题组全体成员积极参与研究，主动开设研讨课，进行研课、磨课。在课题研究过程中，课题组成员在省内外、市内外共同开设聚焦不同写作阶段的研讨课，进行写前语言输入、写中课堂指导、写后评价等课例展示。承担课例展示的成员都认真撰写教学设计和教学反思，其他成员认真议课、评课，提出自己的见解和中肯的改进建议。这些课堂教学案例（课件、教学设计和视频资源）在全市各高中分享交流，成为清远市高中教师宝贵的教学资源。

③《基于教材主题与话题的原创写作情境设计集》

课题组成员在进行写作教学的过程中，基于学生现有的生活经验、学习兴趣、语言水平以及教材单元主题与话题创设真实写作情境，引导学生积极主动地参与对主题意义的探究活动，使学生学会选择得体的语言形式开展有效的交流。在此过程中，学生认识到学习语言的目的是在真实语境中运用所学知识，理解意义，传递信息，表达个人情感与观点。

（3）写后阶段

①《基于教材主题与话题的过程性写作评价生生互评学生作品集》

二语习得理论对英语写作教学的启示是：开展同伴互评，通过示范和指导，让学生明确评价标准和方法，通过评改同伴习作学习自我评改。南京大学丁言仁教授认为，评阅反馈的最终目的是培养学生的自我评改能力。评改可以引导学生关注自己的语言，看到自己语言上的差距。学生要提高自我评改能力，也就是要提高自主学习能力。在此过程中，教师必须起关键作用——帮助学生明白同伴习作的好差之别，帮助他们注意、归纳和纠正习作中的主要错误，包括主题的挖掘、结构问题、逻辑错误、语言错误、细节错误等，并且帮助他们学会自评、互评与修改。课题组重视在写后环节指导学生根据检查列表进行自评和互评。不少学生评改细致，能非常准确地给同伴的习作写出评语，经过长时间反复的训练，学生的英语写作能力有了较大提升。

②《学生优秀作文集》

为了激发学生的写作兴趣，提高学生的写作能力，同时让学生体验和享受"作者"的乐趣，我们在平时的写作教学中，注重收集经过学生自评、生生互评、师评等多次修改润色，并由作者认真誊写的优秀作文，按照教材单元主题与话题汇编成册，并将作文集摆放在教室的英语角供学生学习分享。

③《基于教材主题与话题的高中英语写作教学模式探究论文集》

每个课题组成员就课题研究的相关内容撰写论文、教学设计、教学心得等。课题组编写了一本《基于教材主题与话题的高中英语写作教学模式探究论文集》（包括已发表的12篇论文），在全市高中英语教师中传阅和参考使用。

④《高中英语过程性写作教学效果调查问卷》

为了后续有效地开展研究，课题组在课题结题阶段设计了有关课题研究效果的调查问卷。

二、课题研究取得的成效

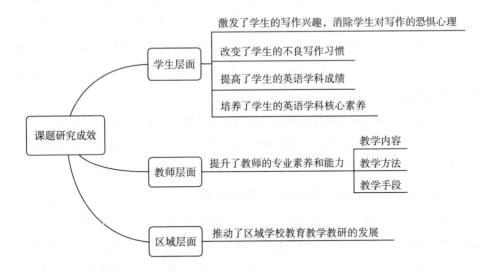

（一）更好激发了学生的英语写作兴趣

3T-3W高中英语过程性写作教学模式营造的轻松的学习氛围激发了学生的英语写作兴趣。因为学生在学习过程中都能有所表现，在课内和课外都能得到展示自己的机会，英语写作的兴趣大大提高，学生不再"谈写作色变"，之前每次作文布置下去只能收到一半作业的现象不复存在。

经过三易其稿，相当一部分学生的作文得以在课堂上、教室里的英语展示栏展示，有的还被收入《学生优秀作文集》在年级分享和传阅。优秀作文的展示更是大大地激发了学生的写作积极性。

（二）有效改变了学生的一些不良写作习惯

3T-3W高中英语过程性写作教学模式的运用激发了学生的积极性、主动性，增强了学生的自主参与意识。学生在参与学习的过程中，互相帮助、互相监督。更重要的是，学生养成了利用思维导图进行词汇积累、写作前认真审题、写后根据评价量表自评互评及找老师面批等良好的英语写作习惯。

（三）有效提高了学生的英语学习成绩

二语习得视角下的写作教学策略有以下几点：第一，激发学生兴趣的任务设计；第二，多阅读输入、范文分析与语块积累；第三，一稿多磨，反复多练；第四，批改归纳、课堂评析和合作互评。本课题研究的3T-3W高中英语过程性写作教学模式就是运用这些教学策略，使学生积极参与，发挥他们的主观能动性的。教师在整个写作教学过程中充分创设条件，刺激学生动眼看、动耳听、动脑读、动口说、动笔写，强化学生的读写过程、听说过程，使读与写、听与说的训练相互结合。同时，从学生的阶段认知水平和接受能力出发，精心设计、选择教学方法与课堂结构，创设有利于学生主动求知的写作情境，使所有学生都能参与学习过程。

实践证明，把3T-3W高中英语过程性写作教学模式应用于写作教学实践中，能够为学生提供有效参与的实践环境，有利于激发学生英语写作的兴趣，学生愿写、乐写，作文成绩自然就能得到提升，英语总分也随之提升。

（四）逐步培养了学生的英语学科核心素养

在课题研究过程中，课题组基于教材单元主题，依托教材多模态语篇，通过学习理解、应用实践、迁移创新等层层递进的语言、思维、文化相融合的活动，使学生听、说、读、看、写的语言技能相互促进，在帮助学生习得语言知识和文化知识的同时，创设基于学生已有知识和生活体验的真实情境，让学生运用语言技能阐释文化内涵、比较文化异同，形成正确的价值观和积极的情感态度，提升分析问题、解决问题的能力和自主学习的能力，从而实现学科育人。

（五）逐步提升了教师的专业素养和能力

在课题研究过程中，课题组成员积极主动地承担各级各类公开课、展示课，参加各种基本功比赛，在银川、武汉、珠海、湛江等地的中学及清远市的多所学校开设展示课和讲座。他们在课题成果推广交流的过程中，自身专业素养得到相应提升，理论研究水平和课程整合能力也有所提高。同时，积极参与课例展示、评课、议课，使他们的课改意识和业务水平在互学互助中迅速提升。因此，本课题的研究及积极实施，不仅提高了教师的各方面素质，而且使教师乐于将更多的时间花在理论的学习与研究、方法的探究与尝试上，他们因此提高了理论水平、业务水平和教研能力，开阔了视野，转变了教学观念，促进了专业发展。

在此过程中，课题组的吴碧华老师成为广东省特级教师、广东省"百千万人才培养工程"名教师培养对象，主持市级工作室和市级课题；张伟娟老师成为清远市教坛标兵、清远市"最美教师"，主持省级课题；叶青容、黄茗旎、廖敏、郭秀云等老师主持省、市、校级课题。

（六）有效推动了区域学校教育教学教研的发展

课题组积极向上的教育教研氛围极大地影响了区域各学校的教师，尤其是成员所在的八所学校的英语学科教师，同时给区域学校英语学科积累了大量的关于英语写作教学的教研资料和学习资料。构建的3T-3W高中英语过程性写作教学模式，使教师们优化了教学内容，改革了教学方法，创新了教学手段。

总之，经过不懈努力，课题组各阶段的各项研究工作均顺利完成。参与课题的学生写作兴趣大大提高，成绩明显提升，养成了良好的英语写作习惯（包括词汇积累、审题、自评、互评等），学会了在老师的引领和指导下描述身边熟悉的事例，会对单元主题与话题语篇进行模仿训练和情境创设训练。参与课题的教师构建了3T-3W高中英语过程性写作教学模式，探索出了SPORTS审题法，创建了课堂和课后评价量表，自身专业素养和教学教研能力都得到大大的提升。本课题取得了丰硕的研究成果，达成了预期目标。

第二章
实践探索

第一节　人教新课标版教学设计

Book 1 Unit 1 Friendship (Pre-writing)

设计者姓名：叶青容

设计者所在单位：广东省清远市源潭中学

一、教学材料分析

授课年级：高一

教材内容：人教新课标版 Book 1 Unit 1 Friendship

主题：人与社会——人与人之间的友情

课型：读后续写（写前指导）

课时：1课时

二、教学内容分析

【**What**】

这是一个关于友情的惊心动魄的故事。主人公坐飞机从San Francisco（圣弗朗西斯科）去New Orleans（新奥尔良）出差，中途会在Dallas（达拉斯）转机，所以打电话给在Dallas的朋友Luke（卢克），约他出来吃个饭。谁知道飞机在San Francisco晚点了。主人公只能在Dallas停留半个小时，就要转机去另外一个地方，这使得他们的晚餐几乎泡汤。然而Luke是个热情又做事周密的人，他在得知飞机晚点之后，提前为他们的晚餐安排好了一切。饭后，为了赶飞机，两人狂奔。

【Why】

这个故事仿佛是一部美国大片，情节一波三折。在我们平淡无奇的生活中，拥有美好心灵的人往往给我们带来惊喜，留下一辈子都无法忘怀的记忆。文中暗含了"友谊"的真正含义和意义。通过这个故事，我们知道了在这个世界上没有什么是不可能的，处处都有奇迹。

【How】

本文是一篇故事类记叙文，基于"人与社会——人与人之间的友情"的主题语境，以时间、地点、事情经过、人物感受为线索展开，文中的语言彰显了人物的个性特点及心理变化。

三、学情分析

高一年级的学生已在初中的英语学习中积累了一定的词汇量，并掌握了一些简单的学习策略和技巧，初步具备英语听、说、读、看、写能力。但学生的英语水平参差不齐，教师在教学中既要进一步培养尖子生的学习能力又要保证能力稍弱的学生能听懂，调动他们的积极性，使他们愿意学，并在学习过程中享受到乐趣。同时，高一的学生刚入学不久，渴望与同学相互了解、进行沟通，建立新的友谊。本节课的话题贴近学生的生活，既可以引导学生树立正确的交友观，也可以引导学生在原有的知识经验的基础上通过合作探究学习，构建新的知识经验。

四、教学目标

单元目标：

（1）围绕"友谊"的话题，让学生学习有关"朋友"的知识，启发学生对朋友和友谊的思考。

（2）让学生在语篇阅读学习中感受外国文化，深刻理解主题内涵，提高学生的文化意识。

（3）训练学生的阅读技巧，使其养成一定的自主学习能力、语言交际能力等。

（4）让学生通过了解有关友谊的各个方面，学会如何与朋友相处，知道世界各地有关友谊的风俗习惯。

课时目标：

（1）让学生学会从宏观上把握读后续写的方向以及要求，从微观上对读写文本进行基本内容和框架、主要人物的性格特点和情绪发展的分析。

（2）让学生学会从人物、修辞、对话内容等方面对所给文本进行深入分析。

（3）培养学生利用逆推法进行问题假设进而合理推测故事情节的思维品质。

（4）通过拓展延伸主题，让学生形成正确的价值观。

五、教学重点、难点

重点：让学生学会从宏观上把握读后续写的写作方向，从微观上对读写文本进行基本内容和框架、主要人物的性格特点和情绪发展的分析。

难点：让学生学会利用逆推法推测故事情节，设计符合故事情节的合理问题。

六、教学过程

Step 1. Warming-up

1. Brainstorm: Why do we need friends?

2. Play a game: What are the qualities of a good friend?

Purpose：围绕主题创设情境，激活学生已有的知识经验。通过希沃白板5软件系统的"趣味词汇判断游戏"，激活学生对主题认识和已有的知识的，为接下来的人物性格特点分析中的词汇运用做好铺垫。

Step 2. Read for the requirements of writing

Purpose：让学生明确读后续写的要求及特点，明确写作方向及步骤。

Step 3. Read for the basic elements

Activity 1: Ask Ss to judge the type of the text.

Activity 2: Ask Ss to get the basic elements.

Purpose：引导学生分析文本的主题思想、文体，让学生初步了解叙事语篇的基本要点，为下一步梳理故事情节做好铺垫。

Step 4. Read for the plot

Ask Ss to read the events of the story and then keep them in the place of the Story Mountain.

Purpose：以"故事山"（Story Mountain）的形式让学生对故事情节的起伏、走向有形象化的理解。

Step 5. Read for the detailed description

Ask Ss to analyze the author's feeling and Luke's character through the detailed description in the text.

Purpose：引导学生从对故事人物性格和心理的分析切入，对语篇中的细节描述、修辞、对话等方面进行分析，为后面的情节推测做好铺垫。

Step 6. Group work: Predict the plot by raising more questions

Ask Ss to predict the plot by using inverse method to raise more questions.

Purpose：在分析人物性格和心理的基础上，引导学生运用递推法对故事情节进行问题假设并回答问题，以此培养学生的思维品质，丰富续写的内容，使故事变得更加耐人寻味。

Step 7. Post-reading

Q: What theme does the story show?

Purpose：引导学生思考，挖掘文本的深层内涵，强化情感，从而使学生形成正确的价值取向。

Step 8. Post-activity after class

(1) Oral story solitaire. Tell the story in pairs.

(2) Put your oral story into a written one.

Purpose：对课堂学习内容进行延伸拓展，渗透技巧，培养学生的口头表达能力和写作能力。

七、主要教学活动

在课堂上，教师主要通过以下几种方式开展教学：一是围绕"Friendship"的主题创设情境，激活学生已有的知识和经验，并通过"趣味词汇判断游戏"激活课堂；二是在引领学生明确写作要求、写作步骤之后开启文本解读，培养学生获取记叙文基本要点的能力；三是以Story Mountain的形式让学生对故事情节的起伏、走向有形象化的理解，让学生掌握情节梳理方面的技能；四是引导学生从对故事人物性格和心理的分析切入，对语篇中的细节描述、修辞、对话等方面进行分析；五是引导学生用逆推法对故事情节进行问题假设，指导学生如何设问和回答；六是通过设问，引导学生思考，挖掘文本的深层内涵，强化情感，从而使学生形成正确的价值取向，同时在续写中注意主题的升华。

八、板书设计

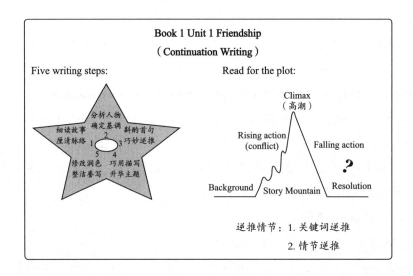

九、教学特色

特色1：教学任务设计巧妙，连贯性强。首先，授课老师围绕"Friendship"的主题创设情境，激活学生已有的知识和经验，并通过希沃白板5软件系统的"趣味词汇判断游戏"激活课堂，为后面的文本人物性格特点分析做好词汇铺垫，巧妙地达成前后融会贯通之效果。其次，以Story Mountain的形式让学生对故事情节的起伏、走向有形象化的理解，让学生掌握了情节梳理方面的技能。最后，引导学生从对故事人物性格和心理的分析切入，对语篇中的细节描述、修辞、对话等方面进行深入分析，为续写奠定基调，让学生在续写时有意识地运用相应的语言特点、修辞手法等，使得前后内容衔接自然，连贯性强。

特色2：方法指导到位，有深度。首先，授课老师引导学生采用逆推法对故事情节进行问题假设，指导学生如何设问和回答，逐步推出合理的故事情节，在预测故事情节发展方面培养学生的想象力和思维能力。其次，通过问题引导学生进一步思考，挖掘文本的深层内涵，强化情感，从而让学生形成正确的价值取向，在续写中注意主题的升华。整节课下来，学生顺利掌握了续写前应具

备的文本解读能力及故事情节预测技巧，也为课后的口述故事接龙活动及续写
任务做了充分的准备。

附1：学生学习资料

Step 1. Warming-up

1. Brainstorm

...

2. Play a game：What are the qualities of a good friend?

Step 2. Read for the requirements of writing

高考全国新课标I卷题型：读后续写（满分25分）

阅读下面材料，根据其内容和所给段落开头语续写两段，使之构成一篇完
整的短文。

Airport Dining

Several years ago, as I was on a business trip from San Francisco to New
Orleans, I noticed I would have some time at the airport in Dallas before catching my
connecting flight. So I called my friend Luke who lived in Dallas, "Luke, I've got an
hour-and-a-half stop at the airport. If you come out and meet my plane, I'll treat you
to dinner." Luke enthusiastically agreed.

When the pilot announced that our flight would be delayed an extra few minutes
in San Francisco, I became upset. Every minute that passed was one minute less that
I would be able to spend with my friend. The plane arrived in Dallas an hour late.
That left me only half an hour to stay with Luke and I still needed time to catch my
connecting flight. At this point, I knew our having dinner together was totally out of

the question.

When I stepped off the plane, Luke was there, waiting for me. "Hey, Luke," I said apologetically, "Thanks for coming out to meet me. I hope you didn't have to wait here too long."

"Oh, no problem," he replied easily. "I called ahead and found out your plane was going to be late."

"Oh, good," I replied. "Look! I'm really sorry about dinner but I'll owe you one next time. Come on, we'll find out what gate my next plane is leaving from. We can head over there together and talk a bit."

"I am very interested in having dinner with you," he said to me.

"The only way you're going to have dinner with me tonight is that you buy a plane ticket to New Orleans!"

"We're having dinner," replied Luke with determination. "Believe me, I have this whole thing arranged. Just follow me."

He picked up one of my bags and carried it out through the security check. The two of us hurried down a short flight of stairs in the parking garage and walked rapidly along several rows of cars until we came to the place where Luke's car was parked.

注意：①续写词数应为150左右；②请按如下格式在答题卡的相应位置作答。

I immediately noticed, in the parking space next to his car, a folding table. _____

_____

With seven and one half minutes to go, we put everything back in the car and ran for my plane. _____

_____

1. Read the requirements of writing above and circle the key words.

2. Write down the five writing steps:

Step 3. Read for the basic elements

1. What type of the text is it?

A. Narration (记叙文).

B. Exposition (说明文).

C. Argumentation (议论文).

2. Get the basic elements.

Step 4. Read for the plot

Read the events of the story and then keep them in the place of the Story Mountain.

Events:

A. Only half an hour was left, which made it impossible for me to have dinner with Luke.

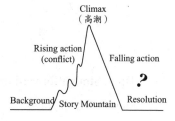

B. I stepped out of the plane and told Luke the fact with apology.

C. I planned to treat Luke to dinner during the connecting flight time.

D. Suddenly, my flight would be delayed an extra few minutes in San Francisco.

Step 5. Read for the detailed description

1. The author's feeling (Use adjectives to describe): _____

2. Luke's character (Use adjectives to describe): _____

Step 6. Group work：Predict the plot by raising more questions

Tip 1: Backward thinking (逆向思维): from result to cause

Paragraph 1：I immediately noticed, in the parking space next to his car, a folding table.

↑

Q4:

↑

Q3:

↑

Q2:

↑

Q1: What did Luke prepare for the dinner?

Paragraph 2: With seven and one half minutes to go, we put everything back in the car and ran for my plane.

Q1:

↓

Q2:

↓

Q3:

↓

Q4:

...

Tip 2: Straightforward thinking (顺向思维): from cause to result

Step 7. Post-reading

Q: What theme does the story show?

_____

_____

Step 8. Post-activity after class

(1) Oral story solitaire. Tell the story in pairs.

_____

_____

(2) Put your oral story into a written one.

I immediately noticed, in the parking space next to his car, a folding table. _____

_____

_____

_____

With seven and one half minutes to go, we put everything back in the car and ran for my plane. _____

_____

_____

_____

附2：写作评价量表（Checklist for Writing）

Items（条目）	Levels（评级）
Cohesion（与所给短文和段落开头衔接融合程度）	☆ ☆ ☆ ☆ ☆
Use of underlined words（下划线词汇使用情况）	☆ ☆ ☆ ☆ ☆
Content（内容的丰富性）	☆ ☆ ☆ ☆ ☆
Accuracy of language（语法和词汇使用的准确性）	☆ ☆ ☆ ☆ ☆
Variety of language（语法和词汇使用的丰富性）	☆ ☆ ☆ ☆ ☆
Coherence（上下文以及语句间的连贯性）	☆ ☆ ☆ ☆ ☆

Book 2 Unit 2 The Olympic Games (My Favourite Sport)

设计者姓名：郭秀云

设计者所在单位：广东省清远市第二中学

一、教学材料分析

授课年级： 高一

教材内容： 人教新课标版 Book 2 Unit 2 The Olympic Games

主题： 人与社会——我最爱的运动

课型： 应用文写作

课时： 1课时

二、教学内容分析

【What】

本节课是把说与写结合在一起的写作技能课。它把口语练习和写作过程相结合，以说促写。首先，教师通过视频引入本单元的主题——奥林匹克运动会，激起学生的同理心。视频中出现的有关运动的词汇，也为稍后展开的口语练习打下基础，使学生变得有话可说，能积极思考他们喜爱或擅长的运动是什么、自己是如何喜欢上某项运动的，以及为此做过什么努力。其次，教师将全班学生分成八个小组，让他们利用教材中提供的语言结构，描述自己喜欢的运动项目。同时，以小组合作的形式开展自由表达训练。最后，教师让学生整理好自己的思路，拟定提纲，写出短文。

【Why】

小组合作的方式在某种程度上降低了教学的难度，也能在一定程度上调动学生的积极性，促进学生主动学习，获取相关英语知识。让学生置身于真实情境中，更有利于自主写作的开展。

【How】

本课从2012年伦敦奥运会剪辑视频入手，激起学生的学习兴趣。接着通过小组合作学习，解决词汇和句型的难点。在搭建好"脚手架"的基础上，学生最终顺利完成本课的写作任务，并对奥运精神有了更深一步的了解。

三、学情分析

授课班级学生是本校高一年级体育特长班的学生，他们入学时英语基础较弱，对英语学习缺乏兴趣和信心，甚至部分学生对英语写作感到恐惧。对于体育特长生来说，他们对本节课的内容——"最喜欢的运动"这个话题应该会感兴趣。本课写作内容难度不大，但要求学生能够用英文表达出来，教师需要加强对学生词汇和句型的输入。

四、教学目标

单元目标：

（1）本单元的中心话题是奥运会——世界上非常重要的体育盛会。通过本单元的学习，学生能了解奥运会的起源、宗旨以及比赛项目。

（2）了解古代希腊的一些神话传说和著名人物。

（3）在写作方面鼓励学生表达自己在体育方面的兴趣爱好，让学生说明最喜欢的运动项目及喜欢的理由，并写成短文。

课时目标：

（1）引导学生分析自己的兴趣爱好，结合说明文文体写作特点，说明自己最喜爱的运动项目及喜欢的理由。

（2）引导学生运用恰当的句型和过渡词，通过小组合作探讨，最终连句成篇。

五、教学重点、难点

重点：引导学生关注说明文篇章结构和文体特点，学会用英语描述自己喜欢的运动，写出100词左右的文章。

难点：让学生学会运用所学句型和写作技巧；通过小组合作探讨，帮助学生理解运动精神并积极参与课题教学活动；让学生学会根据所给的提示和句型，辅以适当的连词写成短文。

六、教学过程

Step 1. Lead-in

1. Watch a video and ask students to think about the sports they like best.

2. Answer the question "What is your favourite sport? ".

Purpose：让学生先进行小组讨论，在写前储备好相关词汇和句型，为写作输出做好充分准备。

Step 2. Writing：描写一项你最喜欢的体育运动（课本第15页）

1. 写作指导

本课时的写作是介绍或描述自己的兴趣爱好，属于描述性文章，本质上属于说明文。写此类文章应注意以下问题：

（1）结构：应采用三段式，即总分总的结构。首先，说明自己最喜欢什么运动以及喜欢此运动的原因；其次，介绍在此项运动中自己最喜欢的运动员并陈述理由；最后，写自己准备如何提高此运动方面的技能。

（2）时态：通常用一般现在时，但具体情况具体分析，应采用恰当时态。

（3）语言：运用生动形象、简洁明了的语言。

2. 常用句型

（1）表示最喜欢：

I like ... best.

Of all the sports, I like ... best.

My favourite sport is ...

I became interested in ... when ...

（2）表示喜欢的理由：

I like it because ...

There is no doubt that ...

The reason why ... is that ...

（3）表示该项运动的优势：

It plays an important role/part in ...

It does us a lot of good.

It is of great benefit to us.

（4）表示结论：

In all, ...

In a word, ...

It can make us healthy and wealthy.

（5）常用的过渡词或短语：

at first, first of all, first(ly), second(ly), finally, at last, in the end however, in addition, what's more, besides, apart from, meanwhile in a word, all in all, in short, in conclusion in one's opinion, as far as sb. be concerned

Purpose：为下面句子翻译做好词汇、短语铺垫，让学生掌握体育类相关短语和表达意见、喜好的句型。

3. 句子翻译

（1）开头部分常用句式。

在所有的运动中，我最喜欢篮球。

_____

我最喜欢打排球。

_____

如果你问我最喜欢哪项运动，我不得不说是游泳。

_____

你对瑜伽（yoga）了解多少？

_____

我第一次看到乒乓球运动，就喜欢上了它。

_____

（2）主体部分常用句式。

我喜欢打篮球的原因是它有很多好处（benefit）。

_____

当我小的时候，我就对它很感兴趣（show great interest in ...）。

_____

瑜伽不仅是一项运动而且是一门艺术。

_____

我喜欢很多乒乓球运动员（athlete），如王楠和王浩。

_____

这项运动需要力量和技术（strength and skills）。

_____

踢足球可以增强我们的体质，使我们保持健康以及训练我们的大脑。

_____

（3）结尾部分常用句式。

我希望将来我能参加奥运会。

_____

总之，我非常喜欢这项运动。

_____

Purpose：通过对三段式各部分常用句型进行分析和归纳，让学生储备写作句型，为下一步写作搭建"脚手架"。

Step 3. Practice

请根据以下要点，以"My Favourite Sport"为题，用英语写一篇100词左右的短文。

（1）我最喜欢的运动是乒乓球。从小我就对乒乓球很感兴趣。

（2）我喜欢打乒乓球的原因是它有很多好处。它可以增强我们的体质，使我们保持健康以及训练我们的大脑。

（3）它是需要力量和技术的运动。

（4）乒乓球不仅是一项运动，还是一门艺术。

（5）我希望我自己能成为一名优秀的乒乓球运动员。

注意：可以适当增加细节，以使短文连贯、通顺。

Step 4. Homework

Share the passage with your classmates and talk about your favourite sport.

七、主要教学活动

本节课是一节写作课，由阅读篇章引入写作。首先，教师通过引入视频，激发学生的学习兴趣。其次，引导学生阅读一篇说明文。学生通过审题分析文体结构，从中找出描述运动的一些常用形容词和常用句型，为下一步写作奠定基础。最后，通过完成句子，积累重点词汇和重点句型，为写作输入搭建好"脚手架"。

通过文本学习，学生基本能了解如何描述人物，并将其应用于之后的写作任务中。本节课上，教师恰当运用启发式教学、任务式教学等方法引导学生一步一步完成学习活动（学生在这节课上学到了什么，学生能够用所学的内容做什么，学生做得如何）。

八、板书设计

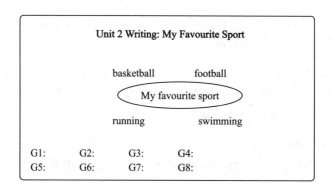

九、教学特色

特色1：充分调动学生情感，以情感人。第一，本节写作课紧扣本单元主题，利用视频导入有效激发学生兴趣，同时为下个教学活动的顺利开展打下扎实的词汇基础。第二，学生的学习热情被充分点燃，学生能够利用视频中出现的与运动相关词汇，大胆开口说英语，表达自己最喜欢的运动项目，这是一个很大的进步。

特色2：基于学情，以学定教。第一，指导学生进行小组合作探讨，从中找到解决问题的办法。第二，鼓励学生积极开展小组活动，既可以消除学生的恐惧心理，增强其锻炼口语的信心，又有利于学生表达自己的兴趣爱好，使其理解奥林匹克精神，理解体育精神。

附：参考佳作

My Favourite Sport

Of all the sports, I like ping-pong best. When I was a child, I showed great interest in it.

The reason why I like playing ping-pong is that it does us a lot of good. It can build up our bodies, keep us healthy and train our brains. Meanwhile, it is a sport that combines strength and skills. In my opinion, ping-pong is not only a sport but also an art.

In a word, I hope I can become an excellent ping-pong athlete in the future.

Book 2 Unit 2 The Olympic Games (Sports and Healthy)

设计者姓名：黄茗旎
设计者所在单位：广东省清远市连山中学

一、教学材料分析

授课年级：高一

教材内容：人教新课标版Book 2 Unit 2 The Olympic Games

主题：人与社会——体育与健康

课型：写作课

课时：1课时

二、教学内容分析

【What】

在学习完Book 2 Unit 2的阅读语篇后，学生对奥运会的起源、宗旨、比赛项目等有了更多的了解。本节课以"人与社会——体育与健康"这一主题为引领，是一节旨在帮助学生巩固、运用本单元话题词汇的写作课。

【Why】

英语写作作为教师教和学生学的重难点，需要教师设计合理、有效的教学活动，搭建足够多的支架，引导学生积累与主题和话题相关的词块来进行应用文写作，同时提高学生的英语综合运用能力，实现学生对知识的学习理解、应用实践与迁移创新。

【How】

基于教材主题和话题，教师运用任务教学法、过程教学法等，通过设计丰富多样的自主学习活动和合作探究学习活动，实现课堂的结构化和情境化，指导学生巩固和运用相关的词汇与表达，最终完成号召信的写作输出。

三、学情分析

连山高级中学位于清远市连山壮族瑶族自治县，属教育薄弱地区。学生英语基础不太好，词汇量普遍不足，在英语口语、写作方面尤为薄弱。因此，本节课的重点为写前词汇、句型等语言知识的输入。

四、教学目标

单元目标：

（1）了解奥运会的起源、宗旨以及比赛项目。

（2）通过学习本单元的两篇阅读文章及配套练习册的一篇阅读文章，掌握与"体育运动"这一话题相关的词汇和句型，增加对奥运会及体育运动的了解，激发对运动的兴趣和坚定坚持运动、锻炼体魄的决心。

课时目标：

By the end of this class, Ss are expected to be able to:

（1）know some sports events in the Olympics.

（2）appreciate the athletes who have made great contributions to our country.

（3）know the benefits of doing sports.

（4）learn how to keep a good balance between study and health.

（5）analyze the features of the letter of appeal and learn how to make the writing more coherent.

五、教学重点、难点

重点：

（1）Get the Ss to know some sports events in the Olympics.

（2）Get the Ss to appreciate the athletes who have made great contributions to our country.

（3）Get the Ss to know the benefits of doing sports.

（4）Get the Ss to learn how to keep a good balance between study and health.

难点：

Guide the Ss to analyze the features of the letter of appeal and learn how to make the writing more coherent.

六、教学过程

Pre-class assignment: Translation - words and phrases related to sports.

运动员 *n.* _____	教练 *n.* _____	露天体育 *n.* _____
比赛 *vi.* _____	比赛 *n.* _____	
比赛选手 *n.* _____	有竞争力的 *adj.* _____	
相似的 *adj.* _____	相似之处 *n.* _____	与……相似 _____
为荣誉而战 _____	渴望竞争 _____	定期地 _____
古代与现代社会 _____	担任裁判 _____	代表国家 _____
提升技能 _____	担任志愿者 _____	打破纪录 _____
赢得第一名 _____	参加 _____	为学校赢得荣誉 _____

Purpose：课前提供翻译练习，帮助学生提前积累单元话题词汇，降低写作难度。

37

Step 1. Lead-in：Individual work

1. Viewing. Get the Ss to talk about the sports events they know: What sports events in the Olympic Games do you know?

2. Speaking. Get the Ss to share their ideas about doing sports.

（1）Are you fond of doing sports? How often do you do sports?

（2）According to the scientific report, a person is supposed to exercise for at least one hour a day. Do you think you spend enough time doing sports every day? Why?

Purpose：基于教材单元主题与话题，通过展示图片与提问的形式导入，激发学生兴趣，帮助学生积累话题词汇，让学生了解中国多个运动项目中为人熟知的奥运健儿，增强其民族自豪感。

话题词汇积累：ping-pong/table tennis, gymnastics, basketball, track and field, athletics, volleyball, badminton, shooting ...

Step 2. Pre-writing

1. Individual work: Listening and paraphrasing

> Emily, a high school student, is being interviewed. Listen and fill in the blanks to see what she thinks of doing sports.

(1) Get the Ss to write down what they have heard about the benefits of doing sports on the handout (Students are divided into two large groups, with different blanks to fill in, one with verbs and the other with nouns).

Handout 1:

> I'm Emily, a high school student from Lianshan Senior High School. I like sports, because doing sports is really a good thing. Firstly, it _____ _____ our physical and mental health. It helps to _____ our body, make us strong and energetic, and _____ too fat. Secondly, doing sports is a good way to _____. When we are busy with our study, sports can _____ our stress. Finally, it's easier for us to _____ when we take part in sport activities, because we _____ the same interest. It's important for making friends. All in all, I get a lot from sports.

Handout 2:

I'm Emily, a high school student from Lianshan Senior High School. I like sports, because doing sports is really a good thing. Firstly, it is good for our _____. It helps to build up our body, make us strong and energetic, and stop us from getting too fat. Secondly, doing sports is _____ to relax ourselves. When we are busy with our study, sports can release our _____. Finally, it's easier for us to make friends when we take part in _____, because we share the same _____. It's important for making friends. All in all, I get a lot from sports.

(2) Get the Ss to exchange their answers with their deskmates and read out the passage.

(3) Paraphrasing. Get the Ss to paraphrase some words and expressions.

Eg.:

like: be fond of

a good thing: useful, helpful, be beneficial to ...

be good for: be beneficial to

energetic: full of energy

when we take part in: when taking part in

important: essential, vital

Purpose：以听促写，通过听录音引导学生掌握与"运动的好处"相关的词汇与表达，为下面的写作做好铺垫；A、B组学生的听力材料设空不同，通过交换答案，学生可以更直观地从不同词性掌握话题语料；教师本人录音，激起学生的学习热情；引导学生使用高级词汇与表达，为作文润色增分。

话题词汇积累：be good for, be beneficial to, build up, stop ... from, relax oneself, release one's stress, make friends, share interests, physical and mental health, sport activity ...

2. Group work：Writing and speaking

Ask the Ss to tell more benefits of doing sports.

Purpose：学生通过小组讨论，了解更多运动的益处。教师将提前准备的和学生提供的较有代表性的词汇及表达写在黑板上，为接下来的写作提供素材。

话题词汇积累：improve our sleeping quality, give us a good appetite, keep us away from diseases, improve our mood, stop us from putting on weight ...

3. Individual work：Listening

> As high school students, we are so busy with our study that sometimes it is difficult for us to find time to do sports. Emily also has the same problem.

Get the Ss to write down what they have heard about the relation of keeping a balance between study and sports.

> I think it is a big problem when it comes to _____ between our study and health. In my opinion, although we are busy with our study, we should _____ some time _____ sports so as to build up our body. All work and no play makes Jack a dull boy. Only when we _____ can we have a good _____ in our study.

Purpose：以听促写，通过听录音引导学生掌握与"平衡学习与运动的关系"相关的词汇与表达，并为下面的写作做好铺垫，同时提倡健康生活、健康学习。

话题词汇积累：keep a good balance between ... and ... , spend ... in doing/on ... , have a strong body, have a good performance ...

Step 3. Writing (Individual & group work)

> 学校即将举办运动会，校广播站英语专栏现征集稿件，号召一些不愿意报名参加的同学积极参加比赛。写作要点如下：
> （1）举办运动会的时间、地点；
> （2）（内容自定）_____ ；
> （3）作为学生，可以做些什么来平衡学习与运动；
> （4）号召同学们积极参加比赛。

（首尾段已给出，针对要点（2）的写作至少须包含以下词组中的5个：beneficial, improve, energetic, physical and mental health, lose weight, sleep, keep away from）

Dear fellows,

Our school is to hold a sports meeting next month on the athletic field, which aims to encourage students to take an active part in doing sports. However, some of us are unwilling to join.

_____

_____

All in all, I strongly call on all of you to participate in the competition!

Yours,

_____

1. Pre-writing：Group discussion

(1) Guide the Ss to discover the features of a writing.

SPORTS

Style (genre) (体裁): _____

Person (人称): _____

Organising (组织): _____

Reader (读者): _____

Tense (时态): _____

Structure (结构): _____

(2) Guide the Ss to use suitable modifiers and linking words to polish a writing.

Firstly, ... / Secondly, ... / Thirdly, ...

First of all ... / Besides ... / Most importantly ...

not only ... but also ... although ... , so ... that ... , so that , in order to

It is ... that ...（强调句）

Only when ... can ...（倒装句）

Purpose：引导学生分析写作要点，培养学生使用修饰语与连接词的意识，为接下来的写作做好铺垫。

2. While-writing

Get the Ss to finish Para. 2 and Para. 3 of the writing in class.

Purpose：要点（2）为自由创作，学生可以随意创设写作内容，以此激发学生对英语写作的兴趣，鼓励学生运用本课时所积累的词汇和表达进行写作，提高学生的应用文写作能力。

3. Post-writing

（1）Assess the Ss' works with a projector.

（2）Guide the Ss to refer to the writing criteria before making comments.

（3）After class, the Ss exchange their works and make assessments on them based on the following checklist.

评价内容 （50分）	标准	自评	他评	师评
卷面 （10分）	The writing looks _____. A. neat B. quite good C. not bad D. terrible			
结构 （10分）	Is the writing is divided into paragraphs? A. Yes B. No			
内容 （信息完整） （10分）	_____ the key points are included. A. All B. Most of C. Some of D. None of			
句式 （10分）	There are _____ good sentences in the writing. A. ≥7 B. 5~7 C. 2~4 D. 0~1			
词汇 （10分）	The vocabulary used in the writing is _____. A. rich B. enough C. limited D. poor			

Purpose：教师在课堂上评价学生习作，与学生共同赏好句、纠错句；利用评价表，引导学生在课后进行习作互改，培养学生的批判性思维；鼓励学生发现同伴习作的亮点并加以学习。

Step 4. Summary

Lead the Ss to summarize what they have learnt in this class.

Purpose：回顾本节课的学习要点。

Step 5. Homework

Get the Ss to complete and polish their writing after class. Get them ready to present their writing in the next class.

Purpose：课后完成整篇习作并加以润色。

七、主要教学活动

本节课的授课过程中，教师共设计了三大语篇：语篇一为看、听、读的输入与说、写的输出，中心词为"运动的益处"；语篇二为听、读、看的输入与说、写的输出，中心词为"学习与运动的平衡"；语篇三为写作输出，融合了"人与社会——体育与健康"和"人与社会——校园生活"两大主题语境，以高考题型——应用文写作的方式呈现。

本节课旨在从听、说、读、看、写等多方面培养学生的英语学科核心素养，具体体现在以下几个方面：

（1）语言能力方面，基于本节课涉及的主题语境"人与社会——体育与健康"，要求学生掌握与体育运动、运动的益处、平衡学习与运动的关系等方面相关的词汇与句式表达，实现从听、读、看的输入到说、写的输出；

（2）思维品质方面，设计有效的教学活动综合培养学生的逻辑思维、创新思维与辩证思维；

（3）文化意识方面，通过了解中国奥运健儿，培养学生的爱国意识与奉献意识；

（4）学习能力方面，学生采用小组合作、创造性写作、写后自评等方式，拓宽英语学习渠道，积极运用和调适英语学习策略。

八、板书设计

Sports events in the Olympic Games:
ping-pong/table tennis
gymnastics
basketball
track and field
athletics
volleyball
badminton
shooting

Keep balance between study and doing sports:
spend ... in doing/on ...
have a strong body
have a good performance

Benefits of doing sports:
keep a good balance between ... and ...
spend ... in doing/on ...
have a strong body
have a good performance

九、教学特色

特色1：在导入部分，教师首先以直观图片展示和提问的形式迅速调动学生的学习热情，激发学生的兴趣；然后通过让学生了解我国奥运健儿，向学生渗透道德教育，增强学生的民族自豪感，同时以主题为引领，提倡和谐、健康向上的价值观。

特色2：语篇设计新颖，听力材料的设空部分存在信息差，引导学生特别留意与话题相关的名词与动词短语。

特色3：写作内容为教师原创作品，让学生参与创设，激发学生对英语写作的兴趣，鼓励学生运用本课时所积累的词汇与表达进行写作，提高学生的应用文写作能力。

十、课例评析

（一）课例评析1：胡翠娥

黄茗旎老师的这节课是基于人教新课标版教材Book 2 Unit 2主题语境"人与社会——体育与健康"的一节应用文（邀请信）写作课，主题"Sports"贯穿整个教学过程，设定的教学目标基本达成。教学活动的设计体现了省级课题研究的过程性写作流程：写前输入——写中教师指导、学生训练——写后展示。单元主题贯穿整个课堂教学。

亮点：

（1）Lead-in环节用音乐、图片等多模态形式，激发学生的学习动机和兴趣。

（2）教师基于学情和教学需要，自录录音进行听力训练，两个语篇的设题意图非常清晰，为后面输出环节（写作要点（2）和写作要点（3））进行充分的语言知识输入。同时，教师用同一语篇进行词汇替换训练，引导学生学会在写作中丰富和优化自己的书面表达。

（3）写作情境创设的第二个写作要点（内容自定）体现了黄老师培养学生思维能力的意识。

（4）整节课较好地践行了新课标所提倡的英语学习活动观：以"Sports"这一主题为引领，依托语篇（2听1写），基于听、说、读、看、写等活动培养学生的英语学科核心素养（语言知识——与"sports"话题相关的语块、文化知识，思维品质——逻辑思维、批判思维和创新思维，学习能力——听、说、读、看、写语言技能都得到训练）。教师能很好地使用激励性评价语。

建议：

要注意合理设计小组合作的讨论任务。

（二）课例评析2：郭秀云

黄茗旎老师的这节课是基于人教新课标版教材Book 2 Unit 2主题语境"人与社会——体育与健康"的一节关于体育运动的应用文（邀请信）写作课。整个教学过程顺利完成，设定的教学目标也顺利达成；各环节设计基于学情，指导细致，注重写前学法指导。

亮点：

（1）教师年轻，课堂充满活力，学生积极参与课堂教学任务。

（2）以听促学，通过播放录音引导学生掌握与本课相关的写作词汇，激发学生学习热情。

（3）教师基本功扎实，用语得体，精心设计课堂练习，体现了课堂的趣味性和层次性。

（4）整节课教学内容丰富，教师评讲、引导恰当，是一节优质展示课。

建议：

本节课以听促学，但听力内容在写前导入部分出现了两次，占用了部分写作时间，让学生误以为是上听说课，建议删减一次听力内容，把精力集中于写前的指导。

（三）课例评析3：何玉琼

黄茗旎老师的这节课是基于人教新课标版教材Book 2 Unit 2主题语境"人与社会——体育与健康"的一节应用文（邀请信）写作课。黄老师在课堂上充满动感活力，语音语调标准，整个课堂张弛有度，板书设计系统、有条理。

亮点：

（1）以直观图片展示和提问的形式导入课堂，激发学生学习热情；通过让学生了解我国奥运健儿，向其渗透德育，增强学生的民族自豪感。

（2）语篇设计新颖，听力材料的设空部分存在信息差，引导学生留意与话题相关的名词与动词短语。此任务的设计不仅能提升学生的听力能力，同时使学生完成了写作句型的积累。

（3）写作内容为原创题型，在写中环节，训练了学生的应用文写作能力，还融入了高考的新题型——故事续写的思维训练，为新题型的教学做好准备，可谓一箭双雕。

（四）课例评析4：陈艳丽

黄茗旎老师基于人教新课标版高中英语教材Book 2 Unit 2 The Olympic Games 文本在清远市连山高级中学高一（1）班（中等生源）设计了以听促写的课例。黄老师的英语口语非常流畅，专业素养高，基本功非常扎实，教学设计别出心裁，其课堂充满活力。

亮点：

黄老师设计的教学活动丰富新颖，听、说、读、看、写活动体现了英语教学的综合性。教学活动过渡自然流畅，每个环节精心设计，很好地践行了新课标六要素整合的英语学习活动观：主题引领，依托多元语篇，巩固语言知识，提升文化意识和学生的思维品质，最终让学生学会学习，真正做到依托语篇、基于活动、发展能力。

（五）课例评析5：张伟娟

黄茗旎老师的这节课是基于人教新课标版教材Book 2 Unit 2主题语境"人与社会——体育与健康"的一节关于体育运动的应用文（邀请信）写作课。

亮点：

（1）导入部分自然流畅。黄老师从学生熟悉的体育运动项目聊起，让学生讨论了一周大概在运动方面花费多少时间、喜欢什么体育运动等问题。学生在轻松自然的状态下进行口语热身，不知不觉便进入写作情境。

（2）以听促学。黄老师巧妙地设计了两份不一样的学案。同桌两人分别拿到两张听力材料设空不一样的学案，学生自然分为A、B两组。在听力结束后，黄老师让同桌交换答案，既使学生直观地从不同词性掌握话题语料，又节省了老师核对答案的时间。

（3）注重培养学生的学习能力。黄老师在点评学生作文后，引导学生欣赏好词好句，并利用评价表，引导学生在课后进行习作互改。同时，鼓励学生发现同伴的亮点并加以学习。

建议：

课堂节奏稍微有点前松后紧的感觉，前面搭建语言支架部分可以再紧凑一些。

Book 2 Unit 2 The Olympic Games (Arts and Sports)

设计者姓名：吴碧华

设计者所在单位：广东省清远市第一中学

一、教学材料分析

授课年级：高一

教材内容：人教新课标版Book 2 Unit 2 The Olympic Games

主题：人与社会——艺术与体育

课型：应用文写作课

课时：1课时

二、教学内容分析

【**What**】

本单元语篇是一篇介绍奥运会的起源、宗旨以及比赛项目的穿越时空的采访稿。学生通过阅读该语篇，对奥运会的发展历程有进一步的了解。本节课是基于教材主题语境和话题的关于体育运动的写作课——邀请信之写前储备的教学活动设计。

【**Why**】

基于教材主题语境和话题，掌握热点话题词汇并运用话题词汇进行交际性强的应用文输出写作是高中写作教学的重难点之一。

【**How**】

基于教材主题语境和话题，运用任务教学法、探究法和过程教学法，指导学生复习和复现所学词汇及句型。通过邀请信写作的形式，输出得体的文章，鼓励学生学以致用。

三、学情分析

从整体上看，学生的英语学习能力和基础属于中等水平。通过前面几节课的学习，学生对奥运会的运动项目及相关知识有所了解，对本节课所讨论的话题比较熟悉。尽管学生已经进入高中学习阶段了，但是学生在英语写作方面应具备的词汇、句型及写作技巧仍比较欠缺。他们对与本节课（写作）相关的知识结构了解得并不系统和全面，这对学生进行迁移性学习产生一定的阻碍，需要教师在写前帮助他们进行充足的语言输入。为此，本节课重点围绕写前储备这一环节设计教学任务。

四、教学目标

单元目标：

（1）了解奥运会的起源、宗旨以及比赛项目。

（2）通过阅读本单元的两篇阅读文章及配套练习册的一篇阅读文章，掌握与体育运动话题相关的词汇和句型。

（3）加深学生对奥运会及体育运动的了解，激发他们对体育运动的兴趣和坚定他们锻炼体魄的决心。

课时目标：

（1）To consolidate some words and phrases concerning sports in Unit 2.

（2）To master some useful expressions used to write an invitation letter.

（3）To learn how to write an invitation letter with the words and phrases learned in Unit 2.

（4）To motivate Ss' love for sports.

五、教学重点、难点

重点：

（1）To consolidate some words and phrases concerning sports in Unit 2.

（2）To master some useful expressions used to write an invitation letter.

（3）To learn how to write an invitation letter with the words and phrases learned in Unit 2.

难点：

To learn how to write an invitation letter with the words and phrases learned in Unit 2.

六、教学过程

Step 1. Lead-in

Get the Ss to watch a video clip about the theme song called "Rise" for Rio Olympic Games in 2016 and answer the following questions after watching it.

Q1: How do you feel after watching the video?

Q2: What sports events can you see in the video?

Purpose：首先，基于教材主题和话题，充分利用信息技术，以多模态的视听形式（视频）创设语境，导入主题，复习本单元关于sports events的词汇。其次，为学生后面的写作做好词汇的铺垫。最后，激发学生对体育运动的热爱。（引导学生用moved、inspired、excited、thrilled等词汇谈观后感）

Step 2. Pre-writing

Task 1：Individual work

Get the Ss to read a passage which contains most of the new words and phrases in Unit 2 and try to figure out the meanings of the underlined words and phrases. Encourage them to recite the passage after class. P90 ~ 91

Purpose：结合本单元话题，挑选一篇含有大部分本单元重点词汇的文章让学生阅读。学生通过阅读有语境的篇章复习词汇，为写中环节词汇的使用做好铺垫。

Task 2：Individual work & Group work

Get the Ss to listen to a letter of invitation from NMET Ⅲ, 2019 (2019年高考英语全国卷Ⅲ), and fill in the missing words. (5mins)

Purpose：第一，挑选高考真题的习作范文，围绕邀请信每个段落的内容进行有针对性的挖空，让学生通过听的输入方式，填写所缺单词或短语，为下一步分析文本的特点与结构做好铺垫；第二，避免单一地直接给学生阅读范文，以求在有限的时间内，多渠道刺激学生的感官，以更好地进行语言输入。

Task 3：Individual work & Group work

Guide the Ss to further analyze the characteristics of the passage.

SPORTS

Style (genre) (体裁)：_____

Person (人称)：_____

Organising (组织)：_____

Reader (读者)：_____

Tense (时态)：_____

Structure (结构)：_____

The outline of the letter of invitation

Beginning：_____

Body：_____

Ending：_____

Purpose：结合学生所填单词或短语，启发学生观察和思考，指引他们归纳邀请信的写作特点和写作内容，为学生自主进行写作搭建必要的知识框架。

Task 4：Individual work & Group work

Get the Ss to choose suitable sentence patterns for each paragraph of an invitation letter, write them down in their handouts and try to recite them. Then the teacher offers suggested samples and get Ss to recite them in class. Then, finish some translation exercises. (7 mins)

Purpose：结合学情，减轻学生的负担，避免大量翻译练习的直接罗列。让学生自主判断，对教师给出的三个段落的套用句式进行归类，并在背诵后做适量的翻译练习，为后面的写作训练做好相关句型的铺垫。

Task 5：Individual work & Group work

Get the Ss to do some exercises to consolidate the words and expressions in Unit 2 as well as the useful expressions of an invitation letter in the form of competition.

Purpose：通过竞赛的形式，激发学生的学习热情，活跃课堂气氛，提高学生对课堂的专注度，测试学生对本节课话题词汇以及邀请信套用句式的掌握情况，进一步为写中环节做好铺垫。

Step 3. While-writing (Designed for homework)（基于单元话题原创题）

Encourage the Ss to finish the following writing task within 20 minutes after class and hand it in tomorrow morning. (Guide the Ss to work out the outline with the guidance learned in Task 3 of Step 2 if time permits)

假设你是李华。为了激发学生对体育运动的热爱，以及坚定学生强健体魄的决心，你校决定于下周末在运动场举行为期两天的校运会。在邻校做交换生的美国朋友Henry对体育运动很感兴趣，本校同学也很期待外国友人的来访。为此，你写信邀请他前来观看校运会比赛。内容包括：

1. 校运会举行的时间、地点和校运会的比赛项目。

2. 参加对象：各班运动员。

3. 奖励情况：各比赛项目前三名颁发奖牌。

4. 班级象征：写有不同格言的班旗。

注意：①词数100左右；②可以适当增加细节，以使行文连贯。

参考词汇：激发对……的热爱：inspire one's love for

强健体魄：build sb. up

Purpose：结合本单元主题语境及话题词汇，围绕本节写作课的技巧指导及写作特点，创设情境，让学生在最大程度上学以致用。鉴于学生整体水平不高且处于高中的起始阶段，在设置作文题目时有意识地给学生提供较多的提示信息。

Step 4. Summary

1. Key words and expressions concerning sports in Unit 2.

2. What makes a good invitation letter?

Purpose：总结本节课两大重点，让学生更清晰地反思本节课的得与失。

Step 5. Homework

1. Finish the writing task using what we have learned in this lesson.

2. Supplementary reading: Read another sample writing of an invitation letter from NMET Ⅱ, 2017 and recite it.

3. Read more sample writings and useful expressions concerning invitation letters in the following WeChat official accounts (微信公众号：夺分英语，爱V高中英语&浪哥英语).

Purpose：鼓励学生自主学习和积累相关词汇，了解实际生活中的邀请信件；鼓励学生通过网络等多种渠道挖掘课外学习资源，自主获取、梳理并学习新知识。

七、板书设计

> **Book 2 Unit 2 The Olympic Games**
> Pre-writing for a letter of invitation based on the unit topic
> Key words and phrases:
>
> Key sentence patterns:
>
> The structure of a letter of invitation
> Beginning:
> Body:
> Ending:

八、教学特色

特色1：教学设计着眼于提升学生的思维品质，在课堂上给学生搭建了充分的学习支架，利用信息技术，以视听形式（视频）创设语境，导入主题，复习本单元关于 sports events 的词汇，为写作部分做好词汇的铺垫。同时，激发学生对体育运动的热爱。

特色2：整节课学生都在参与各类教学活动，师生互动、生生互动都非常充分。教学中，游戏环节把整节课的学习气氛推向高潮，使学生在课后仍意犹未尽。

附：学生学习资料

Book 2 Unit 2 The Olympic Games

Pre-writing for a letter of invitation based on the unit topic

（单元话题下邀请信之写前储备）

Step 1. Lead-in

Watch a video clip about the theme song called "Rise" for Rio Olympic Games in 2016 and answer the following questions after watching it.

Q1: How do you feel after watching the video?

_____

_____

Q2: What sports events can you see in the video?

_____

_____

Step 2. Pre-writing

Task 1：Individual work

Read the following passage which contains most of the new words and phrases in Unit 2 and try to figure out the meanings of the underlined words and phrases. Recite the passage after class. P90～91

A **Fair** Competition

"Swifter, Higher and Stronger" stands for the spirit of the Olympics. But fairness is the basis of this motto. Only when you win fairly will you and your homeland deserve the great glory. But nowadays, unlike the ancient honest slave competitors, some hopeless athletes who can't bear the pain of training cheat when taking part in games. Medals seem to have magical power causing them to cheat, and the prize money has replaced the motto as their only goal.

So, in the gymnastics event to be held in our city next month, one of the host's responsibilities is to keep competitions fair. They advertised on posters outside the stadium to promise that every competitor is to have a regular physical examination in a gymnasium one after another. No one can bargain on this. The volunteers in charge will be very strict. It is foolish to cheat because they won't be admitted to compete and will even be fined as well.

Task 2：Individual work & Group work

Listen to a letter of invitation from NMET Ⅲ, 2019 (2019年高考英语全国卷Ⅲ) and fill in the missing words.

Dear Henry,

Knowing that you are _____ in music, I am writing to _____ you to join in the music festival with me.

Here are some _____ about the music festival. It will be held on the playground from 5 p.m. to 8 p.m. next Sunday. We will see many fascinating _____, like singing and dancing, which can make us _____. _____, we will meet some students there, _____ we can make some new friends. _____, we all expect you to be on the stage.

I will be delighted if you could _____ us. I'm _____ your early reply.

Yours,

Li Hua

Task 3：Individual work & Group work

Further analyse the characteristics (特点) of the passage.

SPORTS

Style (genre) (体裁): _____

Person (人称): _____

Organising (组织): _____

Reader (读者): _____

Tense (时态): _____

Structure (结构): _____

The outline of the letter of invitation

Beginning: _____

Body: _____

Ending: _____

Task 4：Individual work & Group work

Choose suitable sentence patterns for each paragraph of an invitation letter, write them down in your handouts and try to recite them. Then, finish some translation exercises.

Useful expressions for a letter of invitation

1. The party will be held in ... on ...

2. Knowing that you're interested in ..., I'm writing to invite you to ...

3. I believe it will broaden your horizons (拓宽视野) and make a deep impression on you.

4. Here is a brief schedule (安排) about this activity. First, ... Second, ... Finally, ...

5. Your participation (参与) will surely make the activity much more meaningful.

6. I would appreciate it if you could confirm (确认) your participation at your

earliest convenience.

7. There will be many activities, such as ...

8. I'll be extremely delighted/grateful/thankful if you could accept my invitation and I am looking forward to your early reply.

9. Undoubtedly, you will have an enjoyable/unforgettable time there.

10. On behalf of (代表) ..., I am writing to invite you ...

邀请信开头段：

_____

邀请信主体段：

活动细节：时间、地点、内容

_____

活动意义及邀请理由：

_____

邀请信结尾段：

_____

Practice：Translate the following sentences into English.

1. 知道你对体育运动很感兴趣，我写信邀请你来观看我们的校运会。

_____

2. 我是李华，学生会主席。我代表我们学校写信邀请你与我们一起去。

_____

3. 那一天，将会有很多体育项目，如跑步、跳高、跳远等。

_____

4. 你的参与一定会使得该活动更有意义。

_____

5. 如果你能接受我的邀请我将会非常高兴，期待你的早日回复。

Task 5：Individual work & Group work

Do some exercises to consolidate the words and expressions in Unit 2 as well as the useful expressions of an invitation letter in the form of competition. Challenge yourselves and try your luck!

Step 3—Step 5见P51

（2017全国卷Ⅱ）

Dear Henry,

I'm Li Hua, a Chinese student of yours. Knowing that you are interested in traditional Chinese culture, I'm writing to invite you to visit a paper-cutting exhibition with me.

The exhibition will be held in the City Museum next Saturday, lasting for 8 hours—from 9:00 a. m. to 5:00 p.m. During the exhibition, you can have a close look at varieties of paper cuts, such as "Double Happiness" for wedding decorations. Besides, whoever presents at the exhibition will be given a piece of paper-cutting as a gift. I'm firmly convinced that you will have great fun and benefit a lot.

I would be extremely delighted if you could accept my invitation. I'm looking forward to your early reply.

Yours,

Li Hua

九、课例评析

（一）课例评析1：胡翠娥

吴碧华老师的这节课是基于人教新课标版教材Book 2 Unit 2主题语境"人与社会——体育与健康"的一节应用文（邀请信）写作课，主题"Sports"贯穿整个教学过程。教学过程中各环节的设计体现了本节课的重点在于对学生进行写前指导、写前输入充分。

亮点：

（1）因为是借班上课，教师利用课前几分钟与学生进行Q&A的互动，拉近师生距离，消除学生对老师的陌生感，为课堂充分互动打好基础。

（2）Lead-in环节让学生带着任务进行视听（viewing）：How do you feel after watching the video? What sports events can you see in the video? 培养学生边听边记边思的学习习惯。

（3）精选语篇进行语言知识的输入——通过"A Fair Competition"语篇输入sports话题语块、通过2019年高考英语全国卷Ⅲ习作范文（自录音形式播放）输入邀请信模板句式，体现了吴老师基于学情引领学生进行充分的语言输入的意识，为后面输出（写）环节做充分的铺垫。

（4）"Useful expressions for a letter of invitation"的设计有新意，不是直接呈现邀请信开头、主体、结尾的常用句式，而是要求学生根据所给的句式进行重新整理，体现了教师培养学生思辨能力的意识。以竞赛形式进行的"Translation"符合学生的年龄特点，有利于消除学生对写作的恐惧心理，让学生在轻松的气氛中完成学习任务。

（5）基于单元话题创设真实的写作情境，符合高考写作题型的命题特点。

（6）整节课师生互动充分，教师能恰当使用激励性评价语言，使课堂气氛轻松活跃。

（7）"Homework"设计部分给学生提供补充阅读和微信公众号，体现了吴老师培养学生自主学习习惯的意识。

（二）课例评析2：郭秀云

吴碧华老师的这节课是基于人教新课标版教材Book 2 Unit 2主题语境——"人与社会——体育与健康"的一节关于体育运动的应用文（邀请信）写作课。整个教学过程顺利完成，设定的教学目标也顺利达成。各环节设计基于学情，指导细致，注重写前学法指导。

亮点：

（1）教师在课堂上有激情，教学环节紧凑，合理把握教材重点，突破教学难点。

（2）课前注重与学生交流，消除学生紧张感，写前注重多模态教学输入，引入视频教学和一段听力练习，为学生写作搭建"脚手架"。

（3）教师基本功扎实，用语得体，精心设计的课堂练习体现趣味性和层次性。

（4）整节课教学内容丰富，教师评讲、引导恰当，是一节优质展示课。

（三）课例评析3：陈锦春

吴老师的这节课是紧紧围绕工作室的省级课题开展的一节写前知识储备课。教学目标在于通过设计指导写作技巧的教学活动，实现"输入（input）—内化（intake）—输出（output）"的教学过程，并通过设计真正体现以学生为主体、教师为主导的小组合作的课堂活动，让英语学科核心素养在写作课中真正落地。为此，在授课过程中，吴老师给学生提供了五个与本节课授课重点相关的语篇，包含口头和书面等多模态语篇。语篇以整体感知、具体分析、实践操作（结合高考真题进行应用文写作及听力训练）等形式呈现，为学生深入探讨在学习生活中遇到的问题及相应的解决方案提供素材。基于语篇，学生开展了听、说、读、看、写等学习活动，顺利地达成了本课的教学目标。

本节课的教学设计与课堂教学均达到了很好的效果。比较成功的地方有：①素材选择有代表性，教学设计创新，教学重点突出，教学效果明显；②教师教态亲切自然，全英文授课，口语标准流利，师生互动良好，课堂气氛活跃；③全方位对学生进行写作技能指导，结合单元话题和词汇，多维度对学生进行强化训练，学生参与课堂的积极性高。

（四）课例评析4：廖敏

吴碧华老师依托人教新课标版教材Book 2 Unit 2 The Olympic Games的主题，进行了单元主题下的邀请信写前写作指导的课例展示。基于课题研究的写作教学模式，吴老师以一曲激情高昂的里约奥运会的主题曲导入新课，成功地点燃了学生的热情，自然地引出了写作主题。在授课过程中，吴老师给学生提供了五个与本节课授课重点相关的语篇，包含口头和书面等多模态语篇。语篇以整体感知、具体分析、实践操作等形式呈现，为学生深入探讨在学习生活中遇到的问题及相应的解决方案提供素材。基于语篇，学生开展了听、说、读、看、写等学习活动，顺利地达成了本课的教学目标。

吴老师的课堂通过精心设计的教学活动，实现了"输入—内化——输出"的教学过程，并通过设计真正体现以学生为主体、教师为主导的小组合作的课堂活动，让英语学科核心素养在写作课中真正落地。

附：学生习作

学生习作1：

Dear Henry,

How are you doing? In order to inspire students' love for sports and build everybody up, our school decides to hold the school sports meeting next week. I know you are interested in sports, so I'm writing to invite you to watch the games.

Here is a brief schedule about it. The meeting will be held in the school stadium from Dec. 3rd to Dec. 10th. There will be many sports items to be held, such as running, basketball game, high jump. Athletes from different classes are to take part in it. Every class will design a class flag with a special motto to stand for their class. The Top 3 will be awarded with gold, silver and bronze medals in every event.

We will be very happy if you could join us. I'm looking forward to your early reply.

Yours,

Li Hua

学生习作2：

Dear Henry,

How is everything going? In order to stimulate students' love for sports and strengthen their bodies, our school will hold a sports meeting. I know you are interested in sports, so I am writing to invite you to watch the games.

The school sports meeting will be held on the playground next weekend for two days. There are many events to be held, such as running, long jump, high jump. Athletes from each class will compete in the games. Gold, silver and bronze medals will be awarded to the top three in each event. Each class has its own symbol which is shown through the class flag with a specific motto on it. I believe your presence will add more fun to the activity.

I would be more than happy to see you on that day. I am looking forward to your early reply.

Yours,

Li Hua

学生习作3：

Dear Henry,

In order to inspire our love for sports and build us up, our school is going to hold the school sports meeting in the stadium next weekend. Knowing that you are interested in sports, I'm writing to invite you to join us.

Here is a brief schedule. The opening ceremony starts at 7:30 a.m. next Saturday. After that, various sports events like running, high jump, long jump will begin as scheduled. Athletes from each class will compete in different events. Only the top 3 will be awarded with gold, silver and bronze medals. The class flags with different mottoes stand for different classes. Your participation will surely make the activity much more meaningful.

I would appreciate it if you could confirm your participation at your earliest convenience. We are all looking forward to seeing you!

Yours,
Li Hua

Book 3 Unit 2 Healthy Eating

设计者姓名：廖敏

设计者所在单位：广东省清远市第二中学

一、教学材料分析

授课年级：高一

教材内容：人教新课标版Book 3 Unit 2 Healthy Eating

主题：人与自我——健康的生活方式

课型：应用文写作

课时：1课时

二、教学内容分析

【What】

本节课的活动设计是写中和写后综合，重点在于通过写中的各项活动激发学生进行英文输出的热情。本堂课的主题是"写一封建议信"，介绍"healthy eating"的相关知识，如"junk food""green food"等，并且学习建议信"hamburger"结构，开头、结尾句式，以及主体段的组织方式。

【Why】

启发学生从人与自我、人与社会的角度思考"healthy eating"对健康生活方式的意义。

【How】

本堂课首先通过单元话题导入，用旧知识带出新知识，接着组织学生以头脑风暴的方式储备与本次应用文写作主题相关的词汇，激发其写作兴趣。在充分做好词汇铺垫的基础上鉴赏范文，引领学生观察并总结建议信的主体段落结构。其次，本堂课的重点是让学生观察图片，按照给出的写作要求进行分组讨论，并给出减肥的可行性建议。再次，各个学习小组分工合作，分别负责开头段、中间段和结尾段的写作。各自完成之后，同学们开始玩"拼文游戏"，即拿着自己的段落去寻找"文友"，三人一组，凑成一篇完整的建议信。最后，教师点评2~3组的作品，先由该小组选出代表朗诵全文，教师再展示建议信评价量表，引导学生领会一篇好的应用文应达到什么样的写作标准。

三、学情分析

学生通过对本单元前面板块的学习，对"healthy eating"已经有了一定的了解。大部分学生已经掌握了本单元的相关词汇，并初步懂得了这些词汇的含义和基本用法，但也有部分同学对建议信这一文体还不熟悉，不知如何动笔。以上情况决定了教师需要搭建一些"脚手架"，通过教学活动的设计，为学生提供一些词汇、句型和写作技巧上的支持。在写作活动写后评价环节，教师还设计了小组合作、师生合作、生生合作的活动，最终让学生顺利完成写作任务，并达成完成写后评价与拓展的任务目标。

四、教学目标

（1）Master some useful expressions concerning the topic of "healthy eating".

（2）Master the skills of writing a letter of advice.

（3）Take action to keep a balanced diet in your daily life.

五、教学重点、难点

Important points：

（1）Stimulate students to have a good understanding of how to write a letter of advice.

（2）Cultivate students to write a letter of advice properly and concisely.

Difficult points：

（1）Discover the structure of the letter of advice.

（2）Master some useful expressions concerning the letter of advice.

（3）Develop students' writing ability.

六、教学过程

Teaching Activities	Activity Designs		Purposes
	Teacher's Activities	Students' Activities	
Lead-in	1.Present a short clip of video and ask Ss to brainstorm some words 2.Check the homework	1.Watch the video and brainstorm some words about junk food and green food 2. Blank filling What's a "balanced diet"	To let Ss be prepared for the vocabulary related to healthy eating
Activity 1: Fast reading	Present Ss a sample essay and instruct them to notice the structure	Individual work: Read the essay and discover the structure of the advice letter	To highlight the structure
Activity 2: Detailed reading	Guide Ss to study the key points in letter writing	Individual work: Read, discover and think	To let Ss know and notice the main tense, person and the word limit of the advice letter
Activity 3: Study the organization	Ask Ss to discuss "What suggestions would you like to give Brown？"	Group work: Discussion	To let Ss think about possible, reasonable and practical suggestions
Activity 4: Writing	1.Ask Ss to write their respective parts 2.Ask Ss to combine their own writing parts with other two partners and make them a whole	Individual & Group work: Groups 1 & 2: Para. 1 Groups 3 & 4: Para. 2 Groups 5 & 6: Para. 3	1. To apply the words and phrases to writing 2. To use the right structure and the suggestions they discussed before 3. To develop expressing skills in writing 4. To develop the ability of using language

续 表

Teaching Activities	Activity Designs		Purposes
	Teacher's Activities	Students' Activities	
Activity 5: Show time	1.Choose and show some groups' writings 2. Show Ss the checklist of writing	Share their writing with the whole class	To learn how to appreciate and access a writing
Summary and homework	1.Summarize what has been learned in the class 2.Assignments: 【Must】(1) Polish your writing (2) Assess another group's writing according to the given checklist 【Optional】Development reading		1.Develop students' ability in while-writing and post-writing 2.Consolidate what has been covered in the class
Blackboard design	Struture of a letter of advice { beginning: writing purpose main body: specific advice + supporting reasons ending: hope/expectations Uscful expressions of a letter of advice: 1. I am writing to express my views concerning ... 2. My suggestions are as follows. 3. I hope you will find these suggestions/proposals helpful/practical/useful.		

七、教学特色

特色1：写中课堂活动丰富多彩，小组合作学习形式多样。讨论、拼文、小组报告等课堂活动充分调动了每一个学生的枳极性。

特色2：写后引入写作评价量表并引导学生进行同伴互评，有效地提高了学生的写作能力。

特色3：渗透生活常识，倡导健康生活理念。

附：参考佳作

Dear Brown,

I am writing to express my views concerning your obesity, which disturbs you so much. I hope you could lose some extra calories after taking my suggestions.

First, you should have a balanced diet, which generally includes proper amounts of fish, meat, vegetables, fruit as well as main food. Second, remember to eat less snacks and junk food because they contain much sugar and fat and make you fat and weak. Besides, you had better have meals regularly, and don't skip breakfast.

I hope you will find these proposals useful and I am ready to see you become healthy and build up a strong body soon.

Yours,

Li Hua

Book 3 Unit 5 Canada— "The True North"

设计者姓名：胡翠娥

设计者所在单位：广东省清远市第二中学

一、教学材料分析

授课年级：高一

教材内容：人教新课标版Book 3 Unit 5 Canada— "The True North"

主题：人与自然——自然生态［主要国家（城市）地理概况］

课型：写作课

课时：1课时

二、教学内容分析

本节课是基于人教新课标版教材Book 3 Unit 5 Canada— "The True North"阅读文本 "A Trip on 'The True North'" （Page 34）的写作课。写作的话题是 "地点介绍（how to introduce a place）"。

教师基于教材单元主题与话题给学生播放了一个3～4分钟的介绍加拿大的

自然地理和人文地理的视频（观中任务：快速记录视频中介绍了加拿大的哪些自然地理和人文地理），作为写前Lead-in的口头语篇；把教材语篇改编成一篇介绍加拿大的短文，同时把介绍地点的重要短语设空，作为写前Lead-in的书面语篇；结合学生亲身经历（新西兰姐妹学校师生交流活动）原创一个真实的写作语境。

《高中英语课标》指出，语言教学中的语篇通常以多模态形式呈现，既包括口头的和书面的，也包括音频的和视频的。不同的语篇类型为学生接触真实社会生活中丰富的语篇形式提供机会，也为教师组织多样的课堂学习活动提供素材。

教师在认真研读和分析教材语篇后，根据学情和教学内容的需要科学处理和改编课内教材，大胆选择课外视频形式的语篇，灵活选用另一版本（北师大版）的教材相关主题与话题的语篇，通过一系列的听、说、读、看、写活动，使学生接触真实多样的语篇材料和语篇形式，实现了引导学生整合语言知识、发展语言技能、形成文化意识、运用学习策略的目标。

三、学情分析

学生来自高一年级，整体水平为中等。学生通过对本单元教材语篇的听、说、读课型的学习，已对加拿大的自然地理和人文地理有了比较清晰的认知，也从阅读语篇中获取了大量的语言知识信息。绝大部分学生作为清远人，对清远的自然地理和人文地理很熟悉，在学习理解上基本没有困难，但是学生对与本节课（写作课）相关的知识结构的认识并不系统和全面，运用英语连贯性地介绍、评价事物的能力普遍较弱。这对学生实现语言知识和文化知识内化，巩固新的知识结构，基于新的知识结构通过自主合作探究的方式综合运用语言技能进行迁移创新有一定的阻碍，需要教师进行更进一步的语言输入和学法指导。

四、教学目标

1. 语言能力

（1）通过本节课的学习，学生能够运用常用的介绍地点的重要短语及词语：be located in, largest, cover an area of, cold/ warm, be rich in, have a population of, be famous for ...

（2）学生能够运用常用的"回复信件"的句式结构：

I'm glad to receive your letter saying ... / I'm glad to know from your letter that ...

I'm writing to introduce it to you.

I sincerely invite you to come to Qingyuan again

I can't wait to see you here again.

I am looking forward to your coming here.

If time permits, I will go to New Zealand to see you./Time permitting, I will go ...

Best wishes to you.

（3）学生能够掌握日常生活中常见应用文（回复信）的基本格式、结构及语言特点。

（4）学生能够通过多模态（视频，改编、原创、教材精选的语篇，思维导图，鱼骨图，照片等）发展听、说、读、看、写的语言技能。

2. 学习能力

学生能够强化良好的学习习惯（如写前观看视频并快速记笔记的习惯）；学会通过观察语篇自主发现有用信息；学会制作思维导图（如何介绍加拿大）或鱼骨图（回复信结构）使知识结构化；通过小组合作学习的方法开展学习（写后互评和修改）。

3. 思维品质

学生能够通过所听、所看（视频）、所读（教师根据教材语篇改编）梳理语篇、概括有用信息（介绍地点）；能够分析、推断逻辑关系，建构新概念（介绍清远）；能够结合回复信的语言特点大胆、创造性地表达自己的观点（清远很美，值得再来等）；能够通过评判同伴的作品，指出其优点和不足之处，以形成批判性思维。

4. 文化品格

通过三个语篇，学生能够更多、更全面地了解加拿大、新西兰和自己的家乡清远，拓宽国际视野；通过比较异同（新西兰的奥克兰和中国的清远），能够认同优秀文化，增强国家认同和家国情怀。

五、教学重点、难点

重点：学会运用语言知识以回复信的形式向外国笔友介绍自己的家乡。

难点：在运用语言知识的同时拓展相关信息，体现回复信文体和作者的读者意识。

六、教学设计理念

本节课的设计理念是：基于教材主题与话题和英语学习活动观，依托多模态话语进行高中英语过程性写作教学。

《高中英语课标》指出，主题为语言学习提供主题范围或主题语境。主题语境不仅规约着语言知识和文化知识的学习范围，还为语言学习提供意义语境，并有机渗透情感、态度和价值观。多模态形式呈现的语篇承载着语言知识和文化知识，传递着文化内涵和价值取向，不同的语篇类型为学生接触真实社会生活中的语篇形式提供机会。

《高中英语课标》还指出，英语学习活动的设计应注意以下几个问题：情境创设要尽量真实，注意与学生已有的知识和经验建立紧密联系；教师要善于利用多种工具和手段，如思维导图或信息结构图，引导学生完成对信息的获取与梳理，教会学生归纳和提炼基于主题的新知识结构；教师要善于提出从理解到应用、从分析到评价等有层次的问题；教师要根据所学主题内容、学习目标和学生经验等，选择和组织不同层次的英语学习活动。

20世纪80年代，研究第二语言教学的学者，如美国的瑞姆斯（Raimes）、扎姆（Zamel）和英国的赫奇（Hedge）都倡导将"过程法"应用到第二语言的写作教学中。过程教学法的理论基础是交际理论（Interaction Theory），它认为写作实际上是一种群体间的交际活动，而不是写作者的单独活动。它将教学的重点放在学生的写作过程和写作能力上，充分培养学生的思维能力，强调教师对学生写作策略的培养和对学生写作过程的全程指导。过程性写作（Process Writing）教学一般分为写前准备阶段、写中阶段、写后修改（Revising）和编辑（Editing）阶段。它是针对传统的无自由创作空间、机械输入输出的结果教学法而产生的。

基于这几点，教师在本节课中，基于教材主题与话题，通过几个语篇（视频、教材改编、原创和选自北师大版教材的语篇）创设与主题内容［人与自然——自然生态：主要国家（城市）地理概况］和学生生活（与新西兰姐妹学校师生交流、向笔友介绍自己的家乡清远）密切相关的语境，激发学生参与活动的兴趣，调动学生已有的基于该主题的经验，以思维导图（如何介绍加拿大）和鱼骨图（回复信结构）的形式帮助学生建构和完善新的知识结构。整节课Pre-writing — While-writing — Post-writing环节任务设计层层递进，通过一系列关联主题的语言学习和思维活动，培养学生的语言理解和表达能力，推动学生的深度学习，实现知识迁移。

七、教学过程

Stage	Activity	Activity Aims	Activity Description
I. Warming-up	1. Watch the video 2.Talk about what is mentioned about Canada in the video	通过视听形式（视频）创设语境，导入主题，激活学生已有的关于"加拿大的自然地理和人文地理"的认知和经验，帮助学生进行充分的写前语言输入；同时帮助学生更进一步地了解加拿大的自然地理和人文地理，拓展学生的知识面	Ss watch the video and talk about what they watched in the video about Canada's geography and humanity
II. Revision	1.Complete the passage adapted from the reading passage on Page 34 and the video 2.Make up a mind map of how to introduce Canada according to the adapted passage and the video	基于教材语篇原创一道填空练习，激活学生已有的认识和经验。其一，帮助学生进一步熟悉教材语篇；其二，引导学生重点关注通常从哪些方面描述地点和描述地点（加拿大）的常用表达；其三，引导学生关注如何围绕话题把各种细节有序地组织起来。引导学生学会在学习活动中发现、理解并处理重点信息，建构对加拿大国家概况的整体认知，为下面环节学生运用所学知识创造性地介绍清远（写作任务）奠定语言、思维和文化基础	Ss complete the passage, check up the answers and make up a mind map in groups

Stage	Activity	Activity Aims	Activity Description
Ⅲ. Pre-writing	1.Show some photos taken at the Exchange & Sharing Session of New Zealand Sister School 姐妹学校师生交流 2. Create the writing situation	展示2019年××新西兰姐妹学校师生到清远市第二中学交流的照片。直观的照片里学生熟悉的人物（同学和自己）一下子吸引了学生的注意力，使学生倍感亲切和兴奋。这时老师不失时机地引出写作材料，创设真实的写作情境	1.Ss watch the photos and feel excited 2.Teacher leads the Ss to create the writing situation
Ⅳ. While-writing	1.Analyze of the writing material —SPORTS (Style, Person, Organizing; Reader, Tense, Structure) 2.Make the outline of the writing (the beginning, the body and the ending) Beginning　Body　　Ending 3.Two Ss deal with the beginning and the ending orally (How to begin and end the response letter) 4. The body part (Show Ss some photos of Qingyuan before their parctice)	1.帮助学生在正式写作之前认真思考作文的文体、人称、时态、写作对象、写作要点，根据文体和写作要点以图示形式（鱼骨图）构思文章结构并确定各部分的写作要点信息，给予学生充分的写作指导 2.引领学生重建对回复信的开头结尾、写作意图、邀请、承诺、祝愿的已有记忆性知识，为完成完整的写作做铺垫 3.用学生身边熟悉的事物（家乡清远）创设真实的写作情境，让学生人人有话可说，激发学生参与写作的兴趣，引领学生了解和掌握写作任务（介绍清远）应该从哪些方面展开、按照什么方式呈现	Ss analyze the writing material and deal with the beginning and ending of the response letter with the help of the teacher. And then begin to practise writing alone after enjoying some photos of Qingyuan's geography and humanity

Stage	Activity	Activity Aims	Activity Description
Ⅳ. While-writing	 chicken　　hot spring Body: Humanity history　language　population 　　　Cantonese （PPT展示）	4.学生根据从前面层层铺垫的各环节中获取的知识开始写作。基于课堂时长的考虑，学生只需完成回复信主体部分（介绍清远）。但是，学生要注意根据文体和写作对象来取舍前面铺垫过的写作内容（是写信给笔友，而不是单纯地介绍清远），培养学生获取信息、整合内化信息的能力，让学生学会分析问题和解决问题，发展学生的语言能力和学习能力	
Ⅴ. Post-writing	1. Revising (Checklist—PANTS: Person; Agreement; Number; Tense; Structure, Sentence patterns & Spelling) 2. Presentation （学生的课堂生成） 3. A student's commenting on the writing 	1.学生根据给出的提示以自改、同伴互改的形式从语言和内容方面进行修改和检查，成为习作训练的主人。在这个评价过程中，学生自我反思、自主学习和合作学习的能力得到提升 2.展示学生课上即时生成的作文并由一名学生从语言方面进行点评（好的方面和需改进的地方），教师进行辅助点评，最后全班在教师的引领下从内容方面进行点评。作文被当堂展示，学生的自信心和写作积极性可以得到极大的提高。有机会当"点评师"，学生口头表达、分析判断和解决问题的能力也得到培养	Ss revise the writing for a few minutes. Teacher presents a student's writing and gets another student to comment on the writing

续 表

Stage	Activity	Activity Aims	Activity Description
VI. Homework	1.Finish the whole writing in the composition exercise-books 2. Extended learning A reading passage from Module 2 Unit 4 Lesson 4 (北师大版) in the hand-out: 1）Underline the useful expressions used to describe Auckland 2）Compare Auckland with Qingyuan (a table for Ss) 3）There is a beautiful and most famous university in Auckland called Auckland University. Would you like to study there after graduating from our school? Why?	1.课上重点完成回复信的主体部分，课后学生需把课上学到的知识内化成整体，达成语用目标 2.用北师大版教材Module 2 Unit 4 Lesson 4语篇让学生进行拓展阅读，同时设计三个学习任务。第一，学生在比较新西兰奥克兰和中国清远异同的过程中延伸学习，体会文化差异。第二，学生通过完成第一个学习任务，强化课堂所学重点之一：语言知识——描述地点的常用表达。学生在完成第一和第二个学习任务后，通过阅读、比较、分析，加深对文化差异的理解，正确认识和对待他国文化，坚定文化自信，增强国家意识，拓宽国际视野	Ss finish the homework after class
VII. A project（Group work)	Suppose your hometown plans to develop tourism. Please make a poster for your hometown to attract more tourists	第一，学生分组（来自同一个地方的分为一组）利用教材、网络等资源收集自己家乡的概况及值得宣传的地方；用自己喜欢的方式把收集到的信息以地图、照片、文字等形式在海报上呈现出来。第二，学生通过参与制作海报，进一步巩固本课的学习内容（话题词汇、如何介绍地点等）。第三，学生在教师的指导下，为家乡的发展出谋划策。学生的语言能力、思维品质、文化意识、学习能力的发展融入学习的整个过程	Ss finish the project in groups in two weeks

八、板书设计

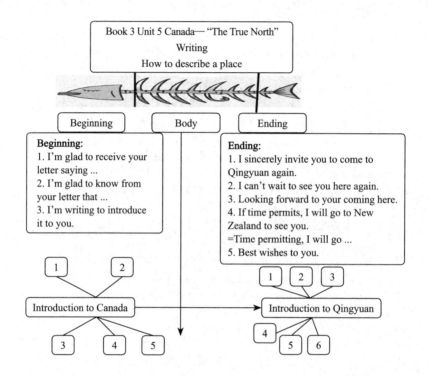

九、教学特色

特色1：基于教材主题与话题的多模态话语

多模态话语分析理论兴起于20世纪90年代的西方国家。多模态话语可以将多种符号模态并用。在多模态教学中，主要强调把多种符号模态（语言、图像、音乐等）引入教学过程，构建完整形象的教学情境，充分调动学生的多种感官，体现了外语教学中注重听、说、读、写、看相结合的特点，激发了学生学习语言的兴趣。正如克雷斯（Kress）所说，在教材、报纸、网络等中，图像正替代语言成为主要的意义构建资源，在"视觉文化的影响下"，动态图像逐渐取代文本用来传递信息。

本节课中，基于教材主题与话题，教师运用多模态话语包括口语、视频、图像等"视听动态资源"和教材改编语篇、原创语篇、选自北师大版教材的语篇等，创设与主题内容［人与自然——自然生态：主要国家（城市）地理概况兰〕和学生生活（与新西兰姐妹学校师生交流、向笔友介绍自己的家乡清远）密切相关的语境，激发学生参与活动的兴趣，调动学生已有的基于该主题的经验，以思维导图（如何介绍加拿大）和鱼骨图（回复信结构）的形式帮助学生建构和完善新的知识结构。教师全程指导、帮助学生完成语篇输出。

特色2：体现过程性写作教学模式

过程教学法的理论基础是交际理论，它认为写作实际上是一种群体间的交际活动，而不是写作者的单独行动。它将教学的重点放在学生的写作过程和写作能力上，充分培养学生的思维能力。教师的指导也始终贯穿整个写作过程，包括构思、写提纲、写初稿和修改等各个写作环节，直至最后成文。

整节课，教师设计的Pre-writing—While-writing—Post-writing等环节层层递进，巧妙铺垫，通过一系列关联主题的语言学习和思维活动，培养学生的语言理解和表达能力，推动学生的深度学习，帮助学生实现知识迁移。

附1：写作情境

假设你是李华，上个星期新西兰姐妹学校Kaikorai Valley College到你校交流。你交到的笔友Jenny回国后写信给你，说她非常喜欢清远以及在清远吃过的美食，她想更多地了解清远，并邀请你去新西兰。请你用英语给她写一封回信，内容包括：

（1）清远的地理（位置、气候、自然资源等）；

（2）清远的人文（历史、旅游、人口、语言等）；

（3）邀请她再来清远并答应有机会一定应邀。

附2：参考佳作

Dear Jenny,

I am glad to hear that you like our Qingyuan and that you'd like to know more about it. Now I will tell you something I hope you will be interested in.

It is located in the north of Guangdong Province and it is a large city. It is young, only about 30 years old and has a population of about 3.87 million. It is neither too cold in winter nor too hot in summer. Much of the city is covered with trees and grass so you can enjoy the beautiful scenery all the year round. If you come here in spring you can see our special city flower which is like a bird. As for food, our Qingyuan is famous for its chicken. Once you taste it, you will never forget it. Of course there are many other kinds of delicious food. It is also known for its hot springs which will make you relaxed mentally and physically. Interestingly, most people here speak a dialect called Cantonese just like your Maori. In a word, Qingyuan is really a place worth your visit.

Book 4 Unit 5 Theme Parks

设计者姓名：何玉琼

设计者所在单位：广东省清远市第三中学

一、教学材料分析

授课年级：高一

教材内容：人教新课标版Book 4 Unit 5 Theme Parks

主题：人与社会——主题公园

课型：写作课

课时：1课时

二、教学内容分析

【What】

本单元以主题公园（Theme Parks）为话题，旨在通过单元教学，使学生了解世界各地的各种各样的主题公园，学会向别人介绍某个主题公园的大体情况，以及设计各项活动，同时培养学生热爱生活的情感。

【Why】

主题公园这一话题贴近学生生活，在现实生活中，学生有向外国友人交流、介绍主题公园的需要，因此，有必要培养学生的这一语言能力，并使学生能通过写作，表达与主题公园相关的内容。

【How】

本节课以单元整体教学为主要设计思路，设计了基于本单元话题的写作课——How to describe a theme park，与应用文（推荐信）写作相结合，让学生在巩固话题相关内容、语块、句型的同时，搭建推荐信的写作框架，提高写作能力。

三、学情分析

学生英语基础一般，作文平均分为9分（满分15分），有一定的语言表达能力，思维比较活跃，大多数学生在课堂上的参与度较高。由于基础不够扎实，学生在进行书面表达时往往存在审题不仔细、信息点不完整、表达不准确、行文不够流畅等问题。

学生通过对本单元教材语篇的听、说、读课型的学习，已对单元主题——Theme Parks有了比较清晰的认知，也从阅读语篇与单元学习中获取了相关的语言知识信息，有一定的话题词汇与背景知识储备。

四、教学目标

单元目标：本单元主题是"人与社会——主题公园"。主题公园作为当今社会人们主要休闲、娱乐场所之一，是一个非常贴近生活、具有时代性、可深度挖掘的教学主题。本单元以主题公园为背景，围绕"a world of fun"开展听、说、读、看、写多种教学活动，贴近学生生活，鼓励学生探索人与自然、人与社会的和谐发展，有利于培养学生积极的生活态度。阅读部分"Theme Parks—Fun and More Than Fun"围绕主题公园展开，需要学生阅读一篇包含三个主题公园宣传介绍的语篇，学生读后完成介绍公园的短文，通过写作表达与公园主题意义相关的内容。

本节目标：到本节课结束时，学生能够：

（1）掌握与单元主题"人与社会——主题公园"相关的背景知识、词汇、句型。

（2）能够运用与本单元主题相关的表达完成一封推荐主题公园的信。

（3）能够了解并欣赏国内外著名的主题公园，并有条理地介绍主题公园。

五、教学重点、难点

重点：

（1）掌握与单元主题"人与社会——主题公园"相关的背景知识、词汇、句型；

（2）描写主题公园和写一封推荐信。

难点：

在介绍主题公园的习作中运用一些写作技巧来优化句子。

六、教学过程

Step 1. Lead-in

1. Get Ss to know about the learning objectives of this lesson.

2. Get Ss to enjoy pictures of different types of theme parks and summarize the different themes.

（amusement theme park，marine/wild animal theme park，history/culture theme park，science theme park，movies/cartoons theme park）

Purpose：导入教学目标；通过图片，直观呈现主题公园的不同主题，激发学生回忆起本单元主题：theme parks 带给人们的不仅仅是娱乐，还有各种各样的知识和激动人心的新体验。

Step 2. Pre-writing

Task 1: Guide the Ss to analyze the paragraph (Paragraph 2 on P34) selected from the text.

The theme park you are probably most familiar with is Disneyland. It can be found in several parts of the world. It will bring you into a magical world and make your dreams come true, whether you are travelling through space, visiting a pirate ship or meeting your favourite fairy tale or Disney cartoon character. As you wander around the fantasy amusement park, you may see Snow White or Mickey Mouse in a parade or on the street. Of course Disneyland also has many exciting rides, from giant swinging ships to terrifying free-fall drops. With all these attractions, no wonder tourism is increasing wherever there is a Disneyland. If you want to have fun and more than fun, come to Disneyland!

Information we can get: name, location, theme, activities, feelings

Task 2: Guide the Ss to draw a mind map of how to describe a theme park.

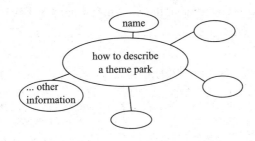

Task 3: Review some useful expressions used to describe a theme park.

1. 主题公园_____

2. 过山车_____

3. 刺激的游乐设施_____

4. 令人恐惧的跳楼机_____

5. 海盗船_____

6. 欢乐公园_____

7. 巡游_____

8. 各种各样的_____

9. 因……而出名_____

10. 熟悉_____

11. 使你实现梦想_____

12. 尽情玩乐并有更多收获_____

13. 最独特的主题公园之一_____

14. 模仿_____

15. 在室内外剧场_____

Purpose：这三个写前任务旨在让学生回归课本、回顾话题。课文中三个 theme park 的介绍段落结构都很对称。课中引导学生对课文阅读文本的段落进行分析，用思维导图呈现介绍theme park所要包含的信息，并引导学生关注选取段落的语言特色。引导学生回顾、掌握本单元话题的写作语块（基于学情，本话题useful expressions 中的单词、短语全部来自P34课文），为之后的写作活动做好词汇铺垫。

Step 3. While-writing

1. Ask Ss to read the writing background.

2. Guide Ss to discuss in groups and decide what information they will choose to write in their letters, sharing their own reasons.

Writing Task:

Suppose you are Li Hua and your American pen pal Jenny sent you a letter telling she plans to travel to Guangdong next summer holiday. She really wants to pay a visit to one of the theme parks in Guangdong, and she is asking you to recommend one theme park for her.

Now you decide to recommend the Shenzhen Happy Valley to her.

> **深圳欢乐谷**
>
> 占地面积35 000平方米，融参与性、娱乐性、趣味性为一体，中国最佳主题公园之一，共分为西班牙广场、卡通城、冒险山、欢乐岛、金矿镇等八大主题区。有100多个老少皆宜、丰富多彩的游乐项目，还从美国、荷兰等国家引入众多全国乃至亚洲独有的项目。连续四年荣膺亚太十大主题公园，是中国主题公园行业的领跑者。拥有如中国第一座悬挂式过山车"雪山飞龙"、亚洲最高过山车"全球至尊弹射式过山车"等项目。
>
> 开放时间
>
> 09：30～22：00；停止售票时间：20：30；停止入场时间：21：00（1月1日～12月31日，周一～周日）；tips：夜场开放时间18：00～22：00
>
> 门票信息
>
> 全价票：230人民币；夜场票：100人民币（1月1日~12月31日周一~周日）
>
> 游玩时长
>
> 1天
>
> 地址
>
> 广东省深圳市

Purpose：通过小组讨论，让学生就写作材料（深圳欢乐谷的相关信息）进行交流，选择、梳理写作要点，并以思维导图的形式呈现出来，为接下来的个人写作确定写作内容。

Task 1: Guide the Ss to think about the style, the person, the writing contents, the language style, tense and the structure, using "SPORTS" rules.

SPORTS

Style: _____   Person: _____

Organizing: _____   Reader: _____

Tense: _____   Structure: _____

Task 2: Guide the Ss to make an outline of the whole letter.

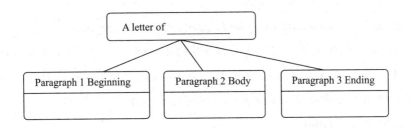

Purpose：以图示形式帮助学生在正式开始写作之前认真思考作文的文体、人称、时态、写作对象、写作要点，让学生根据文体和写作要点构思文章结构，确定各部分的写作要点信息。

Task 3: Beginning & Ending

1. Ask the Ss to fill in the blanks using the correct forms of given words.

2. Help the Ss work out the useful sentence patterns written in the beginning or ending of a recommendation letter.

Beginning:

1. _____ that ..., I'd like to _____ ... to you. I hope you'll be interested in it.

2. _____ (delight) to know that you are coming to visit China, I think _____ a good choice to ...

3. I'm happy to learn that you show great _____ (prefer) for ..., I strongly recommend ... to you.

Ending:

1. I do hope that you can consider my _____ (recommend) and it can be of great help for your decision.

2. I'll be _____ (extreme) delighted if you can take my recommendation into consideration.

3. I hope you will find my recommendation _____ (help).

Purpose：学生在之前已经接触过推荐信，对推荐信的内容框架和常用句式已有印象。因此，本节课引导学生回顾推荐信的开头和结尾需要用到的范式句型，为完成完整的写作做铺垫，提高学生的语用能力。挖空处是学生的易错点或句型中的核心词汇，设空以加强学生记忆。

Task 4: Writing (the main body)

Get the Ss to finish the writing individually in the limited time.

Purpose：让学生独立完成本次推荐信的主体部分——介绍深圳欢乐谷。在写前环节，完成本节课话题的写作词汇、相关表达的积累，以及推荐信写作框架的搭建之后，让学生限时完成主体段落的输出写作。

Step 4. Post-writing

1. Present several students' writings.

2. Ask the Ss to focus on the contents and language and choose the best one they think.

3. Lead the Ss to have a discussion and summarize the ways of writing impressive sentences to introduce a theme park.

Tips: Use adjectives to provide details, use modifiers (修饰语) to emphasize and echo the topic.

Purpose：借助希沃授课助手直观展示学生习作，引导学生通过评价他人的作文，关注写作内容的逻辑性、合理性，以及在关注语言的正确性的基础上发现优秀习作中的亮点，提升学生的鉴赏、辨析、判断能力。同时，提醒学生关注并思考"how to write impressive sentences to introduce a theme park"，为下节课引导学生润色习作做铺垫。

Step 5. Homework

Task 1: Get the Ss to finish or polish their writing.

Task 2: Get the Ss to exchange their writing with other group members and make comments. Ask the Ss mark at least three good expressions while checking.

Offer the Ss an optional project: Make use of Automatic Speech Recognition (ASR) to transfer the letter to words.

Purpose：根据学情，让部分学生完成课堂上未写完的文章，写完的同学则完成作文的润色。一方面，让学生组内交流互改，培养学生的批判性思维，鼓励学生发现并学习他人写作中的亮点（至少找三处好词好句）。另一方面，为学有余力的学生提供选做作业，让学生利用一些能识别语音的App或技术手段，如讯飞输入法，把自己的作文经由口头语言转化成书面语言，让写作变得更加好玩，激发学生学习英语的兴趣，全面提高学生的英语综合能力。

七、主要教学活动

写前环节：立足学情，通过对课文中描写迪士尼乐园（Disneyland）段落的分析及思维导图引导学生归纳介绍主题公园所需要涵盖的主要内容。此外，回顾单元话题词汇，帮助学生检测话题词汇的掌握程度，扫清学生写作障碍。

写作环节：创设"为美国笔友珍妮（Jenny）推荐一座广东的主题公园——深圳欢乐谷"这一写作情境。大部分学生都有去欢乐谷游玩的体验，因此对这一写作情境有共鸣。在引导学生分析写作材料和搭建推荐信的写作框架后，要求学生在文体写作（推荐信）的框架下结合"主题公园"话题内容进行限时语言输出。本次写作采用开放式命题，给学生提供的是深圳欢乐谷的相关信息，兼顾学生的不同学情。对于英语基础好的学生，为他们开发个人主题（决定个人写什么）留有较大的余地；对于基础不佳的学生，需要他们根据写前归纳的思维导图进行写作内容的整合。

写后环节：展示一至两篇学生习作（初稿），在课堂上给予口头反馈和全班集体讨论反馈。

八、板书设计

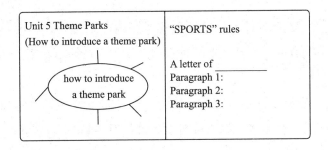

九、教学特色

特色1：其一，本节课是基于人教新课标版教材Book 4 Unit 5主题语境"人与自然——主题公园"的一节应用文（推荐信）写作课，主题贯穿整个教学过程。其二，设定的教学目标基本达成，各环节设计基于学情，指导细致，注重学法指导。其三，基本符合过程性写作流程：写前输入—写中教师指导、学生训练—写后展示。其四，各个环节的教学任务层层递进，由词到句到篇，由浅入深，由易到难，符合学生语言学习渐进性的特点，为学生进行语言输出（写）做好充分铺垫。

特色2：其一，写前以直观图片、基于教材的语篇、思维导图形式的知识结构图引入，有意识地利用多模态语篇对学生进行看（viewing）和读（reading）等理解性技能训练。其二，注重学生小组合作，让学生根据教师提供的关于深圳欢乐谷的材料选择写作要点，属于半开放式设计，体现了教学民主和以学生为主体的意识，由布置学生写什么转变为学生选择写什么，增强了学生的写作动机和兴趣。

十、课例评析

（一）课例评析1：胡翠娥

何玉琼老师的这节课是基于人教新课标版教材Book 4 Unit 5主题语境"人与自然——主题公园"的一节应用文（推荐信）写作课，主题贯穿整个教学过程。设定的教学目标基本达成，各环节设计基于学情，指导细致，注重学法指导。基本符合过程性写作流程：写前输入—写中教师指导、学生训练—写后展示。

亮点：

（1）各个环节教学任务设计层层递进，由词到句到篇、由浅入深、由易到难，符合学生语言学习渐进性的特点，为学生进行语言输出（写）做好充分铺垫。

（2）写前以直观图片、基于教材的语篇、思维导图形式的知识结构图引入，体现了何老师利用多模态语篇对学生进行看（Viewing）和读（Reading）等理解性技能训练的意识。

（3）学生小组合作，根据教师提供的关于深圳欢乐谷的材料选择写作要点，属于半开放式设计，体现了何老师教学民主和以学生为主体的意识，由布置学生写什么转变为学生选择写什么，增强了学生的写作动机和兴趣。

（4）创设真实的交际情境（写作任务），体现了何老师语用意识强。

建议：

（1）当麦克风出现问题时应该及时应变。

（2）给学生提供的关于深圳欢乐谷的信息最好以英语的形式呈现，并加以简化。

（3）最后展示环节可以由学生口头展示改为借助希沃授课助手等信息技术手段进行直观展示，更有利于学生发现和反馈问题。

（二）课例评析2：陈锦春

何玉琼老师以单元整体教学为主要设计思路，设计了基于人教新课标版教材Book 4 Unit 5 Theme Parks的写作课——How to describe a theme park。在写后环节，展示学生习作，提醒学生关注并思考"how to write impressive sentences to introduce a theme park"，为下节课引导学生润色习作留下悬念。

整节课，何老师在每个教学环节都能够密切关注学生的学习动态，循循善诱，很好地完成了本节写作课的任务。

（三）课例评析3：郭秀云

何玉琼老师的这节课是基于人教新课标版教材Book 4 Unit 5主题语境"人与自然——主题公园"的一节应用文（推荐信）写作课，主题贯穿整个教学过程，教学目标基本达成。

亮点：

教师年轻，有活力，基本功扎实，教学语言清晰流利；教学案设计得颇有心思，引入思维导图，帮助学生构建写作框架；整个教学过程流畅，初步达成教学目标。

不足：

首先，发给学生的学案比较零散，有三页，建议整合成一页。其次，其中一页给出推荐信话题词汇和句型的学案，教师没有在课堂上提及，但学案的最后一部分有模仿练习，学生不知道要不要完成。最后，教师给出的写作任务是完成推荐深圳欢乐谷的写作，但提供的深圳欢乐谷信息内容都是中文，而且比较长。

建议：

整节课设计得颇有心思，但在细节处仍有可以改进的地方。例如，在思维导图这处，可以给出一些更细微的指导语，让学生知道往哪方面拓展。此外，最后关于写作的题型，建议给出常规的高考写作题型，效果可能会更好。

（四）课例评析4：叶青容

何玉琼老师这节课是基于人教新课标版教材Book 4 Unit 5主题语境"人与自然——主题公园"的一节应用文（推荐信）写作课。何老师基本功非常扎实，语言素养好，教学过程流畅自如，教学目标达成率高。

亮点：

（1）立足学情，灵活处理教材。何老师从教材文本中截取了关于迪士尼乐园（Disneyland）的文段，学生依托文段能更清楚地了解主题公园的写作结构。

（2）教学设计思路清晰，教学方法多样，注重创设适合学生的任务，注重发展学生思维品质和培养其学习能力。例如，写前任务2以思维导图的方式归纳，更加直观，学生更容易理解，记忆更深刻。又如，写中的任务2，也让学生加强了对写作框架的直观理解，为下一步写作做了很好的铺垫。

（3）在语言输入方面准备充分，给予学生关于推荐信的话题词汇、句型参考。

（4）在创设写作任务方面采用开放式命题，符合高考作文命题趋势。同时给学生创设熟悉的写作主题，让学生有话可写。在语言充分输入的基础上，学生顺利输出，效果更好。

建议：

（1）导学案三页印在一起。

（2）设置作文任务时，按照现高考题型设置。

（五）课例评析5：张伟娟

何玉琼老师的这节课以单元整体教学为主要设计思路，基于人教新课标版教材Book 4 Unit 5主题语境"人与自然——主题公园"设计了一节应用文（推荐信）写作课。整个教学过程流畅、自然，教学目标基本达成。

亮点：

（1）导入部分新颖自然，学生易于接受。本节课，教师没有以传统的教学方法引出所讲的主题，而是把课本语篇改写成一篇介绍迪士尼乐园（Disneyland）的小文段，从而引出写作的主题——如何介绍主题公园。

（2）环环相扣，过渡自然。何老师从课文语篇入手，按name—location—theme—activities层层深入，引领学生分析篇章结构。因此，后面完成"how to introduce a theme park"的思维导图就顺理成章了。

（3）创设贴近学生生活的写作情境，学生写起来得心应手。何老师围绕本单元话题，用纯英文的方式命题，创设了"为美国笔友珍妮（Jenny）推荐一座广东的主题公园——深圳欢乐谷"这一写作情境。大部分学生都有去欢乐谷游玩的体验，因此对这一写作情境有共鸣，写作效果良好。

（4）何老师设计开放式命题作文，符合高考的作文命题趋势，兼顾学生的不同学情，对于英语基础好的学生，为其开发个人主题（决定个人写什么）留有较大的余地，对于基础不佳的同学，需要他们根据写前归纳的思维导图进行写作内容的整合。

不足：

提供给学生的深圳欢乐谷的内容比较零散，不便于学生在有限的时间内快速找到所需信息。

建议：

介绍深圳欢乐谷的部分，可以找一张网上的宣传图片，为学生提供视觉上的输入，也可以播放一个1～2分钟的视频，增加写作前的目的语输入，同时能锻炼学生"看"的能力。

（六）课例评析6：陈艳丽

清远市第三中学的何玉琼老师本次授课内容是基于人教新课标版教材Book 4 Unit 5 Theme Parks 话题的写作课——how to describe a theme park。整堂课的设计以单元整体教学为主要思路，循序渐进地推进。

亮点：

（1）教师基本功扎实，口语流畅，表达准确，与学生的互动也非常好。

（2）本堂课对学情的把握准确，充分体现了复习课以旧带新的特点。导入部分通过回顾课文中描写迪士尼乐园的段落复习相关话题词汇，为即将进行的写作搭建"脚手架"。

（3）写中教师创设了"为美国笔友珍妮（Jenny）推荐一座广东的主题公园——深圳欢乐谷"这一贴近学生生活实际的写作情境。利用深圳欢乐谷的中文介绍让学生根据所学知识自主选择写作内容，兼顾了不同层次学生的水平，让个别基础欠佳的同学，也可以根据写前归纳的思维导图整合写作内容。

建议：

（1）导入部分复习主题公园相关话题词汇时可以按描写的类型来分类，同时可以口头操练部分句子，这样能大幅度降低写作难度。

（2）深圳欢乐谷的中文介绍内容太多且部分内容难以用英语表达，因此，教师课前可以适当删减或改编，使之适合学生发挥。

（七）课例评析7：黄茗旎

何玉琼老师这节课是基于人教新课标版教材Book 4 Unit 5主题语境"人与自然——主题公园"的一节应用文（推荐信）写作课。

亮点：

（1）课前进行单词与语篇输入，所选择材料皆是教材内容，能够帮助学生在繁忙的高一学习中快速定位该单元的重点词汇与句型。

（2）头脑风暴部分向学生介绍不同种类的主题公园，以达到激发学生兴趣的目的。

（3）采用创新的SPORTS写前分析法，并将其作为固定模式长期使用。

（4）写作内容为深圳欢乐谷，为学生熟悉且感兴趣的话题，加上写前的大量输入，使得学生有话可写。

建议：

（1）多页导学案可整合为一页。

（2）设置作文任务时，可以按照现高考题型设置。

（3）写作内容应尽量基于写前输入的词汇、句型。

Book 5 Unit 2 The United Kingdom（一）

设计者姓名：陈锦春

设计者所在单位：广东省清远市第一中学

一、教学材料分析

授课年级：高三

教材内容：人教新课标版Book 5 Unit 2 The United Kingdom

主题：人与自然——国家地理概况

课型：写作复习课

课时：1课时

二、教学内容分析

【What】

本单元语篇是两篇介绍英国人文历史、地理以及著名景点的记叙文。学生通过阅读语篇，对英国的历史文化、名胜古迹有了进一步的了解，掌握了一些关于介绍景点的词汇和句型。本节课是基于教材主题语境和话题设计的推荐旅游景点的写作课。

【Why】

本节课是一节写作课，设计的目的是让学生通过复习Unit 2 The United Kingdom，巩固描写旅游目的地的句型和词汇，让学生在学习理解和应用实践后，实现知识的迁移创新，向外国朋友推荐一个有代表性的中国旅游景点。

【How】

本节课采用过程性写作教学模式，遵循写前—写中—写后的写作步骤。教师采用图片、视频导入的方式，激发学生的学习兴趣，再通过自主学习、合作学习、探究学习等学习方法，引导学生认识写作结构和写作特征。最后学生进行小组合作式写作，并通过评价表进行互评。

三、学情分析

高三学生的英语水平较高，学生有很强的自主学习能力，平时的英语写作平均分约11分（满分15分）。学生对写作的步骤很熟悉，能通过分析语篇来归纳写作结构和写作特征，会灵活运用语篇所提供的句型和词汇进行写作，并能在已有的认知基础上，对同伴的作文进行分析和评价。

四、教学目标

单元目标：

本单元主题是"人与自然——国家地理概况"，话题是"The United Kingdom"。学生通过Warming-Up（热身）、Reading and Comprehending（阅读与理解）、Using Language（语言运用）等板块的学习，对英国的历史文化、名胜古迹等有了进一步的了解。学生通过学习，拓宽国际视野，加深国际理解，提升跨文化沟通能力，形成正确的世界观。

课时目标：

本节课是基于教材主题语境与话题设计的推荐旅游景点的写作课。设计的目的是让学生通过复习Unit 2 The United Kingdom，巩固描写旅游目的地的句型和词汇，向外国朋友推荐一个有代表性的中国旅游景点，培育家国情怀，坚定文化自信。

五、教学重点、难点

重点：

巩固描写旅游目的地的句型和词汇，向外国朋友推荐一个有代表性的中国旅游景点。

难点：

学会用思维导图构建写作结构、确定写作内容。

六、教学过程

Step 1. Lead-in

1. Get the students to talk about the places (cities) that they have ever visited.

2. Get the students to watch a video clip and write down the information they hear.

3. Guide the students to think what tourist destinations they'd like to recommend.

4. Get the students to know about the learning objectives of this lesson.

Purpose：基于单元话题创设教学情境，激活相关话题的词汇，导入教学目标。

Step 2. Pre-writing

1. Get the students to complete the passage according to the given Chinese.

2. Lead the students to work out the structure of the passage.

3. Guide the students to discover the writing features.

4. Help the students work out the useful sentences.

Purpose：通过阅读相关范文，让学生发现并了解推荐信的基本结构和写作特点。引导学生掌握本节课话题的写作词汇、写作模板和相关表达，为接下来的写作活动做好铺垫。

Step 3. While-writing

1. Guide the students to discuss with their group members and decide what to write in each paragraph. Work out a mind map.

2. Get the students to finish the writing individually.

Purpose：通过小组讨论，让学生进行思想交流，梳理写作要点，并将其以思维导图的形式呈现出来，为接下来的小组写作活动搭好框架。

Step 4. Post-writing

1. Guide the students to refer to the writing checklist before making comments.

2. The students exchange their writings with their group members and make comments on them.

3. Get the students to present their writings.

Purpose：通过同伴交流互改，培养学生的批判性思维，鼓励学生发现并学习他人写作中的亮点（找好词好句）。

Step 5. Summary

Help the students make a summary of the writing lesson.

Purpose：回顾本节写作课的学习重点，巩固已学的知识。

Step 6. Homework

1. Get the students to polish their writings.

2. Get the students to finish the exercise.

Purpose：给学生提供了2015年高考的语法填空题，其内容是描写桂林旅游的，紧扣本单元的话题。

七、主要教学活动

这节课主要包括三个教学活动：

一是写前的视频导入，激活话题词汇。用学生的旅游视频导入，创设了真实的教学情境，让学生在轻松愉悦的氛围中复习相关词汇。接着，通过外国朋友的英文视频，引入了这节课的教学目标，使学生形成教学期待。

基于本单元的话题是英国人文历史，设计了一篇"到英国旅游"的推荐信来导入，既让学生了解了推荐信的写作结构、写作特征，又加强了学生对课文语篇的了解。在学习语篇的基础上，引入了相关的写作词汇和写作句型，为接下来的写作任务做好铺垫。

二是写中活用思维导图，搭建写作框架。为了让学生有更清晰的写作思路，让他们的写作内容充实有力，教师通过小组讨论的形式，让学生讨论他们会推荐哪个中国旅游景点给外国朋友，梳理写作要点，并以思维导图的形式呈现出来，为接下来的小组写作活动搭好框架。接着，基于思维导图，学生进行写作。

三是写后的评价活动，促进英语学科核心素养有效养成。写作完成后，设计了同伴互改的环节，既培养学生的批判性思维，鼓励学生发现并学习他人写作中的亮点（找好词好句），又加深了学生对写作评价标准的认识，让他们更客观地评价同伴或者自己的写作。

四是展示学生的作品，并做一些点评。点评后引导学生回顾本节写作课的学习重点，巩固已学知识，并紧扣本单元话题，布置了相关作业。

八、板书设计

Unit 5 The United Kingdom

Writing—How to Write a Letter of Recommendation

Basic Structure	Writing Features
Paragraph 1 _____	Tense: _____
Paragraph 2 _____	Person: _____
Paragraph 3 _____	Language Style: _____
	Linking Words: _____

九、教学特色

特色1：根据学生的学情，设计了以思维导图为中心的写作活动，主要目的是教学生学会围绕写作主题，拓展写作内容，并以思维导图的形式呈现出来，让其写作思路更清晰、更有条理。避免学生在写作中陷入"写作要点不全，结构混乱"的僵局，让学生明白，在写作中，有了写作思路框架的支撑，写作就会变得更简单。

特色2：重视现代信息技术的应用，运用多模态教学形式，丰富英语课程学习资源。使用学生拍的三段旅游视频来引入，创设了真实生动的教学情境，激活了学生已有的知识和经验，铺垫了必要的语言和文化背景知识。

附：学生学习资料

I. 课前任务驱动（单元词汇自测）

1. 旅游景点_____
2. 旅游目的地_____
3. 名胜古迹_____
4. 历史名城_____
5. 历史文化古迹_____
6. 被认为是……_____
7. 因……而著名_____
8. 享有盛名_____
9. 地标性建筑_____
10. 是……的象征_____
11. 更加了解当地文化_____
12. 学习中国历史文化_____
13. 欣赏大自然的美景_____
14. 开阔视野_____
15. 吸引海内外游客_____
16. 起源于……_____

Ⅱ. 课堂师生互动

Step 1. Lead-in

Students talk about the places of interest that they have ever visited.

Step 2. Pre-writing

Task 1: Complete the reading passage according to the given Chinese.

Dear Li Hua,

I am glad to know that you are coming to visit the UK. I'd like to ＿＿＿＿＿＿＿
＿＿＿＿(推荐一个热门旅游地) —London to you. I hope you will ＿＿＿＿＿＿＿(对
它感兴趣).

There are several reasons why I think London is ＿＿＿＿＿＿＿＿＿(一个不
错的选择). As we all know, London, the capital of England, ＿＿＿＿＿＿＿＿＿ (吸
引了众多的海内外游客) every year. As one of the oldest cities in the UK, London
has many ＿＿＿＿＿＿＿＿＿＿(古老建筑), ＿＿＿＿＿＿＿＿＿＿(博物馆),
and ＿＿＿＿＿＿＿＿＿(历史文化古迹), among which London Bridge stands
out as ＿＿＿＿＿＿＿＿＿(地标性建筑).

By visiting London, not only can you enjoy the beautiful landscape, but also you
can learn about British history and ＿＿＿＿＿＿＿＿＿(灿烂的文化).

I hope you can take my recommendation into consideration. I believe you
will ＿＿＿＿＿＿＿＿＿(伦敦会给你留下深刻印象的).

Task 2: Work out the structure of the passage.

Paragraph 1 : ＿＿＿＿＿＿＿＿＿＿＿＿＿＿＿＿＿＿＿＿＿＿＿＿＿＿

Paragraph 2 : ＿＿＿＿＿＿＿＿＿＿＿＿＿＿＿＿＿＿＿＿＿＿＿＿＿＿

Paragraph 3 : ＿＿＿＿＿＿＿＿＿＿＿＿＿＿＿＿＿＿＿＿＿＿＿＿＿＿

Task 3: Discover the writing features.

Tense (时态): ＿＿＿＿＿＿＿＿＿＿＿＿＿＿＿＿＿＿＿＿＿＿＿＿＿＿

Person (人称): ＿＿＿＿＿＿＿＿＿＿＿＿＿＿＿＿＿＿＿＿＿＿＿＿＿＿

Language style (语言特征): ＿＿＿＿＿＿＿＿＿＿＿＿＿＿＿＿＿＿＿＿

Linking words (过渡词): ＿＿＿＿＿＿＿＿＿＿＿＿＿＿＿＿＿＿＿＿＿

Useful sentence patterns:

Paragraph 1: ＿＿＿＿＿＿＿＿＿＿＿＿＿＿＿＿＿＿＿＿＿＿＿＿＿＿

（1）得知你将要来……，我向你推荐一处名胜。我希望你会对它感兴趣。

_____

_____

（2）很高兴知道你要来……旅游，我认为……是不错的选择。

_____

_____

Paragraph 2: _____

（1）我认为……是一个不错的选择，原因有几个。

_____

（2）作为……之一，……（城市）有很多旅游景点，其中……最为突出。

_____

（3）通过参观……，你不仅能……，而且能……。

_____

（4）因……而出名，……是一个理想的旅游目的地。

_____

Paragraph 3: _____

（1）希望你能考虑我的建议。祝你旅途愉快。

_____

（2）希望你能考虑我的建议。我相信……会给你留下深刻的印象。

_____

Step 3. While-writing

假设你是李华，你的美国朋友比尔（Bill）对中国文化很感兴趣，他准备下个月来中国游玩，并向你寻求建议。请你给他写一封邮件，向他推荐一个旅游地。要点如下：

（1）推荐的地方；

（2）推荐的理由；

（3）你的祝愿。

注意：①词数100左右；②可以适当增加细节，以使行文连贯；③开头和结尾已为你写好。

Task 1: Choose a tourist destination that you are going to write about.

Task 2: Discuss with your group members and decide what to write in each paragraph. Work out a mind map.

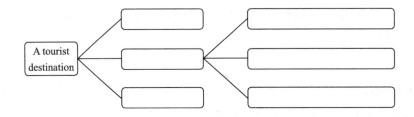

Task 3: Write the main body of the letter.

Dear Bill,

I am delighted to know that you are travelling to China next month. I'd like to recommend a tourist destination—_____ to you. I hope you'll be interested in it.

_____

_____

_____

_____

_____

I hope you can take my recommendation into consideration. And I am sure you will be impressed by its charming beauty.

Yours,

Li Hua

Step 4. Post-writing

Task 1: Peer assessment.

1. Exchange your writing with one of your group members.

2. Make comments on it based on the following criteria.

（1）卷面：The writing looks _____.

A. neat   B. quite good

C. not bad   D. terrible

（2）结构：It is divided into _____ paragraphs.

（3）内容（信息完整）：_____ the key points (写作要点) are included.

A. All of   B. Most of

C. Some of   D. None of

（4）句式：There are _____ good sentences in the writing.

A. many   B. a few

C. few   D. no

Underline two or three good sentences.

（5）词汇：The vocabulary used in the writing is _____.

A. rich   B. enough

C. limited   D. poor

Circle at least five good expressions.

3. Three students form a group. Read out your writing to your group members.

4. Choose the best one.

Task 2: Present your writing.

Step 5. Summary

In this lesson, we have learned ...

1. some useful expressions used to recommend a tourist destination, such

as _____, _____, _____, _____, _____.

2. how to write a letter of _____.

Step 6. Homework

1. Improve your writing.

2. Finish the exercise.

Ⅲ. 课后培育

Yangshuo, China

It was raining lightly when I 1. _____ (arrive) in Yangshuo just before dawn.
But I didn't care. A few hours 2. _____, I'd been at home in Hong Kong, with 3.
_____ (it) choking smog. Here, the air was clean and fresh, even with the rain.

I'd skipped nearby Guilin, a dream place for tourists seeking the limestone
mountain tops and dark waters of the Li River 4. _____ are pictured by artists
in so many Chinese 5. _____ (painting). Instead, I'd head straight for Yangshuo.

95

For those who fly to Guilin, it's only an hour away 6. _____ car and offers all the scenery of the better-known city.

Yangshuo 7. _____ (be) really beautiful. A study of travelers 8. _____ (conduct) by the website Trip Advisor names Yangshuo as one of the top 10 destinations in the world. And the town is fast becoming a popular weekend destination for people in Asia. Abercrombie & Kent, a travel company in Hong Kong, says it 9. _____ (regular) arranges quick getaways here for people 10. _____ (live) in Shanghai and Hong Kong.

十、课例评析

（一）课例评析1：叶青容

陈锦春老师基于人教新课标版Book 5 Unit 2 The United Kingdom的单元话题，结合高考作文题型，设计了一节写作课——how to write a letter of recommendation。教师专业素养高，基本功非常扎实，课堂教学充满激情，课堂气氛活跃。

亮点：

（1）陈老师在导入环节善于创设生活情境，吸引学生的注意力，课堂气氛活跃。

（2）教学设计立足学情，节奏紧张，内容丰富，在写前充分进行语言输入，为接下来的写作活动搭好框架。

（3）写前以思维导图的方式帮助学生梳理写作要点并展示，体现了教师重视对学生思维能力和合作精神的培养。

（4）在写后环节设计了"同伴互改"活动，并给学生提供了作文评价的标准，鼓励学生发现并学习他人写作中的亮点，培养了学生的批判性思维。

（5）在课堂的结尾，陈老师展示了学生的作品，让学生在分享中学到了知识。整节课教学环节设计合理，教学思路非常清晰，课堂活动丰富多彩，使学生积极参与各个教学环节。

（二）课例评析2：张伟娟

陈锦春老师的这节课是基于人教新课标版教材Book 5 Unit 2主题语境——人与自然的一节关于推荐信的写作课，过程性写作贯穿整个教学过程，目标达成度高。

亮点：

（1）注重真实情境的创设，使学生沉浸在话题语境中，体现了英语教学活动观。陈老师先是以学生自己拍摄的"the places of interest that they have ever visited"话题视频巧妙导入这节课，吸引学生的注意力，激发学生的学习兴趣。然后通过播放一段一名美国朋友录制的视频，创设"外国人要来中国旅游，你会向他推荐哪个旅游景点"的真实情境，激活相关话题词汇，导入教学目标。

（2）教学环节设计精妙，一步一台阶，为学生搭建写作"脚手架"。陈老师先让学生读一封推荐去英国旅游的书信，引导学生对范文进行细致、全面的分析，帮助学生掌握本课话题的写作词汇、写作结构和相关表达，为接下来的写作活动搭好框架。

（3）为了让学生的写作思路更加清晰、明确，陈老师让学生进行小组讨论，梳理写作要点，并以思维导图的形式呈现出来，通过可视化方式（思维导图）让学生把写作思路转变为图形图像。最后，学生将其写成一篇完整的文章，使语言得以在输入后继续产出。这样的设计，是相当符合学生的思维习惯的。

（4）陈老师在写作之后，指导学生进行自我评价和小组评价，让学生上台展示了自己的作文。整节课完成得很好。

（三）课例评析3：吴碧华

首先，陈老师以学生自己拍的"他们曾经旅行过的地方"话题视频巧妙导入这节课，激发学生的学习兴趣。其次，陈老师让学生读一封推荐去英国旅游的书信，引导学生以思维导图的形式梳理并呈现写作要点。再次，学生参考思维导图，完成写作任务。最后，在写后环节，陈老师设计了"同伴互改"活动。这节课既充分体现了陈老师所在的清远市第一中学所倡导的"三动教学模式"（课前任务驱动、课堂师生互动、课后培育自动），让学生的学习积极性在每个教学环节都被激发起来，也体现了写前、写中、写后高中英语过程性写作教学模式。

陈老师扎实的教学基本功、别出心裁的教学设计、亲切自然且充满激情的教学风格，给听课者留下了深刻的印象。

附：学生习作

学生习作1：

Dear Bill,

I am delighted to know that you are travelling to China next month. I'd like to recommend a tourist destination—Guilin to you. I hope you'll be interested in it.

There are several reasons why I think Guilin is a good choice for you. As we all know, Guilin is famous for its green mountains and crystal clear water, among which Yangshuo enjoys the highest reputation. As one of the most popular tourist destinations in Asia, it attracts a large number of visitors home and abroad. By taking a boat along the Li River, not only can you breathe in the fresh air, but also you can feel the beauty of nature. Moreover, as the saying goes "East or West, Guilin landscape is the best", Guilin is absolutely a getaway for people.

I hope you can take my recommendation into consideration. And I am sure you will be impressed by its charming beauty.

Yours,

Li Hua

学生习作2：

Dear Bill,

Glad to know that you are paying a visit to China next month. I'd like to recommend a tourist destination—Guilin to you.

As we know, Guilin is a famous city in China. In Guilin, not only can you appreciate the beautiful mountains and clear waters, but also you will see the special karst landform. What's more, Guilin has a famous river, which is called Li River. Boating on it, you will find yourself surrounded by picturesque landscape. The local people are very friendly and they welcome tourists from home and abroad with their hospitality.

I hope you can take my recommendation into consideration. And I am sure you will be impressed by its charming beauty.

Yours,

Li Hua

Book 5 Unit 2 The United Kingdom（二）

设计者姓名：张伟娟

设计者所在单位：广东省清远市第二中学

一、教学材料分析

授课年级：高三

教材内容：人教新课标版Book 5 Unit 2 The United Kingdom

主题：人与自然——国家地理概况

课型：写作课

课时：1课时

二、教学内容分析

【What】

The United Kingdom是人教新课标版必修5第二单元的教学内容。学生通过本单元的学习，可以对英国有一个比较翔实的认识，能够拓宽知识面，更进一步地了解和领悟英国语言和英国文化习俗。"Sightseeing in London"这篇文章安排在这个单元的"Reading"板块。通过前面的学习，学生已经了解了英国的构成、历史和地理位置，尤其是英国的首都城市伦敦以及这座城市的发展和风土人情。"Sightseeing in London"是一篇旅游观光记，主要介绍英国的一些名胜古迹，如大本钟、威斯敏斯特教堂、大不列颠博物馆、圣保罗大教堂等。这篇课文配有漂亮的图片。通过这些图片和作者的描述，学生可以感受异国文化，培养文化意识，加深对英国的了解，拓宽知识面，深入地了解和领悟英国的语言和文化习俗。

【Why】

本文作者通过三天的旅游观光，移步换景、情文并茂，以愉悦的心情、丰富的语言给我们展示了一幅幅美丽的画面。这是一篇很好的写作范文。例如，该文用了delight、fancy、splendid、interesting、famous等形容词去评价每一个旅游景点，仿佛把同学们带入其中，真可谓让人身临其境，增添了一份学习的情趣。在"Using Language"部分，教师带领学生逐步学习该文的语篇结构、措辞和修辞手法，从而帮助学生很好地实现知识的迁移。

【How】

根据课文的主题语境和话题，教师设计了一系列与话题有关的写前教学活动，为后面的写作做好充分的铺垫。

三、学情分析

高三学生的认知能力有了进一步的发展，他们渐渐形成用英语获取信息、处理信息、分析问题和解决问题的能力。学生思维活跃，求知欲旺盛，学习态度明确，自主性强，有一定的自主阅读与表达能力，具备良好的团队协作能力，能进行有效的交流、合作和讨论。但学生个性和英语水平差异大，所以教学设计要有梯度，由浅入深。

四、教学目标

单元目标：

本单元的话题是"The United Kingdom（英国）"，通过阅读使学生了解英国的历史和地理位置、国家的构成及名胜古迹。"Warming-Up"板块要求学生完成一项小测试任务，加深学生对英国的了解，并调动学生的积极思维，激发学生的学习动机。

"Pre-reading"板块通过三个有关英国的小问题，让学生预测该文的内容，使其大概了解阅读内容。

"Reading"（"Puzzles in Geography"）板块从地理、历史、政治、文化等多角度说明了英国的形成、发展，以及它的风土人情和人文景观，使学生对英国有一个比较翔实的了解，拓宽了学生的知识面，帮助学生深入地了解和领悟英国的语言和文化习俗。

"Comprehending"板块通过练习，加深学生对文章的理解，训练其概括总结能力。

"Learning about Language" 板块主要突出通过语境运用本单元生词，设计了有关构词法的练习和各种同义或近义的动词的练习。语法部分引导学生发现课文中的过去分词用作宾语补足语的例句，设计了较为简单的填空练习和具有趣味性的游戏。练习册还设计了具有实际意义的活动——完成一份调查报告。

"Using Language" 板块涵盖了听、说、读、写几个部分。听的部分通过张萍玉与导游的对话使学生亲身体验去伦敦旅行的真实情境，既训练他们的听力，又通过回答问题的方式训练他们的分析能力。读的部分主要介绍英国伦敦的一些名胜。通过图片展示，图文并茂地让学生感受异国文化，增强学生的文化意识，培养学生的跨文化沟通能力。说的部分主要以学生演绎游客和导游之间的对话的形式完成。通过练习，学生可以熟练地掌握因没有听清或听懂而请求别人复述的几种表达形式。写的部分要求学生参考所给的形容词和动词，发散思维，把自己收集到的有关某一建筑物或景观的资料写进学生所在地旅游手册。学生需要用最生动的语言进行描述，以吸引人们前来旅游观光。

课时目标：

语言能力：

（1）能使用单元话题词汇和句型完成一封有关旅行计划的建议信。

（2）能模仿课文的优美句子和词语修改并完善作文。

文化品格：从伦敦的观光游记过渡到写中国北京的名胜古迹，培养学生对祖国大好河山的热爱之情与认同感。

思维品质：能根据老师给出的评价标准客观地评价自己和同伴的作文。

学习能力：在模仿优美句子和词语的过程中，培养学生根据主题语境写出得体的建议信，帮助学生运用评价、反思的方法，调整自己的学习内容和进程。

五、教学重点、难点

重点：

（1）能使用单元话题词汇和句型完成一封有关旅行计划的建议信。

（2）能模仿课文的优美句子和词语修改并提升作文。

难点：

根据老师给出的评价标准客观地评价自己和同伴的作文。

六、教学过程

Step 1. Lead-in

1. Ss watch the video clip and underline:

(1) adjectives the author uses to describe the scenery spots and Zhang Pingyu's feelings.

(2) important phrases.

Ss are supposed to find:

① delight, fancy, splendid, interesting, famous, be worried about, make a list of, remain doing sth., on special occasions, in memory of, hear sb./sth. doing sth., pass through, have a photo taken, see sb./sth. doing sth., enjoy doing sth., on show, feel proud of, leave for, fall asleep ...

② some good sentence patterns:

Comparison	
Because she was worried that there was not enough time, Zhang Pingyu had made a travel list first	Worried about the time available, Zhang Pingyu had made a list of the sites she wanted to see in London
This solid stone, square tower had a history of one thousand years	This solid stone, square tower had remained standing for one thousand years
At the end of the day, she looked at the outside of Buckingham Palace	She finished the day by looking at the outside of Buckingham Palace
It's a pity that the library had moved from its original place into another building	Sadly the library had moved from its original place into another building

2. Make sentences by imitating the sentence patterns in the text.

Purpose：通过回顾本单元课文的重点单词、词汇和句型，激活学生原有的知识，将学生的注意力导向写作词汇和句型的升级上。模仿高级句子的表达，为后面的作文做好铺垫。

Step 2. Pre-writing

Ss get into groups of 6 and brainstorm some tourist attractions in Beijing.

Purpose：通过小组讨论、头脑风暴，让对北京景点较熟悉的学生带动其他学生，为写作做好知识准备。

Step 3. While-writing

Watch a video clip and get ready for writing a letter.

假设你是张萍玉，你的美国朋友杰西（Jesse）寒假要来北京游玩两天，向你征求意见。请根据以下要点提示，为他推荐行程安排。

（1）行程安排及理由。

（2）注意事项。

注意：①词数100左右；②可以适当增加细节，以使行文连贯；③开头和结尾已给出。

Task 1: Choose some tourist attractions in Beijing that you are going to write about.

Task 2: In groups, talk about how to arrange the trip properly and work out a mind map.

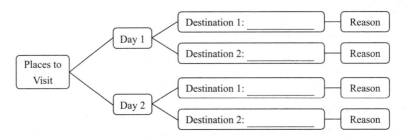

Task 3: Write the main body of the letter.

Dear Jesse,

Delighted to know that you are planning to travel in Beijing for 2 days, I'd like to recommend a travel plan for you. Hope it would be of some help to you.

....

Looking forward to your coming.

Yours,

Zhang Pingyu

Purpose：通过小组讨论，让学生进行思想交流、梳理写作要点，并以思维导图的形式呈现出来，为接下来的小组写作活动搭好框架。

Step 4. Post-writing

Task 1: Self-assessment

Task 2: Peer-assessment

评价内容	自我评价				小组综合评价			
	A	B	C	D	A	B	C	D
1.要点齐全，内容完整								
2.格式正确，结构合理								
3.人称、时态正确								
4.文章自然连贯，连接词使用恰当								
5.单词拼写、句子结构无低级错误								
6.能使用课文中的一些较高级的词汇和句式来增加文章的亮点								
7.断句合理，标点无误								
8.词数恰当，书写整洁美观								
9.本文亮点（用简短的文字表达）								
10.本文不足（用简短的文字表达）								

Purpose：通过自评和同伴互评，培养学生的批判性思维，鼓励学生客观评价自己及他人的作文；通过第6点评价内容，引导学生关注课文中的好词好句。

Step 5. Summary & Homework

(1) Polish your letter according to the assessment form.

(2) Recite the key words, phrases and sentence patterns in this unit.

Purpose：回顾本节写作课的学习重点，布置课后巩固作业。

七、主要教学活动

教师在写前环节，主要安排了以下几个教学活动。

（一）引入课文，关注与话题相关的形容词和短语

教师让学生观看教师制作的一段课文朗读视频，视频中对本单元课文的重点单词、短语和句型都进行了不同颜色的标注，使用多模态手段，让学生在观看的过程中，激活原有知识。看完视频后，教师列出四组句子让学生进行比较。在比较的过程中，学生的注意力也从关注写作词汇过渡到句式的升级上。

（二）模仿高级句子表达，为写作做好铺垫

教师在呈现课文中的优美句式时，也为学生创设了相应的写作场景，要

求学生口头造句。例如，在展示完优美句式"Worried about the time available, Zhang Pingyu had made a list of the sites she wanted to see in London"之后，教师要求学生用相同的句式口头表达"考虑到时间问题，我建议你先把要去的景点写下来"以及"考虑到北京有太多的东西可看，我建议你穿运动鞋"。这不仅在情境中操练了句型，还为后续的写作活动做好了铺垫。

（三）头脑风暴，挖掘写作内容

由于授课班级的学生并不是都去过北京，教师通过小组讨论、头脑风暴的形式，让对北京景点较熟悉的学生带动其他学生一起回忆北京的名胜古迹，让学生可以表达个人观点，同时为写作做好知识准备。

（四）创设真实写作情境，激发写作欲望

为了使学生能带着更明确的目标和理由来表达个人观点，使他们对自己的写作更负责任，更主动地探寻自己思想表达的方法和技巧，教师模拟了一段张萍玉和她的美国朋友杰西（Jesse）的微信聊天记录，创设了以下情境：假设你是张萍玉，你的美国朋友Jesse寒假要来北京游玩两天，向你征求意见。请根据以下要点提示，为他推荐行程安排。

（五）小组讨论，梳理思维导图

在学生明确了写作目的和要求后，教师组织学生进行小组讨论，让学生进行思想交流，梳理写作要点，并以思维导图的形式呈现出来，为接下来的小组写作活动搭好框架。

八、板书设计

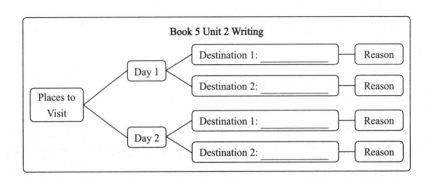

九、教学特色

特色1：

只有单词、短语而没有正确的句子结构，再多、再好的单词、短语也拼不成美妙文章。因此，课文中新的句子结构、表达优美的句子，都是教学中的语言载体，是我们挖掘的训练素材。本课设计的仿句练习，有别于传统枯燥乏味的汉语句子翻译，能让学生在感知句子结构的同时，在真实语境中仿写出句子。如此，既有利于学生创造性思维的训练，又有助于他们写作能力的提高。

特色2：

在写作前，教师引导学生通过思维导图设计旅游路线，帮助学生用英语解决生活中的实际问题，训练学生的深度思维品质。

十、课例评析

（一）课例评析1：胡翠娥

张伟娟老师的这节课是基于省级课题研究项目内容和人教新课标版教材Book 5 Unit 2主题语境"人与自然——国家地理概况"的一节应用文（教学目标写的是建议信，创设的情境是推荐信）写作课，主题贯穿整个教学过程。各环节设计包括写前、写中和写后，都体现了过程性写作教学的完整流程。

亮点：

（1）依托教材，利用教材语篇以听和看的形式进行写前话题词汇和句式的输入。

（2）多模态形式贯穿整个教学过程，尤其是信息技术应用合理，能熟练运用现代化教学手段辅助完成教学任务，使学生的听、说、读、看、写语言技能得到培养和提升。

（3）以听和看的形式创设真实写作情境，让学生了解写作任务，直观生动，体现了张老师的交际语用意识。创设的情境符合高考英语写作的命题特点——提纲式，给学生足够的发挥空间。

（4）设计的基于老师提供的材料小组合作讨论写作要点（行程安排）这一任务，体现了张老师以学生为主体的意识。通过与同伴交流和思考写作内容（如何安排行程），学生的创新思维和批判性思维得到训练。

（5）写后环节设计的评价表（Checklist）给学生提供了自评和互评的标准，引导学生发现自己和同伴作文中的问题，并进行修改和完善。

建议：

（1）在设计听和看的环节时，明确任务，让学生带着任务听和看。

（2）优化句式环节，最好能把参考的句子呈现出来，而不是口头表达。

（3）教师应对学生进行一定的写前指导（信息拓展和文体要求）。

（二）课例评析2：郭秀云

张伟娟老师的这节课是基于人教新课标版教材Book 5 Unit 2主题语境——"人与自然——国家地理概况"的一节写作课。整个教学过程完整，设定的教学目标初步达成，各环节设计基于学情，指导细致，注重学法指导。

亮点：

首先，多模态英语教学模式在这节课上得到充分展现，既改变了传统枯燥的教学模式，又能充分发挥利用数字网络的优势，为英语教育注入新的活力；其次，教师引入的图片和内容都比较新颖，让人有种耳目一新的感觉；最后，在句子比较环节，教师能把好句和一般的句子进行对比，帮助学生写出更多佳句，从而使作文整体提分。

建议：

整节课构思精巧，颇具心思，但内容方面讲得太细，任务设计得比较简单，学生可发挥的地方不多。建议多设计一些环节让学生主动参与、自主探索，从而体现学生的主体地位。

（三）课例评析3：陈锦春

张伟娟老师设计了基于人教新课标版教材Book 5 Unit 2 The United Kingdom话题的写作课——how to write a suggestion letter on trip planning。首先，张老师通过播放一个自己制作的教学视频引入这节课，使学生的注意力迅速被吸引，形成了相应的教学期待。学生在观看视频的同时，在课本上画出描述英国景色的形容词和描写旅游经历的相关词汇。通过观看视频，学生了解了英国的人文地理及历史，增加了对世界的认识。接着，张老师给学生呈现了两组句子，让学生通过观察、比较，发现高级句子里面所运用到的词汇和句型的美，为接下来的写作活动做好铺垫。然后，张老师从英国的人文地理自然过渡到中国的旅游景点，引入了计划到北京旅游这个话题。在进行写作之前，张老师先是组织学生进行小组讨论，对北京的景点做一个合理的旅游计划，为下面的建议信写作提供了要点。最后，学生在单独完成作文后，检查自己的作文，并和另一组的学生交换作文进行互改。为了给学生提供一个客观的评价依据，张老师从写作内容、文章连贯性、词汇运用和书写整洁等角度设计了一个"英语写作自评与互评对照表"。

张老师教学功底十分扎实，能够将现代信息技术融入英语课堂并运用自如，有极强的课堂驾驭能力，在教学中勇于创新，善于观察学生的课堂反应，并灵活做出教学调整。整节课富有层次感，充分体现了多模态教学模式在课堂上的运用。

（四）课例评析4：赖丽萍

张老师课堂把控能力强，基本功非常扎实，教态自然，英语口语流利。

亮点：

（1）课前准备充分。每个环节之间设计紧凑、环环相扣。整堂课下来非常流畅、自然，学生能很好地领会教师的意图，并与教师设计的课堂进程以及提出的各项要求同步。

（2）张老师对多媒体在教学上的应用非常熟练，视频、图文、听力内容都让整节课异常新颖，学生学习的情绪高。

（3）张老师非常有亲和力。上课时，始终面带笑容，平等待人，对学生耐心启发、循循诱导，课堂气氛轻松和谐。在这种氛围下，学生能充分发挥积极性和能动性。

（五）课例评析5：叶青容

张伟娟老师设计了基于人教新课标版教材Book 5 Unit 2 The United Kingdom话题的写作课——how to write a suggestion letter on trip planning。张老师专业素养高，基本功非常扎实，有很强的课堂驾驭能力。本节课设计思路清晰，亮点多。

亮点：

（1）张老师使用多模态输入方式，为写作任务做了充分的准备。

（2）导入视频，图文并茂，听力同步，技术融合有深度。

（3）句型对比后再翻译，马上检测学生学以致用的能力，体现了张老师注重对学生语言能力和模仿能力的培养。

（4）为写作创设真实情境，符合当前高考写作命题要求。

（5）将现代信息技术融入英语课堂并运用自如，体现了张老师将信息技术和学科教学充分融合的能力很强。

（6）张老师在教学中勇于创新，善于观察学生的课堂反应，并灵活做出教学调整。

（六）课例评析 6：陈艳丽

张伟娟老师专业功底深厚，掌握了很新的信息技术手段且能信手拈来地应用于英语课堂教学之中，让学生和听课老师有耳目一新的感觉。

亮点：

（1）导入视频、图文并茂、听力同步，体现了多模态语篇输入，反映出张老师较高的信息技术水平。

（2）张老师通过句型对比，让学生去领悟高级句子里面所运用到的词汇和句型的美，再结合高级句型翻译句子，为后面的写作活动做好铺垫。

（3）布置写作任务能创设真实情境，符合当前高考写作命题要求。

（4）张老师从写作内容、文章连贯性、词汇运用和书写整洁等角度设计了"英语写作自评与互评对照表"，给学生提供了一个客观的量化评价依据，对学生提高写作能力有很大的帮助。

（七）课例评析 7：黄茗旎

张伟娟老师设计了基于人教新课标版教材Book 5 Unit 2 The United Kingdom话题的写作课——how to write a suggestion letter on trip planning。

亮点：

（1）依托教材，选择合适的文本。

（2）将与主题和话题相关的句型进行释义，由易到难，分层教学，引导能力较强的学生运用更好的词汇、非谓语和句式进行表达。

（3）将现代信息技术融入英语课堂并运用自如，体现了张老师极强的将信息技术和学科教学充分融合的能力。

（4）所设的作文题目比较新颖，看似简单，实有奥妙，学生须在多个北京景点中挑选，设计出能在两天内完成的合适的旅行线路，有利于培养学生的审题能力及思辨能力，所设题目接近学生生活，更有意义。

（5）写后的Peer-assessment任务设计较好。

建议：

Step 1中可将学生所归纳出来的形容词及句式与后面的写作进一步衔接，为学生搭建"脚手架"。

（八）课例评析8：廖敏

张伟娟老师专业功底深厚，掌握了很新的信息技术手段且能信手拈来地应用于英语课堂教学之中，让学生和听课老师都有耳目一新的感觉。张老师思维活跃，课堂掌控能力强，在教学中善于进行教学手段的创新，根据学生的情况和课堂反应随机应变，因材施教，使整节课轻松愉悦，很好地达成了教学目标。

首先，张老师通过一个新颖的教学视频来引入这节课，使学生十分感兴趣，并很快进入状态。张老师要求学生一边观看视频，一边在课本上画出描述英国景色的形容词和描写旅游经历的相关词汇。在此过程中，学生了解了英国的人文地理及历史，增加了对世界的认识。其次，张老师给学生示范了如何升级句型。她呈现了两组句子，让学生通过观察、比较，发现高级句子里所运用到的词汇和句型的美。这一设计非常实用，是本课的一大亮点，也为下面的写作活动做好铺垫。再次，张老师从中国的旅游景点，引入北京旅游建议话题，通过布置学生小组讨论任务，让学生对北京的景点做一个合理的旅游计划，为下面的建议信写作提供了要点。最后，学生各自分头写作，并自查自己的作文，同伴进行互改。

附：学生习作

学生习作1：

Dear Jesse,

Delighted to know that you are planning to travel in Beijing for 2 days, I'd like to recommend a travel plan for you. Hope it would be of some help to you.

When arriving in Beijing on the first day, you can go to Tian'anmen Square at 7:00 in the morning to watch the flay-raising ceremony. I consider it is a new experience for you who has never seen a flag-raising ceremony in China. After the ceremony, it is a good choice to visit the Forbidden City, which is very close to Tian'anmen Square. The Forbidden City has many precious cultural relics and grand palaces and buildings. It's extremely worth visiting. In the afternoon, you can also wander around the streets of Beijing to experience the daily life of Beijing people.

The next day, visiting the Great Wall which is one of the world-famous ancient sites would be an excellent choice. Not only can you walk on the Great Wall, but also you can enjoy the sunset. I sincerely hope you can have a good time in Beijing.

Looking forward to your coming.

Yours,

Zhang Pingyu

学生习作2：

Dear Jesse,

Delighted to know that you are planning to travel in Beijing for 2 days, I'd like to recommend a travel plan for you. Hope it would be of some help to you.

As we all knew, there are many tourist attractions in Beijing. First of all, you can go to Tian'anmen Square to watch the flag-raising ceremony. It's relatively late to raise the flag in Tian'anmen Square in winter. You can have a good rest first. Then there are many streets near Tian'anmen Square. You can experience the ancient Chinese culture. Take a look at the Beijing Opera show, have a special snack and fully feel the cultural atmosphere of Beijing. The next day, you'd better not miss the Great Wall. As an old Chinese saying goes, he who does not reach the Great Wall is not a true man. After experiencing the Great Wall, if you still have time, you can visit the place where a famous female emperor in ancient China lived, the Summer Palace. Finally, I hope you can have a good time.

Looking forward to your coming.

Yours,

Zhang Pingyu

学生习作3：

Dear Jesse,

Delighted to know that you are planning to travel in Beijing for 2 days, I'd like to recommend a travel plan for you. Hope it would be of some help to you.

On the first day, it's a good choice to visit the Forbidden City while listening to the guide sharing interesting stories of ancient emperors. We all say, "He who hasn't been to the Great Wall isn't a true man." So the next destination must be the Great Wall. You can finish the day by enjoying the beautiful sunset there.

The second day you can witness the deep blue sky complementing the white ornate ruins in Yuanmingyuan. Then, you can't miss the graceful scenery in the Summer Palace nearby which is one of the most famous royal gardens in the world.

Before your schedule starts, make sure to prepare enough thick clothes and a pair of sports shoes. Don't forget to carry your camera if you want plenty photos that are fancy.

Looking forward to your coming.

Yours,

Zhang Pingyu

学生习作4：

Dear Jesse,

Delighted to know that you are planning to travel in Beijing for 2 days, I'd like to recommend a travel plan for you. Hope it would be of some help to you.

On the first day, you can go to the Forbidden City. The digital Forbidden City, published recently, aims to help visitors admire the splendid building. You can enjoy the tradition and technology being connected perfectly. Besides, if you are hungry, Beijing roast duck is the most delicious food you can't miss. Finally, you can finish the day by walking in the alleyways.

Have you ever heard a proverb, "He who doesn't reach the Great Wall isn't a true man"? I strongly suggest that you spend your second day on it. Words fail to me to describe how grand it is. Only when you arrive by yourself can you understand.

The transports and routines are attached to the email. Remember to bring your sneakers because you can't visit them in a short time.

Looking forward to your coming.

Yours,

Zhang Pingyu

Book 7 Unit 5 Travelling Abroad (Pre-writing)

设计者姓名：黄茗旎

设计者所在单位：广东省清远市华侨中学

一、教学材料分析

授课年级： 高三

教材内容： 人教新课标版Book 7 Unit 5 Travelling Abroad

主题： 人与社会——国内旅行与国外旅行

课型： 话题写作课（写前储备与方案设计）

课时： 1课时

二、教学内容分析

【What】

在学完人教新课标版教材Book 7 Unit 5的语篇后，学生了解了在国外旅行或学习时可能会遇到的一些问题，并学会怎样去解决这些问题和避免这些问题的发生。本节课以"人与社会——国内旅行与国外旅行"这一主题为引领，是一节旨在指导学生学会表达个人观点，用丰富的话题词汇进行写作的写前储备课，并辅以尝试方案设计。

【Why】

学生自初中开始，对"旅行"这一话题，已进行过不少的写作练习，也掌握了一定的话题词汇和表达。但事实上，真正进行国内远途旅行和国外旅行的学生并不多，学生的亲身体验较少。他们更多仍停留在各种书信的练习上，关注点更多放在地点介绍和书信写作模板上，用于写作的话题词汇不够丰富。本节课旨在设计体验式、有一定难度的写作任务，丰富学生的话题词汇，并使学生将其用于口语与写作的输出中。另外，考虑到学生的层次，初步让他们尝试方案设计。

【How】

本课时以"人与社会——国内旅行与国外旅行"的主题语境为引领，依托四大语篇进行教学：语篇一、二为说明文，通过所设计的听、看、读等教学活动介绍了旅行的意义与益处；语篇三为应用文（邀请信），以课后作业的形式完成，要求学生将在本课时积累的旅行的益处、选择的旅行目的地及选择理由通过写作的方式输出，并附上旅行计划询问对方意见；语篇四是应用文（旅行项目设计），要求学生经过学习与小组合作探究，在下一周的课中进行口头展示，并上交旅行方案。

三、学情分析

授课班为清远市华侨中学高二年级的实验班，平时考试，班级平均分大约为115分（满分为150分）。学生的英语语用水平较高，学生能较为流利地用英语传递信息、论证观点和表达情感。另外，学生有一定的利用现代信息技术获取信息的能力，在教师的指导下能够获取与旅游相关的信息。

四、教学目标

单元目标：

（1）了解在国外旅行或学习时可能会遇到的一些问题，并学会怎样去解决这些问题和避免这些问题的发生。

（2）掌握与"旅行"这一话题相关的词汇和句型。

（3）学会表达和支持个人观点，能用所学的词汇描述在国外居住和生活的情况。

（4）在国外旅游时能根据所给的信息选择恰当的旅游线路，并能对有可能发生的事情进行推测。

课时目标：

(1) To get the Ss to know the benefits of travelling.

(2) To instruct the Ss to write letters to invite their friends to go for domestic tours or overseas travels with them.

(3) To instruct the Ss to design a travel schedule.

(4) To improve the Ss' cross-culture awareness.

(5) To build up the Ss' confidence in our country, our culture and our customs.

(6) To integrate patriotism into the class.

五、教学重点、难点

重点：

（1）To get the Ss to know the benefits of travelling.

（2）To instruct the Ss to write letters to invite their friends to go for domestic tours or overseas travels with them.

（3）To instruct the Ss to design a travel schedule.

难点：

（1）To improve the Ss' cross-culture awareness.

（2）To build up the Ss' confidence in our country, our culture and our customs.

（3）To integrate patriotism into the class.

六、教学过程

Step 1. Lead-in

1. Show the Ss the learning objectives of this class.

2. Ask the Ss if they like travelling. Show them pictures taken by the teacher when she went travelling.

3. When presenting the pictures, the teacher briefly explains the culture and customs related to the pictures.

Purpose：在引入部分，教师首先展示了本课时的教学目标，然后展示自己在国内外旅行时所拍的照片，并简单讲解当地的相关文化与习俗。本活动以看、听促学，培养学生的文化意识，激发学生的学习兴趣，为接下来的学习做准备。

Step 2. Learning Activities

Activity 1: Listening and writing (Individual Work）

1. Ask the Ss to listen to the material and fill in the blanks.

2. Ask the Ss to check the answers, and lead the Ss to understand the meaning of travelling based on the underlined words and expressions.

There are plenty of things one can gain from exploring different places. The list includes gaining new friends, new experiences, and new stories.

When you start exploring new places, you get a better understanding of the people living there, including their culture, history and background.

Studies show that travelling can improve your overall health and enhance your creativity. Therefore, you need to take time out from your daily tasks, office responsibilities, hectic schedule, and everyday pressures at least once a year. Plan a tour to a new city with an open schedule and let life present you with the numerous opportunities.

Purpose：教师截取了学案2的阅读文本"10 Wonderful Benefits of Traveling"的前三段，将与主题"travel"相关的表达挖空，并自行录制听力材料。在学生听录音填空并核对答案后，教师引导学生理解文本中所提及的旅行的意义，激发学生对旅行的向往。该活动以听促写，培养学生的自主学习能力，为接下来的邀请信写作做准备。

Activity 2: Speaking, writing and reading (Individual Work & Group Work)

1. Ask the Ss to discuss in groups, list some benefits of travelling and present them in class.

2. Give a requirement that one student at least gives one benefit. Ask them to write all the benefits mentioned down on their learning sheets. 5 minutes for preparation.

3. Ask the Ss to present their opinions in class.

4. Ask the Ss to read the article on another learning sheet and find out the 10 benefits mentioned. Ask them to read the 10 benefits together.

Purpose：学生以小组合作学习的方式，讨论旅行的益处。要求每个学生至少提出一个观点，并把同组其他学生的观点记录下来，在班上进行展示。让学生读与旅行相关的文章，要求找出文中所提及的旅行的十大益处。该活动以说、读促听、写，学生全员参与，能够了解旅行的益处，同时培养概括、分析文章内容的思维品质，创造性思维和合作学习能力，将学习内容应用到实践中。

Activity 3: Speaking and writing (Group Work)

1. Ask the Ss three questions:

Do you like travelling?

Where do you want to go for a tour?

Why do you choose it as your destination?

2. Ask the Ss to share their ideas in groups. Give a requirement that one student of each group write down the opinions of all the group members' and present them in class. 5 minutes for preparation.

Purpose：学生以小组合作学习的形式，讨论想要选取的旅行目的地并说明理由。小组推选一个学生记录并展示。该活动以说、听促写、说，培养学生的创新性思维能力以及合作学习能力，为接下来的应用文写作做准备，并将学生的学习理解深化至应用实践中。

Activity 4: Speaking (T-S Work)

Ask the Ss to share their ideas and tell their advantages and disadvantages.

Purpose：口语活动——学生与教师共同参与，对比跟团游与自由行各自的优缺点。该活动旨在培养学生的口语表达能力与批判性思维。

Activity 5: Project design (T-S Work)

1. Ask the Ss to work in groups and each group chooses one or more provinces of our country or a foreign country as their destinations.

2. Instruct the Ss to design a 7-day tour by themselves from the aspects of clothing, food, accommodation and transportation. Give the Ss some tips on preparations for the tour.

3. Remind the Ss of things to pay attention to for safety during the trip.

4. Provide some help for the Ss to help them design their self-service trip, such as offering some helpful websites and a Chinese travel schedule.

Purpose：学生以小组为单位，选取国内一个或多个省，或选取某一个国家作为旅行目的地，在教师的指导下，设计一个旅行方案。为降低方案完成的难度，教师指导学生从衣、食、住、行四方面入手思考方案设计的思路，提醒学生在安全方面的注意事项，并为其提供一些参考网站。该活动旨在培养学生的探究性思维能力和小组探究学习能力，将学习理解、应用实践上升至迁移创新。

Step 3. Assignments

1. Complete your learning sheet.

2. Write a letter to your best friend and invite him/her to go travelling with you.

The letter should include the following contents: ① the benefits of travelling; ② the destination for your trip and reasons for your choice; ③ show him/her your travel schedule to ask for his/her opinion.

3. Work in groups and design your travel project. Oral presentation for the next Monday and written sheet to be handed in the next Wednesday.

Purpose：作业1要求学生完成导学案，主要强调活动5部分的填空题。教师将课件中"旅行方案设计"环节关于衣、食、住、行与安全方面的与"旅行"主题相关的词汇或表达设计成填空题。学生在上完课后根据自己的理解完成题目。这既是对课堂教学内容掌握程度的检测，也复习了与主题相关的词汇表达，同时为课后的写作和方案设计做好准备。作业2为邀请信写作，学生写信给好朋友邀请他/她一同去旅行，在信中提及旅行的好处、该次旅行的目的地及选择到此旅行的原因，并附上所设计的旅行计划表，征询对方意见。学生通过完成该邀请信的写作，将本课时的教学内容应用到写作输出中，可以有效地检测学习效果。作业3为小组探究学习——完成方案设计，学生通过口语介绍方案设计和书面完成计划表，培养口语技能、创新思维与批判性思维，提升自信心，将所学知识与自身生活经验结合在一起，为未来自身发展做准备。同时，通过设计国内游与国外游路线，学生在了解国外文化的同时，欣赏我国大好河山，探索我国各地人文历史以及优秀文化传统，培养自身文化认同感，增强国家自信与民族自信。

七、主要教学活动

本课时共设计了五个学生活动：活动1以听促写，学生听录音填空。通过该活动，学生了解旅行的意义所在。活动2以说、读促听、写，学生小组讨论旅行的益处，发表自己的观点并记录他人的观点，读与旅行相关的文章。学生全员参与该活动，了解旅行的益处，同时培养自身听、说、读、写的技能。活动3以说、听促写、说，学生小组讨论想要选择的旅行目的地并说明理由，推选一个学生记录并展示。活动2与活动3均培养学生的创造性思维，同时为接下来的应用文写作做准备，将学习理解深化至应用实践中。活动4为口语活动，学生对比团队游与自由行各自的优缺点，培养批判性思维。活动5为方案设计活动，要求学生以小组为单位，选取国内一个或多个省，或选取某一个国家作为旅行目的地，在老师的指导下，设计一个旅行方案。通过该活动，学生从学习理解、应用实践上升至迁移创新。

八、板书设计

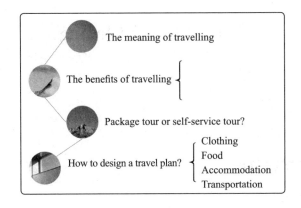

九、教学特色

特色1：本节课有效地落实了指向学科核心素养发展的英语学习活动观，设置了多个学生自主学习、小组合作学习、小组探究学习的课堂活动，包括：①学生自主学习——独立完成听力训练与语篇阅读等；②小组合作学习——共同讨论旅行的益处、旅行目的地的选取及其原因，以口头和书面形式呈现合作学习的成果；③小组探究学习——在老师的指导下，学生通过小组探究学习，课后自主完成书面表达任务，并尝试共同完成一个旅行方案设计。

特色2：本节课将学生所学知识与其生活经验紧密联系在一起，有效培养学生的创造性思维、批判性思维与跨文化交际意识。同时，学生通过设计国内游与国外游路线，在了解国外文化的同时，欣赏我国大好河山，探索我国各地人文历史以及优秀文化传统，培养自身文化认同感，树立国家自信与民族自信。

附：写作情境

Write a letter to your best friend and invite him/her to go travelling with you. The letter should include the following contents:

(1) the benefits of travelling;

(2) the destination for your trip and reasons for your choice;

(3) show him/her your travel schedule to ask for his/her opinion.

Book 8 Unit 2 Cloning

设计者姓名：张伟娟

设计者所在单位：广东省清远市第二中学

一、教学材料分析

授课年级：高三

教材内容：人教新课标版Book 8 Unit 2 Cloning

主题：人与社会——生命

课型：写作

课时：1课时

二、教学内容分析

【What】

教材里本单元的内容、语言技能和语言知识都是围绕"克隆"这一中心话题设计的。课文"Cloning：Where Is It Leading Us?"的主要内容是植物克隆和动物克隆的区别、多利羊的诞生与死亡，以及由此而引发的各种争论。本节写作课是基于Workbook上的一篇阅读材料（关于医疗克隆的辩论"A Debate：Should Medical Cloning Be Allowed?"）。该材料主要介绍了关于辩论的基本规则，以及辩论双方对医疗克隆利弊的不同观点。例如，正方观点：为攻克一些传统方法无法治疗的疾病，帮助那些有行动和思维障碍的人重获正常生活，可用克隆的细胞替换中风病人的神经细胞等，故应该支持医疗克隆。反方观点：从胚胎中提取人类干细胞在伦理上的合理性尚未得到解决，加上人类当前的克隆技术也不够成熟，应采取更为谨慎的态度，故不支持医疗克隆。

【Why】

如何有效地提高学生的英语写作能力一直是高中英语教学中的一大难题。在以往的做法中，教师为学生提供参考词汇、短语句式和万能高分模板，让学生套用成文，然后默写背诵。这种传统的写作教学模式，束缚了学生的创新思维的发展，其写作动机和兴趣也难以持久。另外，写作后，教师往往只能进行一些普遍错误的纠正，再给出相应的例句或者范文，从而指导学生参考修改，学生的写作能力很难得到科学的指导和有效的提高。有效地开展写后活动，对提高学生的写作能力起到关键作用。

【How】

本节课中，教师探索了在学生写作后如何利用丰富的多模态语篇和文字云图、句酷批改网等工具，指导学生反复修改自己的作文，以实现学生写作能力的提高。

三、学情分析

学生对克隆话题、多利羊的诞生与死亡有了初步的认识，并掌握了克隆技术相关话题词汇和句型。而"Workbook"板块关于医疗克隆的辩论，也让学生了解了辩论的基本规则，以及辩论双方对医疗克隆利弊的一些不同观点，为学生提供了表达不同论点的语言形式。然而，学生仍需对克隆话题的语言形式、议论文的逻辑性和语言的准确运用等进一步内化和提升。本节课为学生提供语言表达训练的机会，让学生在复习单元话题词汇的基础上，巩固相关句型和表达，并通过辩论赛的形式进行语言运用。

四、教学目标

单元目标：

本单元的中心话题是"克隆"。"Pre-reading"板块要求学生讨论有关克隆的问题，回答是否能区分自然繁殖与克隆的问题，调动学生讨论的积极性，激发学生对"Reading"板块植物与动物克隆的区别、克隆话题的兴趣，达到热身的效果。通过阅读，在训练阅读方法和技能的同时，帮助学生进一步认识克隆的意义在于为人类服务。本单元的语法是掌握并运用同位语从句及同位语从句与that引导的定语从句的区别。"Using Language"板块包括了读、讨论，写，听三个部分的内容。学生通过学习"恐龙回归"的阅读材料，了解是否能克隆已经灭绝的动物并讨论哪一种动物最值得克隆及其理由。听说板块是听一段关于克隆对动物来说是否残忍的对话并进行讨论，该部分可以激发学生的想象力和培养学生的语言运用能力。本节课是基于"Workbook"上的一篇阅读材料（关于医疗克隆的辩论"A Debate：Should Medical Cloning Be Allowed?"）的语言输出课，旨在培养学生的语言运用能力和思维能力。

课时目标：

（1）语言能力：

① 能利用获得的信息展开辩论——Should medical cloning be allowed?

② 能使用本单元所学的话题词汇、语块和句型将自己对克隆的看法写成一篇议论文。

（2）文化品格：进一步理解克隆技术对人类的重要性以及它可能带来的问题。

（3）思维品质：能根据老师给出的评价标准客观地评价自己和同伴的作文。

（4）学习能力：懂得如何收集优美的词句表达，为议论文的写作积累语言素材。

五、教学重点、难点

重点：根据老师给出的评价标准客观地评价自己和同伴的作文。

难点：能将自己对克隆的看法写成一篇议论文。

六、教学过程

Step 1. Lead-in

The teacher shows students some small video clips about cloning, leading students to have a free discussion: Should medical cloning be allowed?

Purpose：涉及医疗克隆话题的词汇比较生僻难懂，用英语进行辩论难度较大。因此，在呈现辩论议题前，教师通过播放多利羊的诞生与死亡、克隆技术的发展的纪录短片，引领学生观看《中国日报》（*China Daily*）上中国首次成功培育出体细胞克隆猴"中中"和"华华"的新闻视频等导学内容，加深学生对克隆这一写作话题的了解。进一步引发学生思考：Should medical cloning be allowed?

Step 2. Pre-writing

Activity 1: Speaking task-A mini-debate

The teacher organizes a mini-debate, and the rules are as follows:

1. The person who is leading the team that supports/disagrees with the topic will speak first.

2. Then other people can take turns to speak in a free discussion.

3. No one can be rude to other speakers.

4. The chairperson will stop anyone who repeats arguments that have already been made.

5. Anyone can reply to another person's argument.

Activity 2: Listening and writing task

The teacher asks the other students to take notes while enjoying the debate. Then students are going to complete and design the following writing task for today.

写作情境：

今天你们班的同学就"Should medical cloning be allowed?"展开了热烈讨论。请根据表中提示，用120词左右介绍同学们的不同观点，并表达自己的看法。

一些同学赞成的理由	一些同学反对的理由	你的看法
1. 2. 3.	1. 2. 3.	

Purpose：正反方在课堂上进行辩论，其余学生负责记录辩论过程，并进行监督和评判。教师的任务是组织辩论赛，确保辩论赛公平公正地进行。当学生表达不清晰而影响辩论正常进行时，适时提供一些词汇和短语，确保双方有效交流。辩论结束后，全体学生运用本节辩论课所记录的好词好句完成半开放性

写作任务。这一活动为后面的写作提供了内容支撑。

Step 3. While-writing

Activity: The teacher guides students to write the composition

【技巧点拨SPORTS】

1. Style (文体)：属于_____文，要注意_____和_____之间的逻辑性以及不同论据之间的层次性。

2. Person (人称)：_____人称。

3. Organizing (组织)：_____、_____、_____。

4. Reader (读者)：_____。

5. Tense (时态)：通常情况下，使用_____。

6. Structure (结构)：文章一般分_____段：

Paragraphs 1 _____

Paragraphs 2 _____

Paragraphs 3 _____

【写作模板】

Today we had a heated discussion about _____. Opinions are divided.

Some students think that _____. For one thing, _____. For another thing, _____. What's more, _____. However, others hold the view that _____. Firstly, _____. Secondly, _____. Thirdly, _____.

Actually, in my opinion, _____.

Purpose：让学生经历包括主题句、支撑句、体裁、结构等一系列常规写作过程，帮助学生了解写作思维的一般程序，形成写作的思维方法和习惯。

Step 4. Post-writing

Activity 1: Self-evaluation and peer-evaluation.

评价内容	自我评价				互评			
	A	B	C	D	A	B	C	D
1.要点齐全，内容完整								
2.格式正确，结构合理								
3.人称、时态正确								

评价内容	自我评价				互评			
	A	B	C	D	A	B	C	D
4.文章自然连贯，连接词使用恰当								
5.单词拼写、句子结构无低级错误								
6.能使用课文中的一些较高级的词汇和句式来增加文章的亮点								
7.断句合理，标点无误								
8.词数恰当，书写整洁美观								
9.本文亮点（用简短的文字表达）								
10.本文不足（用简短的文字表达）								

Activity 2: Polishing and upgrading

1. Get the Ss to polish and upgrade their compositions paragraph by paragraph.

2. Ask the Ss to update their compositions to *www.pigai.org*, try to polish their compositions according the guidance of the website.

Purpose：通过自评和互评，培养学生的批判性思维，鼓励学生客观评价自己及他人的作文。通过第6点评价内容，强化学生关注课文中的好词好句的习惯。另外，要求学生将习作即时上传到句酷批改网，并根据句酷批改网上的智能提示修改和完善作文，大大提高了写作后反馈的有效性和科学性。

Step 5. Summary & Homework

1. Polish your composition and prepare for a presentation.

2. Recite the key words, phrases and sentence patterns in this unit.

Purpose：回顾本节写作课的学习重点，布置课后巩固作业。

七、主要教学活动

本节课的主要写后教学活动有以下几个。

（一）自我评价和同伴互评

写作后的评价反馈是写作过程的延续，也是高中英语写作教学中非常重要的环节之一。有效的写作反馈能够帮助学生纠正错误，发展学生对写作过程的认知能力，提高学生的写作水平。然而，在传统的写作教学中，写后反馈大多局限于教师的批改，学生被动地接受评价，学生的积极性不高。往往是教师辛辛苦苦地对学生作文精批细改，但是多数学生只草草看一眼分数和教师的评语，很少主动去认真修改错误或重写。而且，学生过于依赖教师的反馈，并将其作为唯一的评价习作好坏的标准，这限制了学生的思维和视野，导致反馈效果低下，不利于学生写作能力的提升。教学中，教师要强调学生在评价中的主体地位，鼓励学生积极参与课堂评价活动，进行自评和互评，使学生认识到自我评价对学习能力发展的意义，从而学会自我评价的方法，并在学习中积极、有效地加以运用，不断提高学习的自主性，达到以评促学的目的。

（二）智能反馈

课堂写作后，学生将作文的初稿上传到句酷批改网。句酷批改网就像一个智能虚拟老师，能与学生实时互动。学生写好作文后只要几秒钟就可以得到分数和评语，其需要巩固的知识点也会被一一指出。这也是一个允许学生"试错"的活动，学生经过自主思考后可对文章进行反复修改并及时得到虚拟老师的指导。在互动中学生的分数会越来越高，文章也会越来越流畅，完成写作任务就像游戏攻关一样有挑战性，这大大提高了学生写作的兴趣。根据句酷批改网收集的数据，教师共收到了76篇学生作文，平均修改次数为7.87次，最高修改次数多达46次，修改次数在5次以上的有33人。从学生的终稿来看，学生采用的高级词汇有所增加，如infertile，使用的从句也更加丰富。

八、板书设计

Book 8 Unit 2 Cloning

Should medical cloning be allowed?　　　　　　SPORTS:

　　　　　　　　　　　　　　　　　　　　　　1. Style:
Approve of the idea:
Reasons:　　　　　　　　　　　　　　　　　　2. Person:

　　　　　　　　　　　　　　　　　　　　　　3. Organizing:
Be against the idea:
Reasons:　　　　　　　　　　　　　　　　　　4. Reader:

　　　　　　　　　　　　　　　　　　　　　　5. Tense:
Your idea:
Reasons:　　　　　　　　　　　　　　　　　　6. Structure:

九、教学特色

特色1:

自我评价和同伴互评相结合的评价模式,为学生提供了真实的读者,鼓励学生有目的地写作并增强他们写作的信心;让学生通过交流、沟通、协商逐步完成并优化写作任务,充分发挥了学生在学习中的主体作用,真正实现了以学生为中心的自主和自助交际法写作模式。

特色2:

以互联网为综合评价手段,对作文进行反复修改,学生写作中使用的高频词、学术词汇、高级词汇逐渐增多,作文中从句的密度逐渐加大,其写作能力也逐渐提高。同时,学生写作的自我效能感也得到加强。

第二节 新人教版教学设计

Book 1 Unit 1 Teenage Life（一）

设计者姓名：张伟娟

设计者所在单位：广东省清远市第二中学

一、教学材料分析

授课年级： 高一

教材内容： 新人教版Book 1 Unit 1 Teenage Life

主题： 人与社会——少年生活

课型： 读后续写

课时： 1课时

二、教学内容分析

【What】

本节课的教学围绕青少年生活展开，在"人与社会——少年生活"的主题下，探讨了中外青少年在学习、课外活动、兴趣爱好、人际交往等方面的状况及面临的问题。本单元旨在帮助学生真实、客观地了解和思考高中生活，让学生能够以积极、阳光的心态规划未来的学习和生活，成就更好的自己。本节课为学习了语法知识后的写作训练课，要求学生使用名词/形容词/副词短语拓展乔伊斯（Joyce）的草稿，锻炼学生的写作能力。

【Why】

为了更好地锻炼学生的写作思维，教师让学生将课文中所学的语篇结构、措辞和修辞手法运用到自己的写作中，以更好地实现知识的迁移。

【How】

教师将新高考写作题型"读后续写"与该训练结合起来，旨在通过增加细节信息，仿写本单元学过的重点句型等活动，引导学生写出有具体细节的句子。再通过引入外研版教材第一册第一单元相同话题的一篇文章"My First Day at Senior High"，引导学生积累有关文章主题、环境，人物心理、神态、动作描写的句子并加以利用，仿照里面的优美句子续写乔伊斯（Joyce）的啦啦队选拔活动日记。

三、学情分析

对于高一新生来说，由于词汇量的不足和写作微技巧的缺乏，读后续写不仅是全新的而且是难度很大的题型，不少同学甚至连读懂原文都存在很大的困难。因此，不宜直接用现有的高考题型。在教学中，应尽量利用好教材里的文本并辅以相关话题词汇、短语、篇章，帮助学生使用阅读记录卡不断积累叙事性文体的词、短语、句型并学以致用。

四、教学目标

单元目标：

本单元的听说板块包括teenage life 中和俱乐部有关的听说部分，导入活动的设计意图是引导学生对不同俱乐部的活动特点或者内容有初步了解。听力板块设计了两个活动：一是判断对话主题；二是捕捉细节信息。"Speaking"板块以pair work的形式引导学生以交流的形式进行信息输出。讨论的内容与本板块中心话题"参加俱乐部"有关。最后，学生需要完成发音练习，以此为基础掌握常见字母组合的发音规律，并且在老师的帮助下巩固语音知识。"Reading and Thinking"板块以"比较不同地方的学校生活(compare school life in different places)"为活动标题，引导学生探讨和比较中外高中新生的生活，了解同龄人的生活状态和情感世界，尤其是在成长过程中克服困难、努力进取的心路历程。语篇的标题是"新生的挑战(The Freshman Challenge)"。文章以第一人称的口吻描述了美国学生亚当（Adam）进入高中后所面临的三个挑战：如何选择课程、如何加入心仪的校橄榄球队、如何适应高中学习生活。文章层次分明、结构清晰，内容符合高中学生的认知需求，能让学生产生共鸣。

具体单元目标为：①学生了解不同语篇的学习目的以及不同语言的结构特征；②学生在语篇学习中理解并学会使用名词性短语、形容词性短语和副词性短语，并运用所学的语法知识描写真实的和想象中的校园生活的不同之处；③学生学习有关校园生活话题的词汇和句式，能够用文字描述自己所选择的俱乐部和在校园中所遇到的困惑、挑战以及美好的校园生活；④拓展学生思维，提高学生思维的批判性、鉴赏性和评价性。

课时目标：

（1）语言能力：

① 使用名词、形容词、副词性短语，增加细节信息。

② 学会欣赏课文 "My First Day at Senior High" 中的优美词汇与表达。

③ 使用本节课所学的结构和句式为给出的阅读材料续写一个通顺、合理的结局。

（2）文化品格：通过本节课的阅读和思考活动，希望学生能够在心理上认识到在高中生活刚刚开始的时候，他们有很多选择要做，有新的压力和挑战要面对，只有把握住机会的人才能为自己的未来负责。

（3）思维品质：能根据老师给出的评价标准客观地评价自己和同伴的作文。

（4）学习能力：懂得如何收集优美的词句表达，为读后续写积累语言素材。

五、教学重点、难点

重点：

（1）使用名词、形容词、副词性短语，增加细节信息。

（2）使用本节课所学的结构和句式为给出的阅读材料续写一个通顺、合理的结局。

难点：使用本节课所学的结构和句式为给出的阅读材料续写一个通顺、合理的结局。

六、教学过程

Step 1. Warming-up

1. Show a picture of "Cheerleaders" to draw Ss' attention.

Q: What is a cheerleader? What do cheerleaders do?

2. Ss watch the video clip and share their opinions on being a cheerleader.

Q: (1) *Do you want to be a cheerleader? Why or why not?*

(2) *What do you think you should learn if you are a cheerleader?*

Purpose：通过视频导入，激发学生的学习兴趣，为本节课的写作创设真实的写作情境。

Step 2. Improving the first draft

1. Guide Ss to improve the draft by asking them these questions.

(1) I've always wanted to be a cheerleader.

(Which school's cheerleader? What kind of cheerleader?)

(2) Yesterday, I tried out for the team.

(What team is it?)

(3) It was hard.

(How hard was it?)

(4) First, we had to dance.

(How? How long? What dance? With whom?)

(5) The teacher showed us how to move, and then we tried.

(How did the teacher show you? How many times did you try?)

(6) Second, we practised singing a song about the school basketball team.

(What kind of song did you sing? How is the basketball team?)

(7) Finally, some girls had to lift their partners.

(Who can lift others?)

(8) The other girls jumped and cheered.

(How did they jump and cheer?)

(9) I think I did well, but the other girls were better.

(How well did you do it?)

(10) I'm not sure if I'll make the team or not.

(What team is it? When?)

2. Get Ss work in groups of six, and improve the first draft together by filling the blanks.

I've always wanted to be a _____ cheerleader. Yesterday, I tried out for a _____ team. It was _____ hard. First, we had to dance _____. The teacher showed us _____ how to move, and then we tried _____. Second, we practised singing _____ song about the _____ school basketball team. Finally, some

_____ girls had to lift their partners. The other girls jumped and cheered _____. I think I did _____ well, but the other girls were _____ better. I'm not sure if I'll make the _____ team or not.

Purpose：通过设问的方式，引导学生添加名词、形容词、副词性短语来拓展文章，掌握第一个读后续写微技能。

Step 3. Improving the second draft

1. Get Ss to review these sentences they've learnt before, then try to imitate these sentences and add two or three sentences to give readers a cleaner picture of what happened during the try-outs.

P4

I'm a little anxious right now. What if no one talks to me?

I didn't feel awkward or frightened at all.

I feel much more confident than I felt this morning.

P12

I've got two left feet!

P13

My friends go to the Ballet Club and I want to be with them.

2. Get Ss discuss in groups of six and then ask some students to show their opinions.

Purpose：通过小组讨论，让学生进行思想交流，学会根据自己学过的课文中的话题语句编写新的句子添加到原文里。要求所添加的句子必须连贯、符合逻辑，从而使学生掌握本节课的第二个读后续写微技能。

Step 4. Continuation writing

1. Show the writing requirement of this period.

［读后续写］

根据以上所给情节进行续写，使之构成一个完整的故事。

注意：①每段续写3～4句，注意连贯性和逻辑性；②续写部分分为两段，每段的开头已为你写好。

After I had pictured it over and over again ... _____

_____

My adviser patted (轻拍) me on the shoulder softly ... _____

_____

Get Ss to discuss in groups of six, brainstorm what would happen next and develop a coherent and logical ending for the story.

2. Before writing, give Ss 5 minutes to read "My First Day at Senior High", try to appreciate the beautiful words and expressions in the text.

3. Guide Ss to imitate sentences ①～⑦ and add more details to develop a coherent and logical ending for Joyce's draft.

4. Finish your own writing.

Purpose：通过头脑风暴，以小组讨论的形式为故事的后续发展设计一个合理的结局。然后引领学生欣赏一篇语言优美的相同话题的文章，让学生学会模仿文章中的句子结构及表达，为自己完成读后续写任务做好充分铺垫。

Step 5. Self-assessment

1. Students can appreciate the beautiful words and expressions in "My First Day at Senior High".

2. Students can use noun/adjective/adverbial phrases to extend sentences.

3. Students know how to collect useful sentences for continuation writing.

4. Students can use the useful structures and sentence patterns they learned in this period to develop a coherent and logical ending.

5. Students believe they can be better at continuation writing if they try hard.

Purpose：通过自评，培养学生的批判性思维。

Step 6. Homework

1. Polish Ss' continuation writing.

2. Collect the beautiful sentences into Ss' reading journal.

七、主要教学活动

教师在写前，主要安排了以下几个教学活动：

（一）视频导入，创设真实的写作情境

在新课导入部分，教师给学生播放了一段有关啦啦队的视频。视频的节拍与韵律贴合时代感，一下子吸引了学生的注意力，教师顺势告诉学生本节课写作的内容与啦啦队有关，激发学生的写作热情。

（二）在情境中运用语法知识，实现知识迁移

在展示本单元语法部分的扩写练习——Cheerleader Try-outs之后，教师设计了十个问题，如Which school's cheerleader? What kind of cheerleader? "What team is it?" "How hard was it?" "How did the teacher show you?" "How many times did you try?" "What kind of song did you sing? How is the basketball team?" "Who can lift others?" "How did they jump and cheer?" "How well you did do it?" "What team is it? When?" 引导学生去思考如何通过添加名词、形容词、副词性短语，增加细节信息，实现语言能力目标1。

（三）小组讨论，学以致用

教师组织学生进行小组讨论，让学生学会根据自己学过的课本中的话题语句编写新的句子并添加到原文里，实现知识的学以致用。

（四）模仿优美句段，积累写作素材

高一学生用外语自由表达个人思想的能力是有限的，他们往往需要借鉴其他材料，其中借鉴的方式之一，就是"直接套用"，如使用课文中意义相近的表达方式或句子。因此，在正式续写前，教师为学生提供了外研版教材第一册第一单元相同话题的一篇文章"My First Day at Senior High"，引导学生积累有关文章主题、环境，人物心理、神态、动作描写的句子并加以利用，让学生仿照里面的优美句子续写Joyce的啦啦队选拔活动日记，为自己完成读后续写任务做好充分铺垫。

八、板书设计

> **Book 1 Unit 1 Teenage (Life Continuation Writing)**
>
> How to edit a draft:
> 1. by using noun/adjective/adverb phrases
> 2. by adding two or three sentences to give readers a cleaner image
>
> (1) "_____" A.
> (2) "_____" B.
> (3) "_____" C.
> (4) "_____" D.
> (5) "_____" E.

九、教学特色

特色1：

本节课能根据学情和话题语境，为学生提供课本外的阅读素材，并引导学生通过仿写的形式把其中的写作手法内化为自己的，充分体现了过程性写作教学的特点。

特色2：

通过分析阅读文本的句子并加以分类，引导学生在阅读过程中透过表面看到更深层次的内容，让学生从遣词造句、主题思想的揭示手法等角度来欣赏文章，促进学生深度思维的发展。

十、课例评析

（一）课例评析1：郭秀云

张伟娟老师的这节课是基于新人教版教材Book 1 Unit 1主题语境"人与社会——少年生活"引领学生探讨中外青少年在学校面临的各类问题的一节读后续写课，主题贯穿整个教学过程。各环节设计基于学情，指导细致，注重学法指导。过程性写作教学写前输入充分。

亮点：

（1）写前通过视频导入，激发学生的学习兴趣，利用多模态语篇输入为学生创设真实的写作情境，体现了张老师基于学情对过程性写作教学的写前输入环节把握准确。

（2）在写前输入环节，张老师设计了一篇基于课文挖空的小短文，引导学生进行细节描写，为下文的拓展续写提供支架，体现了张老师培养学生基于教材（资料）又超越教材的学习能力的意识。

（3）引领学生阅读一篇文章，让学生注意其中的句子描写，并让学生学会模仿文章中的句子结构，为学生接下来的续写做好铺垫。学生通过完成这项任务，语言表达能力得以提升。

建议：

（1）读后续写是写作新题型，要在一节课内完成语言的构建并进行语言输出，难度相当大。教师要思考在有限的时间内如何完成写作任务。

（2）任务2的内容（Choose the sentences you think are useful to add more details to the draft above）由于时间关系，没有进行拓展。

（二）课例评析2：胡翠娥

张伟娟老师基于省级课题"基于教材主题与话题的高中英语写作教学模式探究"和新人教版教材Book 1 Unit 1的主题Teenage Life，结合新高考题型——读后续写，以、听、说、读、看、写等多模态形式设计了一节新型写作课。

亮点：

本节课教学设计突出了几个新：

（1）新教材，新人教版教材内容和外研版教材相关内容巧妙结合，给学生提供大量语言输入。

（2）新学生，首先是新在高一起始年级，学生词汇量和系统写作训练是匮乏的，但是张伟娟老师能在课堂上引导学生基于教材语篇发现有用的语块，进行语块积累并运用，并使师生之间的配合比较默契。

（3）新教法，摒弃传统的写作训练方法，充分利用两种教材相关话题语篇给学生充分的词汇、句型、写作手法等语言输入，同时进行写作技能培养。

（4）新学法，设计阅读记录卡给予学生学法指导，培养学生良好的英语学习习惯，尤其是阅读习惯，设计自评列表，指导学生进行课后反思。

（5）新题型，结合高考新题型巧妙设计"Improving the first draft"和"Improving the second draft"。

建议：

（1）教师的课堂指导语可以更清晰一些。

（2）学生讨论和思考的时间不够充分，可以多预留一些。

Book 1 Unit 1 Teenage Life（二）

设计者姓名：吴碧华

设计者所在单位：广东省清远市第一中学

一、教学材料分析

授课年级：高三

教材内容：新人教版Book 1 Unit 1 Teenage Life（二）

主题：人与社会——学校生活

课型：写作课

课时：1课时

二、教学内容分析

【What】

语篇1：在课前等待正式上课的空隙，给学生播放一段来自TED演讲的视频。演讲者以标准、地道的口语，结合丰富的肢体语言，给学生呈现"如何学习外语才最有效果"的精彩演讲，从视听角度自然地导入了本课关于"英语学习遇到的问题"的话题，同时训练了学生的听力并给予学生学习方法的指引。

语篇2：给学生提供一篇100词左右的、带有下划线标注的有求助信写作特点和结构的范文，让学生整体感知求助信的整体结构和写作特点，指引学生一起去发现并进行归纳总结。教师通过此语篇，训练学生发现问题和分析问题的能力。

语篇3：在学生了解求助信的写作特点和结构之后，及时指引学生初步掌握求助信每一个段落可能用到的相关表达，随后为学生提供实践操作的写作训练。该语篇与本课导入的情境一致，为写作实践做好铺垫。通过此语篇，在激活并检验学生对求助信相关表达的认知的基础上，训练学生解决问题的能力，培养学生的逻辑思维能力。

语篇4、语篇5：首先，在学生实践操作写作训练之后，指引他们从结构、内容、句式、语法等方面进行小组交流并点评组员之间的写作，目的在于让学生在自主、合作、探究的基础上，综合运用语言技能，实现语言的迁移，进行创造性输出。其次，视上课时间灵活处理，给学生提供两篇相同话题的求助信，分别以短文改错和语法填空的形式呈现，供学生在课堂上巩固训练或作为课后作业自测和巩固。两个语篇的提供，旨在通过训练学生已经非常熟悉的高考题型，进一步巩固学生求助信的规范写作，训练学生考试的技巧。

语篇6：给学生提供更多关于高中英语求助信范文的网址，鼓励学生通过网络等多种信息渠道拓展课外学习资源，自主获取、梳理并学习新知识。

【Why】

掌握热点话题词汇并运用话题词汇进行交际性强的应用文写作是高中写作教学的重难点之一。

【How】

基于高考热点话题之一，运用任务教学法、探究法和过程教学法，指导学生复习和复现所学词汇及句型，让学生通过求助信的写作形式，输出得体的文章，鼓励学生学以致用。

三、学情分析

本班学生在该校理科生中整体排名前二，每次大考班级英语平均分约90分（总分150分）。学生整体比较自觉，但性格偏文静的学生比较多，所以上课时的整体氛围稍欠活跃，并且学生的英语基础两极分化严重。对于写作话题词汇，本班学生从高一第一学期开始，就有步骤地在课内和课后按照话题顺序去加强对新课标话题项目涉及的写作词汇的记忆与运用。到目前为止，该班学生已经基本上学完了24个话题相关词汇，并结合话题词汇进行了相关话题的写作训练。但是，由于学生缺乏扎实的语法基础和较为定型的写作模式，提炼信息要点不够精准，他们在习作时往往觉得难以下笔，容易出现信息点遗漏、信息点堆砌、语法错误严重、句式杂乱等现象。这就需要教师及时指导，帮助他们建构相关写作的知识框架，指导他们掌握一定的写作策略并及时进行反思和总结。

四、教学目标

（1）掌握与"学校生活"这个话题相关的一些词汇和短语。

（2）基于自主学习与发现问题，进行小组合作探究学习，并在教师的指导下掌握求助信相关的写作技巧。

（3）通过同伴交流，辨析同伴作文的优劣，学会归纳语言知识，取其精华，培养批判性思维。

（4）学会在学习和生活中遇到问题和困难时主动向别人求助，进而及时有效地解决相关问题，培养积极向上的人生态度。（课堂动态生成）

五、教学重点、难点

重点：

（1）教师以过程法为指导，逐步搭建台阶和知识框架，引导学生按照"发现问题—分析问题—解决问题"以及"input—intake—output"的思路，循序渐进地掌握本节课话题的写作词汇、写作模板和相关表达。

（2）学生通过同伴交流，辨析同伴作文的优劣，学会归纳语言知识，取其精华，培养批判性思维。

难点：

学生通过同伴交流，辨析同伴作文的优劣，学会归纳语言知识，取其精华，培养批判性思维。

六、教学过程

Step 1. Lead-in

1. Ss watch a video about "How to learn a foreign language effectively" during the break as usual.

2. Get the Ss to share their opinions on English study.

3. Brainstorm the possible problems they have in English study.

4. Guide the Ss to discuss the solutions to the problems.

5. Get the Ss to know about the teaching and learning objectives of this lesson.

Purpose：围绕主题创设情境，激活学生已有的知识和经验，导入主题，引出与学生密切相关的待解决的问题，使学生形成教学期待。

Step 2. Pre-writing

1. Get the Ss to read a sample writing and find out the structure and characteristics of a letter of asking for help.

2. Guide the Ss to summarize the basic structure and characteristics of the sample writing.

3. Encourage the Ss to translate some useful expressions for writing a letter of asking for help. Meanwhile, get them to learn more expressions of each part and write them down in their handouts.

Purpose：基于学生的元认知，让学生整体感知求助信的基本结构和写作特点。引导学生按照"发现问题—分析问题—解决问题"以及"input—intake—output"的思路，循序渐进地掌握本节课话题的写作词汇、写作模板和相关表达。通过此语篇，训练学生发现问题和分析问题的能力。

Step 3. While-writing

1. Guide the Ss to read through the writing instructions and review some related words and phrases before writing the letter.

2. The Ss are required to finish their writings on the deliberately-designed answer sheets within 15 minutes.

Purpose：激活并检验学生对求助信相关表达的认知基础，训练学生解决问题的能力，培养学生的逻辑思维能力。

Step 4. Post-writing

Share & Learn:

1. Each of the Ss is required to share his or her writing with at least two different group members by doing the followings:

(1) Read aloud his or her partners' writings.

(2) Use a red pen to mark any problems he or she finds and offer his or her suggestions.

(3) Write down his or her name as well as the score in the blanks for the graders.

(4) Exchange his or her ideas with the group members and recommend the best one to be shared to the rest of their classmates and make comments on it.

2. Before the Ss make comments on their partners' writings, offer them some tips for making comments.

3. Present a possible version of the letter and guide the Ss to pay attention to the structure, characteristics and useful expressions of the writing.

Purpose：学生通过同伴交流，辨析同伴作文的优劣，学会归纳语言知识，取其精华，培养批判性思维；在展示学生优秀作品时，教师与学生一起挖掘亮点，改进不足，并给学生提供凸显写作特点的参考范文，鼓励学生敢于发表见解，培养他们独立思考的习惯，并训练他们的口头表达能力。

Step 5. Further development

(Optional for homework)

If time doesn't permit, the following exercises will be done after class.

1. Proofreading

2. Rational cloze test

Purpose：视上课时间灵活为学生提供两篇相同话题的求助信，分别以短文改错和语法填空的形式呈现，供学生课堂上巩固训练或课后自测和巩固。两个语篇的提供，旨在通过训练学生已经非常熟悉的高考题型，既进一步巩固学生求助信的规范写作，又训练学生的考试技巧。

Step 6. Summary

1. The Ss are encouraged to summarize the key points they have learned in this lesson.

2. The teacher encourages the Ss to learn to effectively solve problems they meet in their study and life.

Purpose：回顾课堂学习重点，升华主题，加强德育浸润，鼓励学生积极对待在学习和生活中遇到的问题。

Step 7. Homework

1. Get the Ss to further polish their writings and hand them in tomorrow.

2. Demonstrate the top 7 writings from seven groups onto the bulletin board in the classroom.

3. Surf the given website to read more sample letters of asking for help.

Purpose：鼓励学生自主学习和积累相关词汇，了解实际生活中的求助信件；展现优秀写作，营造互相学习的良好氛围；鼓励学生通过网络等多种信息渠道拓展课外学习资源，自主获取、梳理并学习新知识。

七、板书设计

The screen shows the main teaching procedures and teaching content of this lesson in the form of PPT.	How to write a letter of asking for help
	Basic structure: Characteristics:
	Para. 1 _____ Tense: _____
	Para. 2 _____ Tone & modal verbs: _____
	Para. 3 _____ Difficult expressions:
	Para. 4 _____ do sb. a favour/give sb. a hand
	be faced/confronted with
	be encountering
	...

八、教学特色

特色1：在整节课的授课过程中，教师给学生提供了六个与本课授课重点相关的语篇，包括口头和书面等多模态形式的语篇。语篇以整体感知、具体分析、实践操作、结合高考题型（短文改错和语法填空）等形式呈现，为学生深入探讨在学习和生活中遇到的问题及解决方案提供素材，开展基于语篇的听、说、读、看、写等学习活动，以达成本课的教学目标。

特色2：教学课程设计非常清晰，逻辑严密，注重细节的描述，整个课堂严谨有序，互动充分。以过程法为指导，逐步搭建台阶和知识框架，引导学生按照"发现问题—分析问题—解决问题"的思路，循序渐进地掌握本节课话题的写作词汇、写作模板和相关表达并进行限时写作与点评。学生在有限的课堂时间里，产出效果明显。

附1：学生学习资料

英语书面表达——求助信

I. Pre-writing

Read a sample writing and find out the structure and characteristics of a letter of asking for help.

Dear Kate,

I am Li Hua, a Senior 3 student. Recently, I have been busy preparing for my College Entrance Exam, but unfortunately I find it quite hard to concentrate on my study. So I am writing to ask you for help.

I am encountering some problems which trouble me a lot. First, I have to spend so much time on my homework that I hardly have time to take sports. Moreover, the high expectations from the teachers and my parents make me extremely stressed. What troubles me most is that it is difficult for me to fall asleep every night.

Could you please offer me some advice on how to solve these problems? Thanks for your kindness in advance.

Looking forward to your early reply.

Yours sincerely,

Li Hua

Basic structure（基本结构）:

Para. 1: _____

Para. 2: _____

Para. 3: _____

Para. 4: _____

Characteristics（写作特征）:

1. 通常使用的时态: _____

2. 阐述要清晰，用词要恰当，注意语气委婉、真诚；情态动词多使用_____

_____

3. 陈述困难或问题要注意使用过渡性词汇，如: _____

_____

Useful expressions for writing letters of this kind:

A. 点明目的

我写信是为了向你寻求帮助。

1. _____

2. _____

More expressions:

3. _____

4. _____

B. 描述困难

我在……方面遇到了一些困难。

1. _____

2. _____

More expressions:

3. _____

4. _____

C. 寻求帮助/建议

你可以给我一些解决这个问题的建议吗?

1. _____

2. _____

More expressions:

3. _____

4. _____

D. 表示感谢

如果你能帮助我/给予我建议,我将不胜感激。

1. _____

2. _____

More expressions:

3. _____

E. 期盼回复

希望尽快收到你的来信。

1. _____

2. _____

More expressions:

3. _____

Ⅱ. While-writing

Practice makes perfect!

假设你是李华，当前你在英语学习方面遇到了一些问题，于是你向你所在学校的外籍老师汤姆（Tom）写一封求助信寻求帮助。要点如下：

1. 本人简介；

2. 求助内容；

3. 希望得到Tom的帮助。

注意：①词数100左右；②可以适当增加细节，以使行文连贯；③开头和结尾已为你写好。

Useful expressions:

1. 英语听力＿＿＿＿＿＿＿＿　　8. 面临＿＿＿＿＿＿＿＿

2. 英语口语＿＿＿＿＿＿＿＿　　9. 不擅长＿＿＿＿＿＿＿＿

3. 英语书面表达＿＿＿＿＿＿＿＿　　10. 掌握＿＿＿＿＿＿＿＿

4. 英语阅读理解＿＿＿＿＿＿＿＿　　11. 寻求帮助＿＿＿＿＿＿＿＿

5. 语法＿＿＿＿＿＿＿＿　　12. 寻求建议＿＿＿＿＿＿＿＿

6. 单词＿＿＿＿＿＿＿＿　　13. 给某人关于……的建议＿＿＿＿＿＿＿＿

7. 词汇量＿＿＿＿＿＿＿＿　　14. 感谢某人某事＿＿＿＿＿＿＿＿

Ⅲ. Post-writing

Share and learn!

Share your writing with at least two different group members by doing the followings:

1. Read aloud your partners' writings.

2. Use a red pen to mark any problems you find and offer your suggestions.

3. Write down your name and the score in the blanks for the graders (评分员).

4. Exchange your ideas with your group members and recommend the best one to be shared to the rest of your classmates and make comments on it.

Tips for making comments on the writing:

1. 卷面：The writing looks ...

2. 结构：It is divided into ...

3. 内容（信息完整）：All the key points are included.

4. 连贯：Linking words are used like ...

5. 语法、句式：There are many good sentence patterns and phrases like ...

附2：学生习作

Dear Tom,

I'm Li Hua, a Senior 3 student in your school. I am writing to ask for your help for I am having trouble in learning English now.

At present, I am faced with two main problems. First of all, I find it quite hard to remember words and put them into use. In addition, I feel so nervous in front of my classmates that I can't say a word in English.

Therefore, I hope you can offer me some advice on how to remember the words and how to overcome my fear of speaking English. I would like to express my gratitude in advance for your kindness.

Looking forward to your early reply.

Yours,

Li Hua

Book 1 Unit 1 Teenage Life（三）

设计者姓名：陈艳丽

设计者所在单位：广东省清远市广州大学附属中学（英德）

一、教学材料分析

授课年级：高一

教材内容：新人教版Book 1 Unit 1 Teenage Life

主题：人与自我——学校生活

课型：Reading for Writing

课时：1课时

二、教学内容分析

【What】

本节课的内容选自新人教版教材Book 1 Unit 1 Teenage Life中 "Reading for Writing" 板块的 "Write a letter of advice"。本单元在 "人与自我——学校生活" 的主题下，探讨了中外青少年在学校、课外活动、兴趣爱好、人际交往等方面的状况及面临的问题。

本课内容为主题语境 "Teenage life" 的读写部分，主要以 "写一封建议信" 为活动主题。首先，阅读文本是一封青少年咨询师罗苏姗（Susan Luo）写给一个因朋友沉迷于电脑游戏和网络而担忧的青少年的建议信。这是一封比较正式的书信，包括日期、称呼、正文、结尾和签名。正文分为两段：第一段说明写信人已经知晓来信人的问题，了解了来信人的感受，即担心朋友上网成瘾；第二段说明了网瘾的害处，并提出解决问题的建议。阅读部分为学生写作的输出环节提供了语言和结构上的支架。其次， "写" 的部分为学生提供了三个青少年青春期烦恼的情境，学生可以分小组进行活动，自主选择其中一个情境，围绕 "问题"

与"建议"展开讨论，并根据提纲独立完成初稿。最后，学生利用评价表进行同伴互评，提出修改意见，并基于同伴的评价做进一步修改，确定终稿。

【Why】

在前面的几个课时，学生已经通过听说和阅读了解了作为一名高一新生可能会面临的挑战。在这个基础上，教师如何给出有用的建议就显得尤为重要。为了更好地锻炼学生的写作思维，教师让学生将在课文中所学到的建议信格式、常见内容构成以及语言特征运用到自己的写作中，能够帮助学生很好地实现知识的迁移。

【How】

本课教学以谈论青少年问题导入，原创一封青少年因担心朋友而写给Susan Luo的求助信，引导学生思考如何回信，再自然过渡到建议信的文本阅读。首先，教师带领学生熟悉信件格式，并理解文本的主要信息。其次，学生再次阅读并整理提建议的相关语言。正式写作之前，学生先浏览教科书提供的三个情境，讨论这些问题，并列出相应的建议及理由，为写作做好准备。最后，学生利用教科书提供的提纲完成初稿，同伴互评并修改、定稿。

三、学情分析

本节课的学习主体是高一新生。学生刚入学一个月，尚处于初高中过渡期。学生对英语写作有畏惧、厌烦心理。学生在初中阶段也接触过建议信，对其基本结构还比较熟悉。但初中所学的建议信偏口语交际，内容简单、词数较少，和高考的应用文写作要求相差甚远。本节课应用文写作属于高中阶段的初次尝试，学生在建议信的语言得体性和如何有理有据地给予建议方面的知识还是很欠缺，所以教师需要有针对性地引导学生逐步提高写作能力。

四、教学目标

该板块设计了读写结合的活动，活动主题是"写一封建议信（Write a letter of advice）"。青少年思想活跃，渴望独立，在"幼稚"与"成熟"之间徘徊，所以在这个特殊的年龄段，青少年会面临各种各样的问题。该板块引导学生思考网瘾、早恋、孤独、与父母之间的代沟等问题，并讨论解决问题的方法，最终让学生将其落实到一封建议信的书写上。该板块由五个活动组成，按照"文本内容理解—文本结构和语言特点分析—写作情境设置—完成写作任务—展示写作成果"的顺序展开。

课时目标：

（1）语言能力

① 通过阅读建议信，厘清建议信的主要内容和结构，把握建议信的语言特征；

② 能够利用写作任务提供的情境，运用提建议的语言写一封语言得体、结构清晰的建议信。

（2）文化品格：该板块引导学生思考网瘾、早恋、孤独、与父母之间的代沟等问题，并讨论解决问题的方法，最终让学生将其落实到一封建议信的书写上。这个活动旨在让学生体会到互相沟通、真诚相助的重要性，并能对照反思自己的行为，解决在现实生活中遇到的问题。

（3）思维品质：

① 让学生对文本中的建议做出评价并阐述原因，以培养他们的批判性思维；

② 让学生针对文本中的问题提出自己的建议，以培养学生的创造性思维；

③ 让学生根据老师给出的评价标准客观地评价自己和同伴的作文。

（4）学习能力：让学生将在课本中所学的语言知识、语篇知识、语用知识、文化知识等运用到新的语境中，去解决与自身生活关系密切的问题，培养学生迁移创新的能力。

五、教学重点、难点

重点：帮助学生掌握建议信的常见结构和语言特征，并使其能写出一封语义连贯、结构清晰的建议信。

难点：学生能够利用写作任务提供的情境，运用提建议的语言写一封语言得体、结构清晰的建议信。

六、教学过程

Step 1. Lead-in

Task: Discuss the questions:

1. When you have some problems in life or in study, what will you do?

2. What is the worried friend's problem?

3. Suppose you were Susan Luo, how would you write the letter back?

Purpose: In this way, the teacher creates a real scene of giving advice, which can not only stimulate students' interest in the topic of writing, but also help students stand in the adviser's shoes to consider what they need to write in their advice letter to make it more persuasive.

Step 2. Reading and thinking

Task 1: Read to discover details concerning advice letters' writing style.

1. How many parts are there in the passage? What are they?

2. What's Para. 1 about?

3. How did the writer present the problem? Can you think of any other expressions?

4. How did the writer express her sympathy?

5. Besides suggestions, what else did Susan Luo say in her letter?

6. What expressions did the writer use to give advice? Can you think of any other expressions?

7. In the last paragraph, how did the writer express her expectation? Can you think of any other expressions?

8. What makes Miss Luo's letter good?

Task 2: Summarize the basic structure of a letter of advice.

The Basic Structure of a Letter of Advice

Beginning: present a problem + express your sympathy

◇ 1. You wrote that ... I understand quite well that ...

◇ 2. I'm sorry you have great trouble in doing ... However, the situation is easy to change if you take my advice. Here are some tips to help you.

Body: suggestions + reasons

◇ I recommend that ... then/that way, ...

◇ Why not/ Why don't you ...? If you do this, ...

◇ It would be a good idea if ... By doing this, ...

◇ I wonder if ... which can not only ... but also ...

◇ What about/How about ...

Ending：expectation

◇ I hope you will find these ideas useful.

◇ I'm sure ...

Purpose： By reading the sample, students can be clear of the structure and characteristics of a letter of advice. In addition, students are encouraged to summarize some useful sentence structures and phrases which can be used in their writings. After that, through oral practice, the teacher can guide students to put the strategies, related sentence structures and phrases into use, which not only helps students grasp them better but also provides a scaffolding for their later writing assignment.

Step 3. Pre-writing

Task: Work in groups. Choose one of the teenagers and discuss his or her problems. List possible suggestions and reasons.

Situation	Suggestions	Reasons
Eric, 15, Chicago My parents won't listen when I tell them things. I guess it's because they're adults and can't understand me. Do you have any suggestions?		
Xu Ting, 14, Hangzhou I always feel lonely after school because my parents work in another city. What can I do?		
Min Ho, 15, Seoul There is a girl I like in my class, but I am too shy to talk to her. Please help me!		

Purpose： Pre-writing consists of three parts. Students read through the three situations and summarize the problems they are facing in their own words. And then discuss the possible suggestions and reasons in pairs or groups. By group work, students are expected to cooperate with each other and enrich their minds.

Step 4. While-writing

Task: Through group work, each group drafts a letter offering advice to any of those students above.

Purpose：This part is to help students put what they have learned into practice and check if they have grasped what they have learned. Since most students find it challenging to finish the letter in such a limited time, the teacher can ask students to finish their writing through group work. Through group work, each member has specific tasks to complete and they need to help each other to finish the writing. By doing so, students' interest in writing can be aroused and they can learn from each other.

Step 5. Post-writing

Task: Present your work and use the checklist to give feedback.

Aspects		Grades		
		A	B	C
Content	Are all the parts of a letter included and organized in a good order?			
	Does the writer give reasons for the advice?			
Language	Does the writer use correct sentences without making mistakes in grammar and punctuation?			
	Does the writer use proper expressions to give suggestions?			
Coherence	Does the writer use effective transitions?			
Handwriting	Is the handwriting easy to read?			

Purpose: Each of the group is required to check their first draft using the questions above as a guide and make some necessary changes. And then the teacher can ask some students to present their group work to the whole class. The teacher is expected to guide the Ss to give feedback on their partner's draft by using the checklist. This activity is designed to help Ss know how to make a self-assessment and comments on others' writings by presenting the checklist.

Step 6. Summary

Ss are encouraged to summarize what they have learned in this lesson.

Purpose: This activity is designed to help students reflect on what they have learned.

Step 7. Homework

1. Revise your letter and put it up in the classroom. (compulsory)

2. Read the four cases of "Talking Teens" on Page 75 of the Workbook, choose one case and write a letter of advice to the parent. (optional)

Purpose: This activity is designed to consolidate students' knowledge they have learned and give a platform for them to show themselves.

七、主要教学活动

教师在写作教学中，主要安排了以下几个教学活动。

（一）创设情境，激发学生思维

通过增设学生给Susan Luo写求助信的环节，引导学生思考Susan Luo如何回信。利用高一学生熟悉的情境，激发学生对这个话题的兴趣，再自然过渡到阅读回信内容，引导学生评价回信是否有说服力。在师生互动环节，教师引导学生以Susan Luo的视角回信，为之后的文本阅读和思考建议有效搭建支架。

（二）设置问题链，促进学生深层理解

在阅读环节，教师通过设置八个问题，层层深入，以问题链的方式让学生了解建议信的基本格式和语言特征。学生了解到：建议信的基本格式一般包括date、greeting、body、close以及signature等部分；建议信的语言要得体；建议信内容要对求助者的问题或困难表示理解和同情。同时，教师通过让学生对文本中的建议做出评价从而提出自己的建议，培养了学生的批判性思维和创造性思维。

（三）小组合作，达成写作任务

小组合作课堂活动贯穿整个课堂，从写前对文本内容、语言特点和建议的得体性方面展开讨论，到写作时小组合作完成一封建议信写作，每个成员都有具体分工与任务，极大地降低了任务的难度，同时有利于各层次学生互帮互助，共同发展。写后让学生利用评价表小组内互改和润色文章，有利于帮助学生进一步关注写作结构和细节上的准确性，进一步提升其写作水平。

（四）写后评价，提高对习作的评判能力

学生利用评价表里的标准逐一对照自己所写的建议信，从而判断这封建议信在内容上是否达到了交际目的，在格式上是否符合建议信的要求。学生交换初稿，利用评价表从内容的完整性、信息之间的逻辑性、语言的准确性和恰当性等方面进行评价，同时反思自己的作品，提高对作品的评判能力，同时提升自身的语言能力。让学生有机会展示自我，从而增强学习动力。

八、板书设计

Book 1 Unit 1 Reading for Writing
The Basic Structure of a Letter of Advice
Beginning: present a problem + express your sympathy
Body: suggestions + reasons
    I recommend that ... then/that way, ...
    Why not/ Why don't you ...? If you do this, ...
Ending: expectation
    I hope you will find these ideas useful.
    I'm sure ...

九、教学反思

本节课是一节读写课，即通过阅读建议者Susan Luo的建议信，分析其文本结构、写信语气、交流有效性等方面的内容，再通过学生建议者角色扮演活动，创设三个常见的学生早恋、孤独、与父母的代沟等问题，引导学生思考并讨论解决问题的办法，最终落实到一封建议信的写作上。因为学生对建议信了解甚少，不清楚建议信的格式、基本结构和语言特征，所以在建议信写作中存在逻辑不通、结构混乱、语气生硬、建议缺乏理由支撑等问题。针对以上问题，本节课运用了情景教学法和过程体裁法，通过小组合作的课堂活动，实现"输入（input）—内化（intake）"的教学过程，从而帮助学生更好地掌握本节课的学习重点。

本节课通过教学设计解答了以上几个重点，达到了较为理想的教学效果。比较成功的地方有：

（1）增设情境。首先，教师通过增设学生给Susan Luo写求助信的环节，引导学生思考Susan Luo如何回信，再自然过渡到阅读回信内容，引导学生评价回信是否有说服力。其次，在输出环节通过创设"I am an adviser"情境，创设三个常见的学生早恋、孤独、与父母的代沟等问题，引导学生思考并讨论解决的办法，体现以英语学习活动观为引领，运用"写前准备—写中指导—写后修改润色"的过程性写作教学法，促进学生自主学习，提升学生思维品质。

（2）小组合作。小组合作课堂活动贯穿整个课堂，从写前对文本内容、语言特点和建议的得体性方面展开讨论，到写作时小组合作完成一封建议信写作，每个成员都有具体分工与任务，极大地降低了任务的难度，同时有利于各层次学生互帮互助，共同发展。写后让学生利用评价表修改和润色文章，有利于帮助学生进一步关注写作结构和细节上的准确性，进一步提升学生的写作水平。

诚然，本节课也存在一些遗憾。首先，课堂容量大，教师的上课节奏快，给予学生反思和内化知识的时间不够，同时对给予建议的不同表达法仅仅停留在口头翻译几个句子上，并未落实到笔头。此外，由于时间关系，在学生作品展示环节，只点评了两篇作文，若能多展示几篇让学生去点评，效果会更好。

十、教学特色

特色1：

以英语学习活动观为引领，运用"写前准备—写中指导—写后修改润色"的过程性写作教学法，促进学生自主学习，提升其思维品质。同时运用了情景教学法和过程体裁法，通过小组合作的课堂活动，实现"输入（input）—内化（intake）"的教学过程。

特色2：

教师通过搭建丰富的语言和结构上的写作支架，简化了写作任务，同时使学生随后的笔头输出进入水到渠成的阶段，达到了较为理想的教学效果。

十一、课例评析

（一）课例评析1：郭秀云

陈艳丽老师的这节课是基于新人教版教材Book 1 Unit 1主题语境"人与社会——学校生活"的一节应用文（建议信）写作课，主题贯穿整个教学过程。设定的教学目标基本达成，各环节设计基于学情，指导细致，注重学法指导。基本符合过程性写作流程：写前输入—写中教师指导、学生训练—写后展示。

亮点：

（1）各个环节教学任务设计层层递进，由语篇导入，引导学生进行主动学习，分析建议信格式，搭建"脚手架"；然后，进一步引导学生根据三个学生的情况，进行头脑风暴，分别给予适当建议，给学生进行语言输出（写）做好充分铺垫。

（2）学生小组合作，根据老师提供的学生所面临的三个问题材料选择其中一个进行任务写作，属于半开放式设计，体现了陈老师教学民主和以学生为主体的意识。本课由布置学生写什么转变为学生选择写什么，增强了学生的写作动机和写作兴趣。

（3）创设真实的交际情境（写作任务）。写作材料符合学生在高中生活中所面临的一些普遍问题。让学生经过讨论得出一些合理的建议，体现了英语核心素养在英语课堂上的具体体现，培养了学生高阶思维能力和写作能力。

建议：

（1）教学内容设计环节较多，导致在学生合作讨论部分时间不充足。

（2）如果在三个设计的情境写作中融入多模态教学，效果可能会更好。

（3）展示环节时间稍显紧凑。

（二）课例评析2：胡翠娥

艳丽老师的这节课基于省级课题"基于教材主题与话题的高中英语写作教学模式探究"和新人教版教材Book 1 Unit 1主题"Teenage Life"的"Reading for writing"，在40分钟的时间里完整地体现了过程性写作教学的写前输入、写中指导和写后反馈，体现了艳丽老师的四个意识。

亮点：

四个意识：

（1）课题研究意识：紧紧把握课题研究的内容，在课堂教学中体现课题研究的主要内容和过程性写作教学的各个环节。

（2）教材处理意识：能修改教材内容，原创一封求助信，创设真实情境引出本节课的主题和教学内容——建议信。

（3）积极评价意识：整节课对学生的课堂表现都能及时做出积极的激励性评价反馈，有利于增强学生的自信。

（4）核心素养意识：在语言知识方面为学生搭建支架。

学习能力：以读促写，在语篇中发现有用的信息、拓展、归纳、模仿、合作等。

思维品质：在Post-writing环节的写后反馈中，学生能辨析语言，正确评判。

建议：

（1）教师讲得偏多，建议给学生更多自主思考的时间和发言的机会。

（2）设计的讨论环节有点流于形式，学生并没有积极参与讨论。

（3）在平时的教学中，写作可以分为2～3个课时完成；

（4）建议体现"学用意识"，可以生生或师生以口头形式表演"求助和建议"。

附1：写作情境

附2：学生习作（一稿）

Book 2 Unit 1 Cultural Heritage

设计者姓名：张美仪

设计者所在单位：广东省清远市清新区第一中学

一、教学材料分析

授课年级：高一

教材内容：新人教版Book 2 Unit 1 Cultural Heritage

主题：人与社会——物质与非物质文化遗产

课型：Reading for Writing

课时：1课时

二、 教学内容分析

【**What**】

本节课的活动设计是读写结合，但重在写作，主题是"写一篇新闻报道(Write a news report)"。介绍了文化遗产（cultural heritage）的相关知识，了解"数字敦煌"项目利用先进的科学技术保护文物的理念。

【**Why**】

启发学生从人与自然、人与社会的角度思考"cultural heritage"所蕴含的人文内涵和意义。

【**How**】

本文是一篇有关利用数字技术制作敦煌莫高窟文物图像的新闻报道。报道具有典型的新闻语言特征，结构鲜明。导语部分讲述了该文化遗产保护项目的概况，主体部分报道了莫高窟的重要历史文化价值和制作文物数字照片的重要意义。

三、学情分析

学生通过对本单元前面板块的学习，具备了一定的与文化遗产相关的词汇量，大部分学生已经掌握了单元相关词汇，对词汇的意义和基本用法有了初步了解。但是大部分学生的语言水平不高，加上对该文体不熟悉，对文本信息的理解比较表面、浅层，没有主动整合、分析和深入理解文本结构，需要教师为其提供一些语言上的支持。另外，在最后的写作活动中，学生要以小组合作形式开展，才能完成写作任务。

四、教学目标

(1) Get students to have a good understanding of some features about a news report by reading the text.

(2) Instruct students to write a summary about a news report properly using some newly acquired writing skills in this period.

(3) Develop students' writing and cooperating abilities.

(4) Strengthen students' great interest in writing discourses.

五、教学重点、难点

Important points:

(1) Stimulate students to have a good understanding of how to write a summary about a news report.

(2) Cultivate students to write a news report properly and concisely.

Difficult points:

(1) Improve students' ability of writing and using English by reporting news.

(2) Get the students to have a better understanding of the Chinese ancient culture relics.

六、教学过程

	教学活动		
Teaching Activities	Activity Designs		Purposes
	Teacher's Activities	Students' Activities	
Lead-in	Present a short clip of video of Mogao caves	Watch the video and think	1.To lead to the theme 2.To activate students' knowledge about cultural heritage
Step 1: Fast reading	Ask Ss to read the passage on P 8 and answer questions	Read the passage and find out the answers quickly	To understand the news report
Step 2: Detailed reading	Ask Ss to read the passage again and answer questions	Individual work: Read and think	To have a good understanding of the news report
Step 3: Study the organization	Get students to study the structure	Focus on the structures and try to remember them	1.To understand the structure of a news report 2.Prepare students for writing
Step 4: Writing	1.Guide the students to finish the translation of the phrases 2.Students work in groups to write a news report	Read the writing task quickly and try to work in pairs to finish the writing with the help of the writing tips	1.To apply the words and phrases to writing 2.To conclude the words and phrases and go for in-depth understanding 3.To develop expressing skills in writing
Step 5: Show time	Choose and show some groups' writings	Share their writings with the whole class	To learn how to appreciate and evaluate a good writing
Summary and homework	1. Summarize what has been learned in the class 2. Assignments: 【Must】①Polish the news report ②Remember the phrases that have been learnt 【Optional】Work in groups to revise the news report and then report it to the class		1.To develop students' writing and cooperating abilities 2.To consolidate what has been covered in the class

七、板书设计

新闻报道
- 标题：
- 导语：who
  - what
  - when
  - where
  - why
  - how
- 主体：
- 结语：

附：写作情境

假设你是李华，是北京一所高中的学生。上周末你校组织了一次保护长城的活动。请你用英语写一篇短文报道这次活动，并给校报英文版投稿。内容包括：

（1）向游客宣传保护长城的重要意义；

（2）发起为修复长城做贡献的募捐活动；

（3）本次活动的意义。

Book 2 Unit 2 Wildlife Protection

设计者姓名：陈锦春

设计者所在单位：广东省清远市第一中学

一、教学材料分析

授课年级： 高一

教材内容： 新人教版 Book 2 Unit 2 Wildlife Protection

主题： 人与自然——保护野生动物

课型： 应用文写作

课时： 1课时

二、教学内容分析

【What】

本节课是一节写作课，写作内容是写信给世界自然基金会（WWF），建议如何保护野生动物。主要的阅读文本是一封写给WWF的信，建议如何保护非洲的红疣猴。文本采用了正式的书信文体，由三段内容组成：第一段介绍了写信人的身份和非洲红疣猴的生存现状；第二段主要是提出保护非洲红疣猴的建议和理由；第三段表达写信人的希望。

【Why】

保护野生动物需要全社会的参与，要求对学生进行保护野生动物的教育，唤起青少年保护野生动物的意识和热情，促进学生深入了解和研究濒危动物的状况，并思考其保护措施，培养学生的社会担当和责任感。

【How】

本节课采用过程性写作教学方法，遵循"写前—写中—写后"的写作教学步骤。学生在了解动物的状况和其面临的问题的基础上，以老师在课堂上搭建的词汇、句型为脚手架，学会写一封有关如何保护野生动物的建议信。

三、学情分析

高一年级的学生有了一定的写作基础，学习热情很高，掌握了一定的写作词汇，熟悉各类应用文的格式、常见写作句型。但其在语言的组织和段落的逻辑紧密性方面还要进一步学习。

四、教学目标

单元目标：

本单元的主题是"人与自然——保护野生动物"展开，通过听、说、读、写等多模态语篇的输入，让学生了解人与自然的平衡关系，认识到人类的不正当消费与濒危野生物种的消失有直接关系，进而增强学生保护野生动物的意识和责任感，并使其寻求动物保护的合理方式和策略，培养其批判性思维和创新思维。

课时目标：

本节课是基于教材主题语境和话题设计的写建议信的教学活动。学生通过了解中外野生动物的生存状况和所面临的问题，思考个人参与动物保护的合理方式，学会写一封有关如何保护野生动物的建议信。

五、教学重点、难点

重点：引导学生通过阅读范文，归纳出建议信的结构和语言特点，并能将其运用到独立写作中。

难点：让学生思考动物保护的合理方式，并能用有条理、有逻辑的句子表达出来。

六、教学过程

Step 1. Warming-up

Show a few pictures of animals being hunted to the students. Draw the students' attention to the problem that some wildlife are being threatened.

Purpose：围绕单元主题，以图片导入，让学生了解野生动物的生存状况和所面临的问题，激活学生已有的知识，渗透相关的写作词汇，为学生后续写作做好词汇积累。

Step 2. Pre-writing

1. Get the students to read the letter written to WWF. Help them to work out what is written in each paragraph.

Para. 1: The current situation of the animal.

Para. 2 ~ 3: Suggestions to help the animal.

Para. 4: Wishes.

Purpose：学生通过分析范文，掌握建议信的写作结构，形成语篇意识，为写作搭好框架。

2. Guide the students to work out the useful sentences for writing a letter of advice by referring to the sample letter.

参考句型：

(1) I live in/on ... This is the (only）home of (name of the animal), but there are only ... left/ but the number of ... has dropped. This is my plan to save the ...

(2) I am writing to draw your attention to the matter.

First, I suggest ... / We should ... Second, ...

(3) Please help these poor ... and I am sure they can survive with your help.

(4) I would appreciate it if you could take my suggestions into consideration.

Purpose：学生从语块到句子，积累建议信的写作句型，并在熟记句型的基础上进行练习，做到学以致用，巩固所学知识。

3. Get the students to choose an animal and discuss the questions in groups.

(1) What is the current situation of the animal? (What problems does the animal face?）

(2) What suggestions do you have to protect the animal? (What measures will you suggest?）

Purpose：学生通过讨论，学会分析动物的现状，分享野生动物保护的不同方法和解决问题的方案，思考个人参与动物保护的合理方式，从而实现积累写作材料、激活写作思维、提高写作信心的目的。

Step 3. While-writing & post writing

1. Get the students to work in groups and write a letter to the WWF. Each student writes one paragraph.

2. Get the students to use the checklist to revise the writing.

3. Ask some groups to present their writings.

Purpose：小组合作写作，降低了写作的难度，培养了学生的合作精神。学生有机会展示自己的作品，可以获得更大的成就感，从而增强学习动力。

Step 4. Homework

Get the students to write a letter to WWF about protecting the Chinese Yangtze finless porpoise.

Purpose：鼓励学生积极寻求保护动物的合理方式和策略，培养学生的批判性思维、创新思维以及综合运用语言的能力。

七、主要教学活动

本节课共设计了三个教学活动：

一是"写前"的准备活动。先以视频、图片的形式引入话题，激活学生有关野生动物保护的词汇，然后基于范文的文本（介绍如何保护非洲红疣猴），运用发现式教学法，引导学生进行语篇分析，包括范文分为几段写，每段写了什么相关内容，还可以用哪些写作句型，等等。学生有了词汇和句型的支撑，增强了写作的信心。

二是"写中"的写作活动。学生以小组为单位，首先确定要写保护哪种野生动物，然后进行小组讨论，讨论该野生动物所面临的问题以及保护的合理方式。学生在进行小组写作时，每个学生负责写一部分，完成后小组把几部分作文组合在一起，再进行润色，添加适当的连接词，使文章连贯顺畅。

三是"写后"的评价活动。学生完成写作后，根据写作评价标准，进行小组互评。这样既培养学生的批判性思维，又加深了学生对写作评价标准的认识，促进学生英语学科核心素养的形成和发展，引导学生学会监控和调整自己的学习。

八、板书设计

Unit 2 Wildlife Protection

Writing—How to write a letter of suggestion

The endangered animal: _____

Para. 1 _____ Current situations: _____

Para. 2 _____ Suggestions: _____

Para. 3 _____

九、教学特色

特色1：这节课教师运用了过程性写作教学方法，结合写作主题和话题，一步一步引导学生从相关词汇、写作句型入手，积累保护动物的相关词块和建议信的写作句型，并在熟记句型的基础上进行练习，为顺利开展写作搭好脚手架。学生通过小组讨论，进行思想交流，思考保护野生动物的合理方法，最后进行语言的输出。整个教学环节紧凑，循序渐进，符合学生的认知水平。

特色2：这节课遵循新课标的理念，以发展学生的英语学科核心素养为目的，实践英语学习活动观，着力提高学生的运用能力。课堂上教师设计了多种学习方式，如自主学习、合作学习、探究学习等。学生通过表达个人观点，发展多元思维和批判性思维，提高英语学习能力和运用能力。

附：写作情境

调查显示，中国长江江豚(Chinese Yangtze finless porpoise)因受人类活动影响而濒临灭绝，目前总数不足1000只。假设你是李华，现请用英文给WWF写一封信，请他们关注这一状况并提供帮助。内容包括：

（1）说明写信目的；

（2）简述江豚现状；

（3）希望WWF如何帮助；

（4）表示感谢并期望回复。

注意：①词数100左右；②可以适当增加细节，以使行文连贯；③开头语已为你写好。

Dear Sir or Madam,

I am a student from Chongqing, China. _____

_____

_____

Yours sincerely,

Li Hua

Book 2 Unit 5 Music (Reading for Writing)

设计者姓名：胡翠娥

设计者所在单位：广东省清远市第二中学

一、教学材料分析

授课年级：高一

教材内容：新人教版Book 2 Unit 5 Music

主题：人与社会——音乐对人类的影响

课型：读写课

课时：1课时

二、教学内容分析

本单元的主题是音乐，属于主题语境"人与社会"下的"文学、艺术与体育"主题群。听、说、读、看、写等所有部分的材料都与音乐有关，涉及的主题是欣赏音乐、音乐的纽带作用、策划音乐节、音乐的疗愈功能、音乐鉴赏与评论以及音乐家。学生通过学习意识到音乐是人类共同的语言，可以把地球村各地的人联系起来。

【**What**】

本节课是基于新人教版教材Book 2 Unit 5 Music的"Reading for Writing"板块

"Write a speech"的读写课。写作的话题是How to write a speech。

本读写板块的语篇是萨拉·威廉姆斯（Sara Williams）发表的一篇演讲。她以自己的亲身经历告知人们："美好的音乐可以疗伤治病（Music is the medicine of the mind）。"

【Why】

以演讲稿的形式有力地说明音乐不仅可以陶冶情操，还可以疗伤治病（Music is the medicine of the mind.）。

【How】

演讲稿是一种常见文体，有独特的组织结构，包括welcome the audience (Good morning!)、introduce yourself (My name is Sara Williams)、propose the topic (It's an honor to be here and to share with you ...)、personal anecdote、personal feeling、close the speech和thank the audience。为了让演讲内容打动人心、有说服力，Sara Williams在演讲中采用了很多修辞手法，包括设问、引用、明喻、暗喻、重复、拟人等。

三、学情分析

（1）知识储备：学生处于高一年级第二学期，整体程度为中等。学生通过本单元"Listening and Speaking""Reading and Thinking""Discovering Useful Structures"等板块的学习，对熟知的音乐这一话题有了更清晰的认知，积累了大量的语言知识（语音、语块、语法），对学习理解类活动没有困难。

（2）学习能力：学生对与本课写作任务"Write a speech"相关的知识结构并不系统和全面，运用英语连贯性地进行演讲的能力普遍较弱。

（3）素养提升：学生对实现语言知识和文化知识内化、巩固新的知识结构、基于新的知识结构通过自主合作探究的学习方式综合运用语言技能进行迁移创新类学习会有一定障碍，需要教师进行更进一步的语言输入和学法指导，引领学生通过体验探究、沟通交流、迁移运用、评价等深度学习活动来实现素养提升。

四、教学目标

通过本节课的学习，学生能够实现以下目标。

（1）语言能力

① 学会与音乐有关的有用表达：have an impact on, listen to music, make me feel ..., help me ..., give me ..., make my spirits fly like ..., treasure music, make it a part of ... ；

② 掌握演讲稿的结构特征和语言特征，写演讲稿初稿。

（2）学习能力

学会通过快速阅读语篇，找主旨句和归纳每个语段的关键词；学会制作思维导图（演讲稿的结构）形成知识结构图；运用小组合作学习方法开展学习（拼文、写后互评和修改）。

（3）思维品质

① 能够通过所听所看（视频）所读（语篇）梳理、概括有用信息，能分析、推断信息逻辑关系建构新概念；

② 结合演讲稿的语言特点创造性地表达自己的观点；

③ 通过评判同伴的作品，指出优点和不足之处，形成批判性思维。

（4）文化品格

通过欣赏视频和阅读语篇，形成"音乐是世界通用的语言，可以把地球村各地的人联系在一起（Music is the universal language of the world and it can bring people all over the world together）"的世界共同体意识。

五、教学重点、难点

重点：学会运用所学的语言知识进行演讲（How music influences my life）。

难点：运用所学的语言知识，采用修辞手法进行演讲（How music influences my life）。

六、教学设计理念

（1）单元整体教学：《普通高中英语课程标准（2017年版2020年修订）》强调"以学科大概念为核心，使课程内容结构化，以主题为引领，使课程内容情境化"。本节课所有环节都围绕"音乐"主题，深入解读、分析、整合和重组教材等教学资源，结合学生的需求，搭建语言支架，引导学生通过本节课的学习，提炼知识并建立关联，生成作品（演讲稿）。

（2）英语学习活动观：《高中英语课标》还指出，英语学习活动的设计应注意：情境创设要尽量真实，注意与学生已有的知识和经验建立紧密联系；要善于利用多种工具和手段，如思维导图或信息结构图，引导学生完成对信息的获取与梳理，教会学生归纳和提炼基于主题的新知识结构；要根据所学主题内容、学习目标和学生经验等，选择和组织不同层次的英语学习活动。

（3）过程性写作教学：20世纪80年代研究第二语言教学的学者，如美国的Raimes、Zamel和英国的Hedge都倡导将过程法应用到第二语言的写作教学中。过程教学法将教学的重点放在学生的写作过程和写作能力上，充分培养学生的思维能力，强调教师对学生写作策略的培养和对学生写作过程的全程指导。过程性写作教学一般分为写前（Pre-writing）（准备阶段）、写中（While-writing）、写后（Post-writing）修改（Revising）和编辑（Editing）阶段。本节课的重点是写前的语言输入。

基于这几点，教者在本节课中，基于教材主题与话题，创设与主题（人与社会——音乐对人类的影响）和学生学校生活密切相关的语境，激发学生参与活动的兴趣，调动学生已有的基于该主题的经验，以思维导图的形式帮助学生建构和完善新的知识结构。整节课通过一系列关联主题的语言学习和思维活动，培养学生语言理解和表达的能力，推动学生的深度学习，实现知识迁移。

七、教学过程

Procedures	Activities	Design Purposes & Goals to Achieve	Core Competencies Covered
Step 1. Lead-in	Ss watch the videos and enjoy different kinds of music. 1.Complete some sentences: (1) _____ (dress) elegantly, the old lady is playing the _____. It sounds _____ and _____. (2) The young lady is playing and we feel _____.	语言知识和语言能力目标：视听形式（视频）创设语境，导入主题，激活学生已有的关于音乐的认知和经验，给学生进行充分的写前语言输入；优美动听的音乐激	新旧连接：在观看视频、欣赏音乐的同时，培养学生听、说、看的能力

Procedures	Activities	Design Purposes & Goals to Achieve	Core Competencies Covered
Step 1. Lead-in	(3) The little girl is playing the _____ and it gives us _____. We feel _____. (4) _____ (absorb) in his performance, the man is playing the _____ and feels _____. 2.Ss talk about what influence music can bring to us	发学生的学习兴趣	
Step 2. Reading	1.Reading for the main idea What is the speech mainly about? A.Music and its problems. B.Influence of music on life. C.The medical treatment. D.The value of music. 2.Reading for the topic of each paragraph 3.Reading for the structure 4.Study language features	语言能力、学习能力、思维品格、文化意识目标： 1.学生快速阅读语篇，获取主旨大意 2.设置填空形式而非匹配形式，旨在让学生学会通过阅读对语段进行归纳概括，提取关键词 3.一方面，基于教材语篇帮助学生进一步熟知教材，另一方面，引导学生重点关注语篇的组织结构；引导学生学会在学习活动中发现、理解并处理重点信息，并建构演讲的整体认知，为下面环节学生运用所学知识创造性地写一篇演讲奠定语言、思维和文化基础	把握本质： 培养学生快速阅读获取大意、关键词、语篇组织结构特征和语言特征等语篇分析的能力 形成知识结构： 培养学生归纳概括的能力 活动与体验： 培养学生发现、理解、处理重点信息并建构演讲整体认知的能力；同时培养学生"音乐是世界通用语言""音乐能让我们生活更美好""音乐能治病疗伤"的意识，让学生学会利用音乐来改善生活；提升学生分析问题和解决问题的能力，使他们能够从跨文化的视角观察和认识音乐，对音乐做

续 表

Procedures	Activities	Design Purposes & Goals to Achieve	Core Competencies Covered
Step 2. Reading		4.充分利用教材资源，灵活处理教材，让学生充分认知修辞手法；让学生基于语篇，提炼写作环节必需的语言知识并进行角色（人称）的转换，为写作搭建语言支架	出正确的价值判断沟通交流：提升学生语言表达能力。变式迁移
Step 3. Writing	写作情境： Write a speech about how music has an impact on your school life. 1.Group work Group 1: Para.1 — Introduction Group 2: Para.2 — Your experience Group 3: Para.3 — The impact music has on you Group 4: Para.4 ~ 5 — Your advice/ hope & the ending 2.Presentation & Evaluation	学习能力、思维品格目标： 1.基于学生认知和真实生活创设真实写作情境，使学生有话可说，激发学生参与写作的兴趣，同时重现演讲组织结构图和语言特征结构图，在归纳本节课所学重点的同时，对学生进行写作指导	迁移运用：培养学生获取信息、整合内化信息的能力，让学生学会分析问题和解决问题，发展学生语言能力和学习能力 沟通交流：培养学生口头表达能力和分析判断能力 价值评判：培养学生批判性思维

Procedures	Activities	Design Purposes & Goals to Achieve	Core Competencies Covered
Step 3. Writing	学生生成的作品 A B	2.基于课堂时长的考虑，学生分组分任务各完成一个段落，然后通过"找朋友"的方式拼成一篇完整的作文，这样能在短时间内有完整的作文生成。用微信文件传输即时上传学生的生成，并由其他学生根据checklist对作品进行评价。当堂展出，学生的自信心和写作积极性得到极大的提高；有机会当"点评师"，学生的口头表达能力、分析判断能力和解决问题的能力也得到培养 3.展出A、B两篇内容相当的习作，让学生评析考试中哪篇会得到更高分。向学生强调书写的重要性	培养学生良好的书写习惯
Step 4. Homework	1.Finish and polish the draft according to SPORTS and PANTS and prepare for tomorrow's presentation 2. Extended learning The ① ____ of Listening to Music: A large number of people like listening to music. Listening to music is ② _____ for us in many ways.	语言能力、学习能力、思维品格目标： 1.由于在课堂上分组只完成演讲稿的一部分，学生课后需要把课堂上所学的知识内化成整体，达成语用目标	迁移创新 价值评判 变式运用

续 表

Procedures	Activities	Design Purposes & Goals to Achieve	Core Competencies Covered
Step 4. Homework	To begin with, since stress is the cause of many ③ ____, we can reduce the risk of getting these ④ ____ by listening to music that we like. Secondly, listening to music is an ⑤ ____ way to remove worry and it is also ⑥ ____ to a good night's sleep. In addition, listening to music can provide us with ⑦ ____ and help develop our ⑧ ____, which will ⑨ ____（填短语）in our future success. In general, listening to music will make us live ⑩ ____.	2.以填空的形式拓展一个课后阅读语篇，强化本节课主题；答案是开放的，以强化所学语言知识和"用英语"改善生活 参考答案： ①Benefits ②good ③illnesses ④diseases ⑤effective ⑥helpful ⑦inspiration ⑧creativity ⑨play an important role ⑩better	学生通过评价同学的和自己的作品，其自我反思、自主学习和合作学习的能力得到提升 培养学生根据语境分析问题、逻辑思维的能力

八、教学流程图

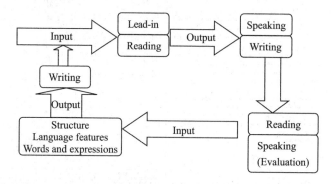

九、板书设计

十、评价设计

	Aspects	A	B	C
Structure	Clear structure and opinion (段落清晰，主题句突出)			
	Convincing facts (支撑句)			
Language	Words and expressions concerning music used (准确运用单元主题"音乐"词汇)			
	Rhetorical devices used (准确运用修辞手法)			
Communication	Appropriate language (符合演讲文体要求)			
Handwriting	Neat and beautiful (工整美观)			

十一、教学特色

特色1：创设基于教材单元主题意义的多模态话语情境

多模态（modality）话语可以将多种符号模态并用。在多模态教学中，主要强调把多种符号模态（语言、图像、音乐、网络等）引入教学过程，构建完整、形象的教学情境，充分调动学生的多种感官，体现了外语教学中注重听说写练相结合的一大特点，激发了学生学习语言的兴趣。本节课中，基于教材主题与话题，教师运用多模态话语，包括口头、视频、结构化知识图、图像、图表等视听动态资源，创设与主题意义（How music influences our life）和学生生活密切相关的语境，激发学生参与活动的兴趣，调动学生已有的基于该主题的经验，以思维导图、图表、符号等形式帮助学生建构和完善新的知识结构。

特色2：体现过程性写作教学模式

过程教学法将教学的重点放在学生写作过程和写作能力上，充分培养学生的思维能力。教师的指导始终贯穿于整个写作过程，包括构思、写提纲、写初稿和修改等各个写作环节，直至最后成文。

整节课层层递进，巧妙铺垫，通过一系列的关联主题的语言学习和思维活动，培养学生语言理解和表达的能力，推动学生的深度学习，帮助学生实现知识迁移。

特色3：巧设问题链实现深度学习

Q1: What influences do you think music can bring to us? (Lead-in)

Q2: What problems does Sara meet? (Reading)

Q3: How does she solve the problems? (Reading)

Q4: What influence does music bring to her? (Reading)

Q5: What advice does she give to us? (Reading)

Q6: If you met the same problems as Sara, how would you deal with them? (Thinking)

Q7：How do you think music influences your school life? (Writing)

整节课的活动设计基于主题（How music influences our life），依托教材语篇，在"Lead-in""Reading""Thinking""Writing"环节设计层层递进的问题形成问题链，引领学生由近（自己）及远（语篇主人公Sara）地深入思考"音乐的治愈功能"，最后在语言输出环节再回到近（自己），思考"如何有效利用音乐的治愈功能"，做到欣赏音乐，享受音乐，享受生活！

附：写作情境

Write a speech about how music has an impact on your school life.

学生习作（小组合作完成的一稿）：

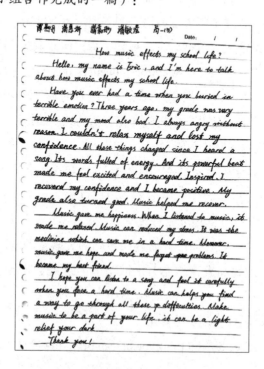

Book 3 Unit 3 Diverse Cultures（Pre-writing）

设计者姓名：赖丽萍

设计者所在单位：广东省清远市佛冈中学

一、教学材料分析

授课年级：高一

教材内容：新人教版Book 3 Unit 3 Diverse Cultures

主题：人与社会——多元文化

课型：读写课

课时：1课时

二、教学内容分析

This teaching period mainly deals with reading for writing an introduction of a place. Students are expected to learn some knowledge about how to write an introduction of a place. The teacher is expected to enable students to master some writing skills concerning information about introducing a place and learn to write one.

三、学情分析

During this period, the class will focus on reading for thinking. Students are expected to get the skills to write an introduction of a place. However, due to their lack of the vocabulary about the introduction of a place, they have difficulty in description. Therefore, the teacher would inspire students to master the skills to get the framework for writing.

四、教学目标

(1) Let students learn the key words and phrases concerning how to introduce a place.

(2) Train the students' ability to write an introduction of a place.

(3) Enable the students to know about brainstorm ideas and get the framework for writing.

(4) Encourage the students to know more about cultural diversity.

五、教学重点、难点

(1) Let students master the key words and phrases concerning how to introduce a place.

(2) Improve the students' ability to write.

(3) Let students master how to write an introduction of a place.

六、教学过程

教学环节		教师活动	学生活动	设计意图
Daily routine and Lead-in	Step 1	Lead-in Teacher greets the whole class as usual		Activate students and remind them to concentrate
	Step 2	Review & check: Teacher asks students to review Li Lan's travel journal learnt last lesson and asks: 1.Where did Li Lan have her dinner in San Francisco? 2.Where was it?	Students answer the questions loudly together	1.Check the teaching situation of last lesson quickly 2.Lead in the topic of Chinatown to be learnt today
Pre-writing: Reading	Step 3	Go through the text and predict: 1.What is the text type of the passage? A. A news report. B. A travel journal. C. A travel guide. D. A letter. 2.What's the main idea of the passage? The passage is mainly about _____.	Read the text in 5 mins and finish the questions	Practise and improve Ss' ability of prediction

教学环节		教师活动	学生活动	设计意图
Pre-writing: Reading	Step 4	Textual pattern analysis: 1. Divide the text into three parts and then match the general meaning of each part. (1) Part 1 (Para. _____) _____ (2) Part 2 (Para. _____) _____ (3) Part 3 (Para. _____) _____ A. The general introduction of the Chinatown in San Francisco. B. Chinatown's cultural influence. C. The specific information of the Chinatown. 2. What information is included in the introduction? Tick the items. 3. Underline the sentences that are used to describe the items above. 4. Make a mind map for an introduction to a city/town.	Read the text again, find out the information mentioned and underline the sentences or the phrases in the text	1.Familiarize Ss with analysis skills 2.Let Ss master what information will be needed to introduce a place
	Step 5	Topic-related lexis 1. Chinatown _____ (locate) in ... is the biggest in America, ... （1）佛冈位于广东省中部。 （2）佛冈的面积约有1300平方千米。 （3）佛冈是广东最吸引人的县城之一。 （4）佛冈的天气很宜人，吸引了很多游客。 _____ _____ _____ 归纳：（位置+面积） _____ _____ _____	1.Fill in the blanks and translate the sentences into English 2.Write the conclusion down	1.Review the usage of the participle and the attributive clause 2.Let students know how to use these words, phrases and sentence patterns

教学环节		教师活动	学生活动	设计意图
Pre-writing: Reading	Step 5	2.This house has a history of several hundred years, _____ (date) back to the Qing Dynasty. （1）佛冈的人口约有32万人。 （2）佛冈的历史约有2000年。 _____ 归纳：（人口+历史） _____ 3.The majority of residents in Chinatown are still ethnic Chinese. (用 be home to同义转换句子) _____ 4.Chinatown _____ (被认为是) an important part of the diverse culture of the USA.		Have Ss familiarize the phrases that will be used in the writing later
	Step 6	Summary: 	Style (体裁)	an exposition
---	---
Tense (时态)	(mainly) the present tense
Organizing Structure	an introduction of San Francisco's Chinatown
Person (人称)	the third person
Readers (读者)	visitors / tourists		Be able to get a clear understanding of the structure of the text, including its style, tense, theme, person and target readers	1.Consolidate students' knowledge 2.Form knowledge system of writing
Writing practice	Step 7	Creative thinking: Use what you have learnt to write an introduction of your hometown. 1.Brainstorm information about Fogang; 2.Useful sentence patterns for writing: (1) There are many <u>places of interest in</u> <u>sp.</u> , such as/like... (2) Fogang is <u>famous for</u> oranges, Zhushan kudzus <u>as well as</u> Sijiu prunes	1.Write down the information that will be needed in the writing on the Ss' paper 2.Write down the useful sentence patterns for writing	1.Make Ss be familiar with the topics they will use later 2.Let Ss have enough writing materials so as to write the introduction

续 表

教学环节		教师活动	学生活动	设计意图
Writing practice	Step 8	Pair Work: Suppose you are a guide. Write down all the information about Fogang in 3 minutes first, and then introduce Fogang to your partner (tourist). (Show time) Ladies and Gentlemen, Welcome to Fogang. I'm glad to be your guide. ... Finally, I hope all of you will enjoy yourselves here. Thank you.	1.Write down all the information in right sentences 2.Introduce your town to your partner	1.Practice their fast-writing skill 2.Share their ideas and broaden their horizons 3.Practice their team-work spirit
Home-work	Step 9	Assignment: Modify your introduction of your town and polish it	Take notes	Consolidate students' knowledge and prepare for the following lesson

七、板书设计

Unit 3 Diverse Cultures
Period 4 Reading for Writing

Brainstorm

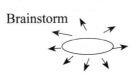

Others：

附：学生习作

Ladies and Gentlemen,

Welcome to Fogang. I'm glad to be your guide.

Located in the center of Qingyuan, Guangdong Province, Fogang covers an area of 1,300 square kilometers. With a population of about 320,000, it has a history of over 2,000 years. You can enjoy some special ancient buildings here. Fogang is famous for oranges, Zhushan kudzus as well as Sijiu prunes which will make you mouthwatering. Besides, there are many places of interest in it, such as Shampoola, Wangshan Temple, Dragon Bay and Country Garden.

I hope all of you will enjoy yourseves here. Thank you!

Book 4 Unit 1 People of Achievement（Pre-writing）

设计者姓名：郭秀云

设计者所在单位：广东省清远市第二中学

一、教学材料分析

授课年级：高一

教材内容：新人教版Book 4 Unit 1 People of Achievement

主题：人与自我 —— 我最钦佩的人

课型：应用文写作

课时：1课时

二、教学内容分析

【**What**】

阅读语篇是一篇记叙文，基于"人与自我——我最钦佩的人"的主题语境，介绍了"The woman I admire most"，让学生了解女性在社会生活中的地位、价值和贡献，讴歌女性在社会各个领域的成就。写作部分由此引入，要求学生运用所学的描述人物品质和个性的形容词和重点句型，把所选人物的故事、品质和个性用英语流利地表达出来。

【**Why**】

基于阅读文本提升学生的高阶思维能力，从而提高学生对女性的社会角色的认识，培养学生（尤其是女学生）的自信心、事业心和社会责任感，使学生建立正确的性别观和社会观。

【How】

写作是语言学习的输出形式，是语言表达能力和思维能力的综合体现。首先，为了创设真实的写作情境，本课以视频引入，让学生了解姚贝娜的生前事迹。其次，对文本进行分析，让学生了解写人的相关词汇和重点句型，为下文写作输出打好基础。最后，通过重点句型的练习，让学生能够熟练运用多种句型对人物进行描写，从而将其运用到写作中去，最终达成本课教学目标。

三、学情分析

授课班级学生是本校高一年级中间层次的学生。他们的英语基础不算特别好，但经过上学期一个学期的学习，他们已经初步接触高中英语写作要求。本节课内容，主要是引导学生描述一个自己钦佩的人物。写作内容难度不大，但要求学生能够用流利的英文表达出来，尤其是要获得高分，需要特别加强对学生词汇和句型多样性的指导。

四、教学目标

单元目标：本单元紧扣"人与自我——我最钦佩的人"这一中心话题，通过介绍几位生活在不同国度的伟人，探讨他们在社会生活中的地位、价值和贡献，讴歌他们在社会各个领域的成就。写作部分要求学生恰当运用介绍人物品质和个性的形容词，把所选人物的故事、品质和个性写出来。

课时目标：引导学生通过阅读介绍伟人事迹的文章，掌握该语篇类型应具备的要素和常用表达手法，探寻和理解语篇蕴含的主题思想，关注人物介绍的应用文语言特点，并最终将其运用到记叙文写作中。

By the end of this period, you will be able to:

—know more about people of achievement;

—grasp some useful words and sentences used to describe a person;

—learn how to describe a person;

—learn how to write a descriptive passage.

五、教学重点、难点

重点：引导学生梳理语篇结构，关注人物描述的语言特点、词汇和常用句型，并能将其熟练地运用到描述性写作中。

难点：让学生能运用多种句型，如定语从句、强调句或倒装句等描述人物性格特征，用地道的英语描述出一个栩栩如生的人物，提高学生对他人的社会角色认知，培养学生的事业心和社会责任感。

六、教学过程

Step 1. Lead-in: Present a video about Yao Beina

Purpose：基于单元教材主题和话题，进行多模态导入，让学生了解本课的学习目标，为课型的开展做好铺垫。

Step 2. Pre-writing

The Woman I Admire Most

The woman I admire most is a singer, whose name is Yao Beina.

She was such a talented singer, who won lots of awards and sang several theme songs for hit movies and TV series. She was interested in music when she was young, and devoted all the time to learning it. It was hard work and determination that made her succeed. In addition, she is optimistic and unselfish. She had breast cancer in 2011. But she was still brave and optimistic to fight against the cancer. She even wrote a song *Heart Fire*, which describes her struggle and pain. After she died, her corneas were donated to the persons who needed.

Such is Yao Beina, the woman I admire most. Her determination and bravery will always inspire me.

1. Finish the outline.

Title: _____

Para. 1: _____

Para. 2: _____

Para. 3: _____

2. Underline some useful sentences in the reading text. (At least 5 sentences)

3. Practice with words and sentences.

Words to describe people:

strong　坚强的；强壮的

smart　聪明的

honest　诚实的

friendly　友好的

generous　慷慨的

warm-hearted　热心的

hard-working　努力工作的

popular　受欢迎的

brave　勇敢的

modest　谦虚的

confident　自信的

considerate　考虑周到的

determined　坚决的

unselfish　无私的

energetic　充满活力的

devoted　有奉献精神的

Sentences:

（1）她是一个伟大的科学家，发现了镭元素。

She is a great scientist _____ discovered radium.

（2）正是她的坚定和勇敢使她成为一个伟大的人。

_____ her determination and bravery _____ made her a great woman.

（3）宋庆龄就是这样的人，一位无私且慷慨的女性。

_____ Song Qingling, an _____ and _____ woman.

Purpose：写前让学生回忆本单元话题，导入一篇优秀范文，让学生从中发现写作时所需要的词汇和句型。一方面为写作做铺垫，另一方面让学生了解到写人作文的框架，为下一步写作做好充足的词汇积累和句型输入。

Step 3. Writing

写作情境：

假如下周日是母亲节，某英语刊物正在进行"我的母亲"征文比赛。请按照下面所提供的主要内容，以"我的母亲"为题，写一篇短文。

主要内容：

（1）母亲住在农村，50多岁，没有文化，但她很关心你的学习情况；

（2）探望母亲的一次经历；

（3）归纳总结母亲的品行。

注意：可适当增加细节，以使行文连贯。

审题

（1）确定体裁：本文为_____。

（2）确定人称：本文应用第_____人称。

（3）确定时态：本文应以_____和_____时态为主。

构思

第一部分：简要介绍_____。

第二部分：探望母亲的一次经历。

第三部分：我眼中的母亲——_____。

词汇参考

（1）in one's fifties　五十多岁

（2）add up to　总共，加起来等于

（3）aware　有意识的

（4）attach importance to... /pay attention to... /take... into account　重视

（5）ensure/insure/guarantee/make certain　确保

（6）concentrate on/focus attention on/devote oneself to/be absorbed in　集中精力

（7）move/touch/affect　感动

（8）burst into tears/be filled with tears/cry one's eyes out　热泪盈眶

句子翻译

（1）我的母亲五十多岁了，住在农村。（who引导定语从句）

（2）尽管她仅仅受一年的教育，但她深刻意识到知识对年轻人的重要性。(although引导让步状语从句)

_____

（3）她非常重视我的学习，鼓励我努力学习。（attach great importance to）

_____

（4）母亲竭尽所能确保我能全身心地学习。（whatever引导宾语从句，in order that引导目的状语从句）

_____

（5）有一次她病重，大夫让她在床上休息几天。（once ...）

_____

（6）我回家看望她时，我看到她在地里干活。（when引导时间状语从句）

_____

（7）我深受感动，禁不住热泪盈眶。（so ... that...）

_____

（8）这就是我的母亲，一位简朴、诚实、勤劳的人。（such is ...倒装句式）

_____

Purpose：通过对写作任务进行篇章结构分析，导入词汇、短语和练习相关句型，让学生组织好作文语言，为学生写作进一步扫清语言障碍。

限时训练：请根据以上所学，以"My Mother"为题，用英语写一篇100词左右的短文。

Step 4. Summary

(1) Learn to describe someone you admire.

Opening: Who is she/he?

Body: Her/His character, personalities, achievements, career, life...

Conclusion: What's her/his spirit?

(2) Some useful expressions and sentences.

(3) Use the checklist to give comments on your writing.

Step 5. Homework

Share the passage with your classmates and talk about someone you admire.

七、板书设计

Unit 1 People of Achievement
（Writing—How to describe someone you admire）
SPORTS

Style (体裁)：_____

Person (人称)：_____

Organizing (组织)：_____

Reader (读者)：_____

Tense (时态)：_____

Structure (结构)：_____

Words to describe people:

strong 坚强的；强壮的	smart 聪明的
honest 诚实的	friendly 友好的
generous 慷慨的	warm-hearted 热心的
hard-working 努力工作的	popular 受欢迎的
brave 勇敢的	modest 谦虚的
confident 自信的	considerate 考虑周到的
determined 坚决的	unselfish 无私的
energetic 充满活力的	devoted 有奉献精神的

八、教学特色

特色1：学生通过文本分析人物特征，培养高阶思维能力。本写作课例教学过程完整，既有写前的铺垫，也有写中的指导，还有写作完成后的自我评价。本课从明星姚贝娜患病一事的视频导入，激起学生的同理心；再根据文本介绍了该女性的事迹，让学生分析该文本写作特色，以及人物特征，学习并拓展描述人物的相关词汇和句型，过渡自然。

特色2：注重价值引领，提升文化意识的获得感。本课落实了新课标中的"立德树人"的宗旨，从情感上提高了学生对女性社会角色的认识和尊重，培养了学生（尤其是女学生）的自信心、事业心和社会责任感，同时使学生树立正确的性别观和社会观。

附：参考佳作

My Mother

My mother, who is already in her fifties, lives in the countryside. Although her schooling adds up to no more than one year, she is quite aware that knowledge is important to young people, so she attaches great importance to my study and always encourages me to study hard.

To ensure that I can concentrate on my study, my mother does whatever she can do for me. Once she was badly ill and the doctor asked her to stay in bed for several days. But when I got home, I found her working in the fields. So deeply moved was I that I couldn't help bursting into tears.

Such is my mother, a simple, honest and hard-working person. She is the person I admire most.

Book 4 Unit 3 Fascinating Parks

设计者姓名：叶青容

设计者所在单位：广东省清远市源潭中学

一、教学材料分析

授课年级：高二

教材内容：新人教版Book 4 Unit 3 Fascinating Parks

主题：人与自然——主题公园的意义

课型：应用文写作

课时：1课时

二、教学内容分析

【What】

阅读语篇是一篇说明文，基于"人与自然——主题公园的意义"的主题语境，介绍了"A Theme Park—Chimelong Paradise"，突出"好玩，不仅仅是好玩（fun and more than fun）"这个主题，让学生了解主题公园存在的价值，在

"人与自然"这个主题下，探索城市主题公园对自然保护、人类生存和发展的意义。

【Why】

启发学生从人与自然、人与社会的角度思考主题公园所蕴含的人文内涵和意义。

【How】

阅读语篇采取了"总—分—总"的写作结构，先从概要介绍入手，再详细介绍长隆欢乐世界有代表性的游玩项目；其语言风格简练有力，笔调轻松，在结尾用了吸引人们前来游玩的句式，直接发出号召。这样的叙述方式是在直接与读者交流，容易感染和打动读者。

三、学情分析

高二年级的学生已多次接触过应用文写作，对应用文写作的结构有一定的了解，但在语言表达的特点、突出主题思想的写作手法方面还需要教师加强引导和锤炼。

四、教学目标

单元目标：

（1）让学生了解并欣赏国内外著名的国家公园、城市公园、主题公园，并能够从人与自然、人与社会的角度了解它们所蕴含的意义和人文内涵。

（2）让学生能掌握介绍国家公园、城市公园、主题公园等的语篇类型应具备的要素和常用表达手法，能模仿范文，结合公园主题，有条理地介绍公园。

课时目标：引导学生通过阅读介绍主题公园的文本，掌握该语篇类型应具备的要素和常用表达手法，探寻和理解语篇蕴含的主题思想，关注地点介绍应用文的语言特点，并能将其运用到自己的写作中。

五、教学重点、难点

重点：引导学生梳理语篇结构，关注主题公园介绍的语言特点，并能将其运用到自己的写作中。

难点：让学生能有条理地表达主题公园的特点特色及其主题意义；能运用

独特的准确的写作手法突出主题公园"fun and more than fun"的主题意义；能自我辨析作文的优劣，培养批判性思维。

六、教学过程

Step 1. Warming-up

Show some pictures about Chimelong Paradise. Get Ss to understand what a theme park is.

Purpose：围绕主题创设情境，激活学生已有的知识和经验，通过图片和提问导入主题，调动学生对阅读文本的阅读兴趣。

Step 2. Pre-writing

Activity 1: Ask Ss to read the text title and predict what will be told in the text.

Purpose：通过主题预测，让学生在接下来寻找描述主题公园要点的活动中理解更加深刻。

Activity 2: Ask Ss to skim the text and then choose the information told in the passage.

A. The location & size.   B. The theme feature.

C. The way to the scenic spot.   D. The writer's feeling.

E. The significance.   F. The typical local handicraft.

G. The tourist attractions.

Purpose：通过快速浏览，让学生在语境中理解主题公园介绍的要点，为下一步的教学活动做铺垫。

Activity 3: Ask Ss to work out the structure of the text.

Para. 1 _____

Para. 2 _____

Para. 3 _____

Purpose：让学生初步整体感知描述主题公园的写作结构，引导学生注意写作逻辑顺序。

Activity 4: Ask Ss to discover the writing tips to describe a theme park.

Tense (时态): _____

Person (人称): _____

Language (语言特征): _____

Linking words (过渡词): _____

Text structure (文本结构): in a _____ order (顺序)

Purpose：以阅读文本为依托，引导学生分析阅读文本的写作技巧，体会和感悟介绍主题公园的文体的特点：通常是以从外至内、从上至下的顺序介绍地点的。培养学生发现问题和分析问题的能力。

Activity 5: Draw a conclusion on sentence patterns from the text.

Purpose：引导学生在语境中理解介绍地点（主题公园）的一些句型，归纳可以运用的相关语言知识，为写作做好语言输入的准备。

Activity 6: Ask Ss to discuss what differences there are between ordinary parks and theme parks.

Purpose：引导学生结合实际生活中普通公园与主题公园的不同，进一步理解主题公园所蕴含的人文内涵和意义。同时启发学生在介绍主题公园的写作手法上要突出"fun and more than fun"的主题思想。

Step 3. While-writing

Write a letter of invitation, inviting your pen friend Peter from America to visit the Old Sod Neighborhood in Qingyuan.

假设你叫李华，你想邀请你的美国笔友彼得（Peter）这个寒假来清远玩，并向他介绍故乡的主题公园。请根据以下要点，写一封邀请信。

1. 故乡的概况。

2. 故乡的具体特色（有八大区，简单介绍建筑风格、蜡像馆、百艺坊、游乐场、农场等）。

3. 参观故乡的文化意义。

注意：①词数100左右；②可以适当增加细节，以使行文连贯；③开头语和结束语已给出。

参考词汇：岭南文化 Lingnan culture

中国岭南民间故宫 the Lingnan Folk Palace of China

百艺坊 the Art Museum

手工艺 handicraft

蜡像馆 the Wax Museum

岭南水乡史 the history of Lingnan Watery Region

Activity 1. 写作思路

1. SPORTS审题法。

Style (体裁): _____

Person (人称): _____

Organizing (组织): _____

Reader (读者): _____

Tense (时态): _____

Structure (结构): _____

2. 谋篇：要点重组。

A letter of invitation about a theme park

Para.1 (beginning): _____

Para.2 (body): _____

Para.3 (ending): _____

3. 行文：运用不同的句型进行翻译。

4. 润色：在文中使用一些非谓语动词，巧用同位语，活用从句，巧用连接词。

Purpose：引导学生养成设计写作思路的习惯，为初稿的形成做好结构和内容方面的铺垫。

Activity 2: Get Ss to discuss what sentence patterns can be used in writing. Ask Ss their different opinions.

Purpose：帮助学生回顾写前文本阅读输入的句型，让学生学以致用，为自己在写作中尽可能多地使用不同句型做好铺垫，并通过让学生发表不同观点，培养学生的批判性思维。

Activity 3: The Ss are required to finish their first draft within 10 minutes.

Activity 4: Ss are required to ask themselves the questions of the checklist and make comments on their draft. Then, Ss revise their first draft using the checklist as a guide.

Purpose：引导学生借助批改和评价工具，关注写作结构的合理布局、语言的适切性和规范性。通过自我评价表，学生可以对初稿进行修改润色，从而培养自主学习能力和辨析写作优劣的能力。

Activity 5: Summary

1. "一问":

What have I learned in the class?

（1）_____

（2）_____

（3）_____

（4）_____

2. "二看":

Did I reach my learning targets in the class?

3. "三做":

(1) Review the content in the class.

(2) Finish the homework actively.

Purpose：回顾课堂学习重点，学会自我反思学习目标达成情况，从而有针对性地加强复习，认真完成课后作业。

Step 4. Homework

Task 1: Exchange your writing with your group members, make comments on it and polish the writing with each other.

Task 2: Recommend the best writing to the rest of your classmates.

Purpose：加强小组合作评价，学会为写作提升档次的润色技能，营造互相学习的良好氛围；通过展现优秀写作，增强学生的写作信心；通过展示评价标准及优秀写作，让学生对自己的写作有明确的定位，找到距离和努力的方向。

七、主要教学活动

本节课共设置了两大教学任务：一是写前通过情境创设，依托阅读文本（介绍长隆欢乐世界），运用任务式教学法、启发式教学法，引导学生进行语篇分析（写了什么？怎么写的？可以获取什么语言？主题公园的意义何在？），让学生掌握主题公园介绍的结构、要点、技巧、语言等，为后面的写作任务做好写作结构和语言输入的铺垫；二是以写作任务（介绍故乡的主题公园）为例，引导学生设计写作思路，掌握谋篇的技巧，使学生能根据阅读文本所学到的去完成写作任务，注重句型的积累和学以致用。

八、板书设计

Fascinating Parks
（Writing—How to describe a theme park）
SPORTS

Style (体裁): _____

Person (人称): _____

Organizing (组织): _____

Reader (读者): _____

Tense (时态): _____

Structure (结构): _____

句型积累:

1. ... located in ... covers a total area of ... _____

2. _____

3. _____

谋篇布局:

A letter of invitation about a theme park

Para. 1 (beginning): _____

Para. 2 (body): _____

Para.3 (ending): _____

九、教学特色

特色1: 写前指导细致, 导向性强。在写前, 依托教材主题与话题开展文本分析, 精选文本素材, 让学生在语境中获得写作语言和写作技巧, 积累万能句型, 为写作做好铺垫。与传统的写作课相比, 依托文本分析和语境指导的写作课既有利于学生领悟写作的要领和谋篇技巧, 也有利于学生更好地积累语言知识, 掌握语言知识在文本中的应用, 还有利于培养学生的英语核心素养。

特色2: "授人以鱼, 不如授人以渔。"授课老师在学生完成写作任务后, 有意识地培养学生对自己作文进行修改、提高的能力。两个评价表给学生提供自评和互评的评价标准, 让学生能够参照列表发现自己和同伴作文的闪光点和问题, 有利于让学生进一步关注写作细节和结构的准确性。同时, 让学生关注丰富的词汇和高级句型的应用, 有意识地摘录好词好句, 为写作积累素材, 养成良好的学习习惯。

附：学生学习资料

Ⅰ. Warming-up

Talk about Chimelong Paradise.

Ⅱ. Pre-writing

Task 1: Predicting.

Read the title of the text and predict what will be told in the text.

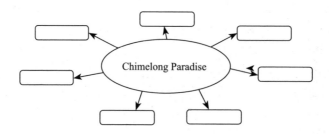

Chimelong Paradise

Chimelong Paradise, located in Yingbin Road Panyu District, covers a total area of 1,000 *mu*. It is famous for exciting rides and is one of the most unique theme parks in China.

There are six zones, so whichever and whatever you like, there is one for you. If you want to experience the terrifying free-fall drops (跳楼机), then the Screaming Zone (尖叫地带) is a good place for you. There are various exciting rides for visitors, such as Diving Coaster (垂直过山车), Ten Inversion Roller Coaster (十环过山车), Motorcycle Roller Coaster, U-Shaped Slide (U型滑板). In performing square, you can see various kinds of shows, some of which are modeled after the films. Besides, you can even see large parades. As you wander around the White Tiger Street , you can do some shopping.

Chimelong Paradise is more than an amusement park. It can provide visitors with a variety of things to see and do. With all these attractions, no wonder more and more visitors come here for a visit. If you want to have fun and more than fun, come to Chimelong Paradise!

Task 2: Read the text and answer the following question.

What information about the theme park can you get from the text?

A. The location & size.

B. The theme feature.

C. The way to the scenic spot.

D. The writer's feeling.

E. The significance.

F. The tourist attractions.

G. The fee.

Task 3: Work out the structure of the text.

Para. 1 _____

Para. 2 _____

Para. 3 _____

Task 4. Discover the writing tips to describe a theme park.

Tense (时态): _____

Person (人称): _____

Language (语言特征): _____

Linking words (过渡词): _____

Text structure (文本结构): in a _____ order (顺序)

Task 5: Draw a conclusion on sentence patterns from the text.

句型:

（1）... located in ..., covers a total area of ... _____

（2） _____

（3） _____

（4） _____

（5） _____

（6） _____

（7） _____

（8） _____

（9）_____

Ⅲ. While-writing

Write a letter of invitation, inviting your pen friend Peter from America to visit the Old Sod Neighborhood in Qingyuan.

假设你叫李华，你想邀请你的美国笔友彼得（Peter）这个寒假来清远玩，并向他介绍故乡的主题公园。请根据以下要点，写一封邀请信。

（1）故乡的概况。

（2）故乡的具体特色（有八大区，简单介绍岭南建筑、小动物园、蜡像馆、百艺坊、游乐场、农场等）。

（3）参观故乡的文化意义。

注意：①词数100左右；②可以适当增加细节，以使行文连贯；③开头语和结束语已给出。

参考词汇：岭南文化　　Lingnan culture

中国岭南民间故宫　the Lingnan Folk Palace of China

百艺坊　the Art Museum

手工艺　handicraft

蜡像馆　the Wax Museum

岭南水乡史　the history of Lingnan Watery Region

Task 1: 写作思路

（1）审题。

SPORTS

Style (体裁): _____

Person (人称): _____

Organizing (组织): _____

Reader (读者): _____

Tense (时态): _____

Structure (结构): _____

（2）谋篇：要点重组。

A letter of invitation about a theme park

Para. 1 (beginning): _____

Para. 2 (body) : _____

A mind map about describing the theme park

Para.3 (ending) : _____

（3）行文：运用不同的句型进行翻译。

（4）润色：在文中使用一些非谓语动词，巧用同位语，活用从句，巧用
连接词。

Task 2: Write your first draft.

Dear Peter,

I am writing to invite you to travel in Qingyuan this winter vocation. Here I
introduce you a very popular park, the Old Sod Neighborhood.

_____

_____

_____

_____

_____

_____

_____

_____

_____

I'm looking forward to your coming.

Yours sincerely,

Li Hua

Ⅳ. Homework

Task 1: Exchange your writing with your group members and make comments on it.

Task 2: Recommend the best writing to the rest of your classmates.

十、课例评析

（一）课例评析1：胡翠娥

叶青容老师的这节课是基于新人教版教材Book 4 Unit 3主题语境"人与自然——主题公园的意义"的一节与何玉琼老师进行同课异构的应用文（邀请信）写作课。主题贯穿整个教学过程；各环节设计基于学情，指导细致，注重学法指导；过程性写作写前输入充分。

亮点：

（1）"Reading for Writing"环节结合教材主题语境与话题和本节课的写作任务的主体部分（介绍故乡的主题公园）选择"Chimelong Paradise"语篇设置四个阅读任务进行相关主题话题词汇、句式、篇章的输入，体现了叶老师基于学情对过程性写作教学写前输入环节的准确把握。

（2）除了基于语篇外，叶老师还设计了让学生分类拓展有用短语的任务，体现了叶老师培养学生基于教材（资料）又超越教材的学习能力的意识。

（3）用不同的句型翻译写作要点的环节，体现了叶老师培养学生多元思维、创新思维的意识。学生完成这项任务，语用能力得以提升。

（4）写后的两个对照给学生提供了自评和互评的评价标准，学生能够参照评价表发现自己和同伴作文的闪光点和问题。

建议：

设定教学目标和学习目标时要基于学情准确把握，避免设定目标不能达成，建议此学案分2个课时完成。

（二）课例评析2：陈锦春

叶青容老师基于新人教版教材Book 4 Unit 3主题设计了一节写前文本输入的"以读促写"的课。叶老师结合学生学情，对本节课进行了精心的设计，从培养学生的写作思路入手，到加强词汇和句型的训练，再到写作思路的回顾，为写作做了一系列的铺垫。首先，在课堂上，她以

"Chimelong Paradise"相关文本解读为切入点，引导学生从内容要点、文本结构、写作技巧三方面进行解读，层层深入，步步为营；其次，通过小组合作活动对介绍主题公园的词汇和句型进行归纳和拓展；最后，在写作任务——介绍"The Old Sod Neighborhood"的写前阶段，她引导学生回顾写作思路，梳理写作技巧。整节课下来，学生较好地掌握了写前思路和介绍主题公园的词汇和句型，为下节课的写作做了充分的准备。

叶老师能根据学生的实际学情，精心设计教学活动，使教学内容由浅入深，课堂内容充实，教学目标完成得比较理想。

（三）课例评析3：张伟娟

叶青容老师的这节课是与何玉琼老师进行同课异构的应用文（邀请信）写作课。她围绕着新人教版教材Book 4 Unit 3主题语境"人与自然——主题公园的意义"展开教学活动。叶老师注重写前的输入，为学生写好这一话题作文提供了大量的知识积累，充分体现了过程性写作的教学方法。

亮点：

（1）课前准备充分。叶老师是一位做事认真、教学严谨的好老师。从叶老师的教学设计、学案等材料来看，她在课前做了大量的准备工作。这种敬业精神值得敬佩。

（2）叶老师善于引导学生，为写作顺利进行搭建脚手架：从训练学生的写作思路入手，到加强学生词汇和句型的训练，再到写作思路的回顾，为学生的写作做了一系列的铺垫。

（3）注重知识的迁移。叶老师从开始的以读促写环节，为学生提供了一篇关于"Chimelong Paradise"的介绍性文章，希望学生能将文章中介绍地点的写作手法迁移到本课的目标中：写一封邀请信，并介绍the Old Sod Neighborhood in Qingyuan的相关信息。另外，叶老师的"Reading for Writing"要求学生总结关于主题公园的话题词汇和语块，并将其迁移到"Pre-writing"环节的Task 2中，设计精妙，适合语言能力弱的学生。

（4）注重学生的形成性评价，符合新课标培养学生学习能力和批判性思维的要求。要求学生在完成一稿后进行自评，在课后作业中要求学生小组评价。评价给出的标准也适合学生的学情，值得推崇。

不足：

整个教学设计内容偏多。

建议：

建议分为3个课时来完成（写前—写中—写后）。

附1：学生习作

学生习作1：

Dear Peter,

I am writing to invite you to travel in Qingyuan this winter vacation. Here I introduce you a very popular park, the Old Sod Neighborhood.

The Old Sod Neighborhood is located in the prince mountains. It has eight attractions. What attracts us most is the Lingnan style buildings. With so many unique architectures, no wonder it enjoys a reputation of the Lingnan Folk Palace of China. There are some scenic spots in the park to let us know about Lingnan culture and history, such as the Art Museum and the Wax Museum. Besides, there is a playground for us to relax. If we want to have a picnic, we also have many cookers available.

The Old Sod Neighborhood not only brings us fun, but also lets us learn Lingnan culture and understand the life of our elder generation. If you visit there, you'll have a good time.

I'm looking forward to your coming.

Yours sincerely,
Li Hua

学生习作2：

Dear Peter,

I am writing to invite you to travel in Qingyuan this winter vacation. Here I introduce you a very popular park, the Old Sod Neighborhood.

The Old Sod Neighborhood is known as the Lingnan Folk Palace of China. It is located in the prince mountains. It is divided into eight parts, each of which has its fun and meaning. Walking in the park, you will find the unique Lingnan architectural design. By visiting the Art Museum and the Wax Museum, you will know more about

Lingnan culture. If you want to experience something exciting, the playground is a good place for you. When you are hungry, you can cook on the farm. What's more, you can appreciate the scene of the farm.

If you come to the Old Sod Neighborhood, you will find it really funny and worthwhile.

I'm looking forward to your coming.

Yours sincerely,

Li Hua

学生习作3：

Dear Peter,

I am writing to invite you to travel in Qingyuan this winter vacation. Here I introduce you a very popular park, the Old Sod Neighborhood.

It is known to all that the Old Sod Neighborhood is one of the most attractive parks in Qingyuan, which is famous for the Lingnan Folk Palace of China. There are eight different areas for visitors to enjoy. Walking in the park, the visitors not only can play, but also can learn a lot about Lingnan culture and history by visiting the Art Museum and the Wax Museum. When the visitors wander around the farm in the park, they will feel very comfortable.

By visiting the Old Sod Neighborhood, the visitors can enrich themselves. It's worth visiting.

I'm looking forward to your coming.

Yours sincerely,

Li Hua

附2：参考佳作

Dear Peter,

I am writing to invite you to travel in Qingyuan this winter vacation. Here I introduce you a very popular park, the Old Sod Neighborhood.

The Old Sod Neighborhood, located in the beautiful prince mountains, covers an area of more than 200 *mu*. It is known for the Lingnan Folk Palace of China.

There are eight parts. Whatever you like, there is one for you. Entering the Old Sod Neighborhood, you will see the unique Lingnan architectures. In the Art Museum, there are many exquisite handi crafts that open your eyes. Besides, the Wax Museum and the magnificent folk art performance will show you an interesting overview of the history of Lingnan Watery Region. If you want to experience something funny, the games on the playground and the picnic on the farm are good choices.

The Old Sod Neighborhood is more than an amusement park. It can also provide you with a chance to learn Lingnan culture and feel the past life scenes of our forefathers. If you visit there, I'm sure you'll have a wonderful trip.

I'm looking forward to your coming.

Yours sincerely,

Li Hua

第三章

教学资源

第一节　基于教材单元主题与话题的写作情境创设（人教新课标版）

（胡翠娥）

Book	Unit	Thematic Context	Topics	Word Bank	Writing
1	1. Friendship	人与自我；人与社会	Friends and friendship; inter personal relationships	*v.*: ignore, calm down, be concerned about, go through, suffer from, recover, get tired of, get along with, fall in love, disagree, dislike, join in, swap, lend a helping hand, understand, communicate, prefer, be fond of, care about *adj.*: upset, calm, concerned, grateful, helpful, determined, reliable *n.*: partner, teenager, friend, friendship	Persuasive writing: a letter of advice 写作情境： 假设你是李华，你的朋友Tom来信说因和朋友产生分歧而感到不快。请你给他回信，内容包括： 1.表示理解并给予安慰。 2.提出具体建议
	2. English around the world	人与社会	English language and its development; different kinds of English	*n.*: language, vocabulary, English, American English, British English, subway/underground, elevator/lift, petrol/gas, spelling, usage, dialect, expression, accent *v.*: come up, enrich, make use of, play a part in, recognize	Persuasive writing: a letter of advice 写作情境： 假设你是李华，你的朋友Tom因受"汉语热"的影响决定学习汉语，来信向你咨询。请你给他

Book	Unit	Thematic Context	Topics	Word Bank	Writing
1	2. English around the world	人与社会	English language and its development; different kinds of English	*adj.*: official, native, Danish, African, French, Chinese, Spanish, Japanese, fluent, frequent, modern	写一封回信，说明汉语流行的原因，并提出几条学习汉语的建议
	3.Travel journal	人与自然	Travelling; describing a journey	*n.*: transport, bus, train, ship, airplane, fare, schedule, journey, travel, trip, atlas, rapids, valley, waterfall, journal, wool, insurance, view, flame, midnight, cave *v.*: prefer, cycle, organize, determine, make up one's mind, change one's mind, forecast, *adj.*: reliable	Persuasive writing: a letter of advice 写作情境： 假设你是李华，你的朋友 Jim 所在的学校要组织学生来中国旅行，有两条路线可以选择："长江之行"或"泰山之旅"。Jim 希望你能给些建议。请你给他回信，内容包括： 1. 你建议的路线 2.你的理由 3.你的祝愿
	4.Earth-quakes	人与自然	Basic knowledge about earthquakes; how to protect oneself and help others in disasters	*n.*: earthquake, quake, typhoon, floods, drought, mud-rock flow, seismic sea wave, windstorm, well, crack, farmyard, pipe, event, nation, steam, dirt, suffering, survivor, dam, track, electricity, disaster, catastrophe, shelter, rainwater, hillside *v.*: burst, ruin, injure, survive, destroy, shock, rescue, trap, dig out, bury, damage,	Persuasive writing: a newspaper article 写作情境： 某地发生地震后，许多互联网科技企业、各大旅游网站和汽车公司等纷纷在第一时间加入抢险救灾行列。请你以灾区学生李华

续 表

Book	Unit	Thematic Context	Topics	Word Bank	Writing
1	4.Earthquakes	人与自然	Basic knowledge about earthquakes; how to protect oneself and help others in disasters	frighten, shake *adj.*: smelly, extreme, useless, frightened, frightening, numerous, countless, homeless, tremendous	的名义给这些企业写一封感谢信，表达你的感激之情
1	5.Nelson Mandela—a modern hero	人与社会；人与自我	The qualities of a great person; the lives of some great people	*n.*: quality, nationalism, livelihood, leap, mankind, lawyer, guidance, passbook, youth, league, stage, vote, violence, equality, relative, terror, cruelty, president, Nobel Peace Prize *v.*: devote, attack, blow up, turn to, lose heart, escape, educate, come to power, reward, be sentenced to death *adj.*: warm-hearted, active, generous, giant, selfless, easy-going, devoted, peaceful, legal, hopeful, equal, willing, educated, mean, unfair, cruel, selfish, anti-black	Descriptive writing: a famous person 写作情境： 假设你是李华，你的英国朋友Tom在给你的邮件中提到他对中国历史很感兴趣，并请你给他介绍一位你喜欢的历史人物。请你给Tom回信，内容包括： 1.该人物是谁 2.该人物的主要贡献 3.该人物对你的影响
2	1.Cultural relics	人与社会；人与自然	Cultural relics protection; famous cultural relics in china and abroad	*n.*: relic, vase, dynasty, design, style, jewel, mystery, worth, painting, castle, art work, rescue *v.*: survive, search, amaze, select, decorate, belong to, remove, rebuild, take apart,	Peraussive writing: a report 写作情境： 某中学生英文报以"保护中国传统文化"为主题举行英语征文活

Book	Unit	Thematic Context	Topics	Word Bank	Writing
2	1.Cultural relics	人与社会；人与自然	Cultural relics protection; famous cultural relics in china and abroad	think highly of *adj.*:cultural, rare, valuable, amazing, fancy, former, local, wooden	动。你阅读了相关要求后，准备给该报投稿，稿件内容包括： 1.保护中国传统文化的重要性 2.谈谈你对文化保护的建议
	2.The Olympic Games	人与社会	Ancient and modern olympic games; olympic spirit	*n.*: competitor, competition, medal, mascot, Greece, volunteer, homeland, athlete, gymnastics, athletics, stadium, gymnasium, responsibility, olive, wreath, motto, similarity, Athens, charge, glory, goddess, pain, striker, beach volleyball, soccer, ice-hockey, baseball, wrestling, badminton, judo, basketball, long jump, swimming, shot-pot, relay race, table tennis, javelin, diving, high jump, running, walking race, fencing, horse riding, sailing, shooting, weight-lifting, pole vault, hurdling, sporting events, Olympic Games, sportsman *v.*: compete, take part in, stand for, admit, host, fine, replace, advertise, deserve *adj.*: competitive, ancient, Greek, magical, regular, swift, physical, hopeless, foolish	Descriptive writing: a favourite sport 写作情境： 假设你是李华。为了激发学生对体育的热爱，强健体魄，你校决定于下周末在运动场举行为期两天的校运会。在邻校做交换生的美国朋友Henry对体育运动很感兴趣，本校同学也很期待外国友人的来访。为此，你写信邀请他前来观看校运会比赛。 内容包括：校运会举行的时间、地点和比赛项目 参加对象：各班运动员 奖励情况：各比赛项目前三名颁发奖牌 班级象征：写有不同格言的班旗

Book	Unit	Thematic Context	Topics	Word Bank	Writing
2	3.Computers	人与社会	Information technology; history and basic knowledge of computers; Robots	*n.*: abacus, calculator, laptop, PDA, sum, operator, technology, revolution, intelligence, reality, designer, tube, transistor, chip, network, web, application, goal, rocket, finance, happiness, human race, programmer, virus, android, teammate, type, coach, appearance, character, robot, monitor, mouse, keyboard, hard disc, floppy disc, printer, scanner, modem *v.*: calculate, simplify, solve, explore, download, arise, signal, deal with, watch over *adj.*: analytical, universal, logical, technological, artificial, intelligent, mathematical, personal, total, mobile, supporting, electronic	Imaginative writing: life in future 写作情境： 某英文报正在举行主题为"畅想未来"的科技创意征文大赛。请你以"… in the Future"为题写一篇英文短文，从功能和用途两个方面描述在日常生活中某件物品的未来
	4.Wildlife protection	人与自然	The importance of wildlife protection	*n.*: wildlife, protection, habitat, loss, reserve, zone, peace, danger, species, fur, relief, laughter, mercy, importance, WWF, insect, income, harm, extinction, incident, tiger, disappearance, animals, monkey, deer, panda, bird, worry, government, porpoise, organization, solution, awareness, environment, research, countryside *v.*: protect, threaten, decrease, increase, endanger, die out,	Practical writing: a letter of asking for help 写作情境： 调查研究显示，中国江豚因受人类活动影响而濒临灭绝，目前总数约1200头。假设你是李华，请用英文给WWF写一封信，请他们关注这个现象并提供帮助。内容包括：

Book	Unit	Thematic Context	Topics	Word Bank	Writing
	4.Wildlife protection	人与自然	The importance of wildlife protection	hunt, affect, pay attention to, appreciate, succeed, bite, rescue, employ, extinct, come into being, inspect, return, disappear, be aware of, take measures, work together, bring ... back to, kill, improve, reintroduce, live in the wild *adj.*: protective, wild, distant, certain, important, fierce, powerful, secure, harmful, harmless, common, unexpected, unfriendly, distant, endangered, local	1. 说明写信目的 2. 简述江豚现状 3.希望WWF如何帮助
2	5.Music	人与社会	Music; different types of music	*n.*: music, musician, rock and roll, orchestra, rap, jazz, karaoke, ballad, fame, instrument, performance, pub, cash, performer, studio, millionaire, actor, actress, addition, excitement, devotion, invitation *v.*: dream of, pretend, attach ... to, form, earn, act, invite, perform, play jokes on, rely on, get familiar with, break up, reunite, sort out, excite, devote, enjoy, prefer *adj.*: musical, classical, folk, choral, famous, extra, happy, humorous, familiar, attractive, excited, exciting, brief, sad, confident, relaxed, relaxing, cheerful, energetic, devoted, sensitive, painful, painless, amazing, wonderful, excellent	Practical writing: asking for advice 写作情境： 假设你是李华，你校将于下个月举办音乐节。作为组织者之一，你遇到了一些问题，写信向你的朋友Tom求助

续 表

Book	Unit	Thematic Context	Topics	Word Bank	Writing
3	1.Festivals around the world	人与社会	Festivals; how festivals begin; how festivals are celebrated	*n*.: celebration, harvest, origin, ancestor, grave, poet, incense, memory, feast, Halloween, Columbus Day, Carnival, belief, trick, arrival, independence, Easter, Christmas Day, the Chinese Spring Festival, the Mid-Autumn Festival, the Dragon Boat Festival, the Lantern Festival, agriculture, produce, award, parade, clothing, Christian, cherry, blossom, custom, rosebud, necessity, permission, holiday, prediction, fashion, parking, apology, sadness, magpie, conversation *v*.: celebrate, dress up, play a trick on, arrive, gain, gather, admire, look forward to, have fun with, fool, permit, predict, turn up, keep one's word, hold one's breath, apologize, weave, weep, set off, remind, forgive *adj*.: religious, seasonal, independent, agricultural, happy, energetic, lunar, worldwide, necessary, sad, obvious	Descriptive writing: favourite festivals 写作情境: 假设你是李华, 你的朋友Tom写信询问你最近开设的有关传统文化的实践课程。请根据提示给他回信, 内容包括: 1. 你喜欢的课程 2.喜欢的原因 3.对你的影响
	2.Healthy eating	人与社会; 人与自我	Problems with diet; Balanced diet and nutrition	*n*.: diet, spaghetti, nut, bean, pea, cucumber, eggplant, peach, pepper, mushroom, carrot, garlic, lemon, mutton, kebab, bacon, muscle,	Persuasive writing: a letter of advice 写作情境: 假设你是李华, 是一名高中生。

续 表

Book	Unit	Thematic Context	Topics	Word Bank	Writing
3	2.Healthy eating	人与社会；人与自我	Problems with diet; balanced diet and nutrition	protection, balance, cola, sugar, sign, vinegar, curiosity, hostess, host, customer, scurvy, fibre, discount, weakness, strength, rickets, obesity, vitamin, protein, debt, benefit, breast, cooperation, ingredient, flavor *v*.: protect, balance, barbecue, fry, lose weight, put on weight, get away with, lie, tell lies, win ... back, consult, digest, earn one's living, glare, spy, limit, sigh, combine *adj*.: protective, balanced, roast, sugary, slim, fat, curious, raw, poisonous, limited	最近你的笔友Amy来信说她因发胖而感到非常苦恼。请根据下列要点给她写一封建议信，内容包括：1.注意饮食合理，营养均衡 2.经常锻炼，保证睡眠充足 3.调整心态
	3.The million pound bank note	人与社会	Forms of literature and art: short story and drama; how to act out a play	*n*.: birthplace, birthday, author, writer, novel, story, boyhood, novelist, narrator, scene, pavement, businessman, bay, nightfall, fault, passage, embassy, patience, charity, envelope, steak, pineapple, desert, amount, manner, rag *v*.: bring up, adventure, phrase, bet, make a bet, wander, permit, stare, spot, account, seek, take a chance, scream, issue, bow *adj*.: penniless, unpaid, contrary, unbelievable, rude, genuine, fake	Descriptive writing: a short article 写作情境：假设你是李华，准备给你校英文报投稿介绍你最喜欢的小说家。请你根据下面提示写一篇短文介绍你喜欢的作家马克·吐温。内容包括：1.马克·吐温是19世纪著名作家，生于密苏里州，当过水手，喜欢写作 2.全世界都有读者喜欢他的作品

续 表

Book	Unit	Thematic Context	Topics	Word Bank	Writing
3	4.Astronomy: the science of the stars	人与社会	Science of the stars; The development of life; space travel and gravity	*n.*: astronomy, astronomer, solar system, religion, theory, atom, billion, globe, violence, carbon, dioxide, nitrogen, vapour, atmosphere, presence, harm, acid, chain, reaction, oxygen, shellfish, amphibian, reptile, existence, mammal, puzzle, biology, biologist, gravity, satellite, geologist, physicist, extinction, climate, comet, spaceship, weight, cabin, mystery, space, astronaut, space travel, training, development, telescope, engine, space suit, oxygen can *v.*: dissolve, react, multiply, lay eggs, exist, give birth to, prevent ... from, puzzle, block out, crash, pull, push, lessen, cheer up, float, get the hang of, break out, exhaust, watch out for, send ... into space, go on a trip into space, develop, feel like *adj.*: solar, religious, global, violent, fundamental, present, harmful, gentle, extinct, weightless, exhausted *adv.*: thus, weightlessly *prep.*: unlike	Expository writing: solving a problem 写作情境： 假设你是李华，你爱好太空探险，但是得不到父母的理解，于是你给英国朋友Stephen发邮件进行交流并请求帮助。要点如下： 1.父母的意见 2.你的观点
	5.Canada— "The True North"	人与自然	Geography of canada; multicultural society	*n.*: trip, journey, travel, voyage, quiz, Canadian, Toronto, beaver, grizzly bear, penguin, eagle, minister, prime minister,	Descriptive writing: a report 写作情境： 假设你是李华，

Book	Unit	Thematic Context	Topics	Word Bank	Writing
3	5.Canada—"The True North"	人与自然	Geography of canada; multicultural society	governor, continent, topic, baggage, scenery, harbour, measure, stampede, cowboy, border, acre, mixture, bush, maple, frost, wealth, distance, mist, schoolmate, booth, pearl, Cantonese, dawn, terror, workplace, buffet, tradition, pleasure, impression, climate, location, population, tourist attractions, food, natural resources, plants, animals, outdoor activities, custom, culture, geography, humanity, beauty, softness, fragrance, faintness, freshness, dewdrop, taste, description, wide rivers, fresh water *v.*: be on a trip to, describe, chat, surround, measure, settle down, manage to do, catch sight of, have a gift for, locate, mix, confirm, broaden, terrify, please, impress, be located in, have a population of, have a history of, have an area of, be covered with, be close to, soar, be surrounded by/with, interest *adj.*: multicultural, polar, prime, eastward, westward, located, northward, southward, upward, downward, slight, urban, mixed, wealthy, distant, misty, broad, traditional, terrified, terrifying, pleased, pleasant, impressed, impressive, natural,	上个星期新西兰姐妹学校Kaikorai Valley College师生到你校交流。你交到的笔友Jenny回国后写信给你，说她非常喜欢清远以及吃过的美食，想更多地了解清远。请你用英语给她写一封回信，内容包括： 1.清远的地理概况 2.清远的人文概况 3.邀请她再来清远

Book	Unit	Thematic Context	Topics	Word Bank	Writing
3	5.Canada— "The True North"	人与自然	Geography of canada; multicultural society	amazing, amazed, beautiful, exciting, excited, worried, tired, surprised, satisfied *adv.*: aboard, slightly, downtown, approximately, nearby, traditionally, terrifically, surprisingly, amazingly	
4	1.Women of achievement	人与社会	Great women and their achievements	*n.*: achievement, welfare, project, specialist, connection, human being, campaign, organization, behavior, shade, observation, childhood, respect, argument, entertainment, crowd, inspiration, support, audience, career, rate, sickness, emergency, generation, determination, kindness, consideration *v.*: behave, move off, observe, argue, lead a ... life, crowd in, inspire, look down upon, refer to, come across, intend to, deliver, carry on, concern oneself with, devote ... to, encourage ... to, work out, communicate with *adj.*: worthwhile, outspoken, considerate, modest	Descriptive writing: short article 写作情境： 你们学校的英文报现征集关于中国杰出女性的英文稿，请你根据以下内容，写一篇短文投稿，介绍科学家屠呦呦。 姓名：屠呦呦 出生：1930年12月30日，中国浙江宁波 职业：科学家 教育：北京医学院（今北京大学医学部） 工作经历：毕业后在中国中医研究院（今中国中医科学院）做研究，1972年发现青蒿素——一种用于治疗疟疾的药物，挽救了数百万人的生命

Book	Unit	Thematic Context	Topics	Word Bank	Writing
4	1. Women of achievement	人与社会	Great women and their achievements		成就：2015年10月，屠呦呦获得诺贝尔生理学或医学奖。她成为首个获科学类诺贝尔奖的中国本土科学家
	2. Working the land	人与社会	Important people, history and methods of agriculture	*n.*: decade, hybrid, output, crop, hunger, freedom, grain, peanut, nationality, occupation, personality, production, bacteria, pest, nutrition, mineral, discovery, focus, soil *v.*: struggle, expand, circulate, rid, be satisfied with, equip, export, confuse, regret, build up, lead to, focus on, reduce, keep ... free of/from, consider oneself ..., graduate from, make it possible to, search for, care about, dream for, avoid *adj.*: sunburnt, super, disturbing, chemical, organic, fertile, industrial	Descriptive writing: a short article 写作情境： 假设你是李华，最近从报刊上了解到袁隆平海水稻研究成功后，你写了一篇英语短文发表在校报上。要点如下： 1. 袁隆平生于1930年，1953年大学毕业 2. 成功研发杂交水稻；在2017年研究海水稻；超级水稻创下新纪录 3. 你的感想
	3. A taste of English humour	人与社会	Different types of English humour	*n.*: humor, mime, comedy, perform, performer, failure, performance, astonishment, teens, tramp, optimism, underdog, snowstorm, leather, mouthful, enjoyment, confidence, costume, gesture, occasion, actress, slide, amusement, explanation, detective, whisper, mess	Descriptive writing: a short article 写作情境： 假设你是李华，你最喜欢的武侠小说家金庸因病去世。请你写一篇短文介绍他，并发表在校报上，内容包括：

续 表

Book	Unit	Thematic Context	Topics	Word Bank	Writing
4	3.A taste of English humour	人与社会	Different types of English humour	*v.*: brighten, astonish, entertain, overcome, pick out, cut off, chew, convince, direct, star in, amuse, react, feel content with *adj.*: verbal, depressed, content, ordinary, astonishing, astonished, fortunate, unfortunate, bored, subtle, entertaining, charming, homeless, worn, worn-out, convincing, outstanding, particular, amusing, amused, mountainous, vast, drunk *adv.*: unfortunately, homelessly, stiffly, particularly	1.他创作了无数武侠小说，很多已被改编成电视剧。 2.英文版《射雕英雄传》已出版，外国友人迷上了中国功夫
	4.Body language	人与社会	Cultural differences and inter-cultural communication	*n.*: statement, association, dormitory, canteen, flight, cheek, defence, misunderstanding, adult, posture, crossroads, employee, function, ease, anger, fist, rank *v.*: greet, represent, approach, defend, misunderstand, dash, be likely to, frown, misread, lose face, turn one's back to, yawn, hug *adj.*: curious, major, spoken, unspoken, likely, facial, false, respectful, subjective *adv.*: curiously, simply, truly	Practical writing: a letter of thanks 写作情境： 假设你是某中学学生会主席李华。上周你校邀请了美国某大学教授史密斯先生来校做一场关于各国身势语的专题讲座。请你代表你校全体学生，用英语给他写一封感谢信
	5.Theme parks	人与社会	Different types of theme parks	*n.*: theme, cartoon, pirate, fairy tale, fantasy, amusement, swing, attraction, tourism, carpenter, craftsman, sword,	Explanatory writing: brochure 写作情境： 假设你叫李华，

续 表

Book	Unit	Thematic Context	Topics	Word Bank	Writing
4	5.Theme parks	人与社会	Different types of theme parks	engine, length, deed, tournament, settler, translator, brand, minority, cloth, jungle, diver, creature, sunlight, outing, admission, shuttle, freeway, souvenir, sneaker, brochure *v.*: be famous for, preserve, be modelled after, advance, get close to, come to life *adj.*: central, various, unique, bald, athletic, advanced	你想邀请你的美国笔友Peter这个寒假来清远玩,并向他介绍故乡的主题公园。请根据以下要点,写一封邀请信。 1.故乡的概况 2.故乡的具体特色(有八大区,简单介绍建筑风格、蜡像馆、百艺坊、游乐场、农场等) 3.参观故乡的文化意义
5	1.Great scientists	人与社会	How to organize scientific research; contributions of scientists	*n.*: scientist, mathematician, biologist, physicist, physician, chemist, expert, painter, conclusion, cholera, cure, clue, outbreak, challenge, victim, enquiry, neighbourhood, pump, investigation, handle, germ, certainty, construction, firework, chart, movement, brightness, universe *v.*: make contributions to, devote oneself to, be expert in, do one's best, invent, discover, put forward, be honored as, be awarded as, put forward, conclude, draw a conclusion, analyse, infect, defeat, attend, expose	Persuasive writing: letter 写作情境: 下周六是母亲节,某英语刊物正在进行"我的母亲"征文活动。请按照下面提供的主要内容,以"我的母亲"为题,写一篇短文 1. 你母亲住在农村,50多岁,没有文化,但她很关心你的学习情况 2. 探望母亲的一次经历

Book	Unit	Thematic Context	Topics	Word Bank	Writing
5	1.Great scientists	人与社会	How to organize scientific research; contributions of scientists	be exposed to, cure, absorb, suspect, foresee, investigate, blame, pollute, link, announce, instruct, construct, contribute, be strict with, make sense, spin, reject *adj.*: scientific, infectious, deadly, severe, responsible, creative, co-operative, positive, revolutionary, enthusiastic, cautious *adv.*: backward, privately	3. 归纳总结母亲的品行
	2.The United Kingdom	人与自然	Countries of the united kingdom; union Jack; famous sites in london	*n.*: province, opportunity, possibility, sightseeing, delight, architecture, food, places of interest, tourist attractions, kingdom, union, credit, currency, institution, convenience, collection, administration, port, countryside, description, fax, possibility, conflict, quarrel, wedding, uniform, statue, longitude, navigation, communism *v.*: consist of, divide ... into, attract, thrill, invite, be located in, unite, clarify, accomplish, break away from, leave out, take the place of, break down, arrange, fold *adj.*: educational, historical, enjoyable, royal, splendid, imaginary, delicious, unwilling, rough, nationwide,	Non-chronological report: tourist guide 写作情境1: 假设你是张萍玉。你的美国朋友Jesse寒假要来北京游玩两天，向你征求意见。请根据以下要点，为他推荐行程安排: 1.行程安排及理由 2.注意事项 写作情境2: 假定你是李华，你的英国朋友Bill对中国文化很感兴趣，他准备下个月来中国游玩，向你征询建议。请你给他写一封邮件推荐

续　表

Book	Unit	Thematic Context	Topics	Word Bank	Writing
5	2.The United Kingdom	人与自然		plus, alike, furnished, original, consistent *adv.*: roughly	一个旅游地。要点如下： 1. 推荐的地方 2. 推荐的理由 3. 你的祝愿
	3.Life in the future	人与社会	Prediction of the good and bad changes in the future; life in the future	*n.*: light rail train, Changlong Zoo, robot, Universities Town, aspect, impression, flashback, guide, tablet, lack, expertise, capsule, steward, stewardess, opening, mask, adjustment, surroundings, combination, carriage, belt, switch, timetable, alien, mud, desert, citizen, typist, typewriter, postage, postcode, button, instant, receiver, efficiency, ribbon, dustbin, ecology, material, goods, representative, settlement, motivation *v.*: attract, integrate into, take up, tolerate, lack, hover, be back on one's feet, press, fasten, lose sight of, sweep up, flash, slide into, speed up, imitate, dispose, swallow, recycle, manufacture *adj.*: convenient, livable, beautiful, comfortable, constant, previous, uncertain, surrounding, exhausted, optimistic, pessimistic, enormous, moveable, efficient, disposal, greedy *adv.*: constantly, sideways	Imaginative writing: life in the future 写作情境： 假设某英文报社向中学生征文，题目是"The House in the Future"。请根据下列要点和你的想象写一篇短文： 1.如何智能化 2.如何服务人

Book	Unit	Thematic Context	Topics	Word Bank	Writing
5	4.Making the news	人与社会	The basic procedure of making the news; newspapers and TV programs	*n*.: the media-news, newspaper, TV, the radio; the jobs-typist, critic, designer, reporter, editor, journalist, photographer, housewife, printer; the qualities-high level of education, a great success assignment, assistant, profession, colleague, activity, amateur, deadline, interviewee, case, accusation, demand, section, crime, edition, department, appointment, dilemma *v*.: be curious, be active, be hardworking, be enthusiastic about, be able to work in a team, be gifted for, involve, be professional in the process-interview, take photos, develop photos, check the report, read and approve, be delivered by, organize, take part in, realize the importance of, raise the awareness of, assist, submit, concentrate, update, acquire, assess, inform, depend on, accuse, deny, publish, polish, approve, process *adj*.: patient, imaginative, well-organized, good, honest, truthful, creative, admirable, careful, eager, successful, meaningful, unforgettable, delighted, unusual, thorough,	Practical writing: a letter of application 写作情境： 假设你是李华，你打算应聘某英文报社招聘记者，请按写作要求写一封申请信。 1.写信的目的 2.自身优势 3.表达愿望

续 表

Book	Unit	Thematic Context	Topics	Word Bank	Writing
5	4.Making the news	人与社会	The basic procedure of making the news; newspapers and TV programs	professional, skeptical, guilty, demanding, concise, gifted, idiomatic, accurate, senior, chief, negative *adv.*: firstly, then, after that, finally, meanwhile, deliberately, technically	
	5.First aid	人与自我	First aid; safety in the home; medicine; medication	*n.*: aid, first aid, injury, nosebleed, ankle, cupboard, skin, organ, layer, barrier, poison, ray, variety, liquid, radiation, pan, stove, tissue, electric shock, blister, nerve, scissors, basin, bandage, ointment, infection, symptom, label, kettle, wrist, sleeve, blouse, throat, ceremony, bravery, pressure, ambulance, scheme, bruise *v.*: fall ill, bleed, sprain, choke, heal, swell, char, squeeze, put one's hands on, treat, apply, make a difference *adj.*: temporary, sprained, essential, complex, mild, vital, swollen, watery, unbearable, pour, damp, tight, firm *adv.*: mildly, tightly, firmly	Instructional writing: first aid instructions for particular injuries 写作情境：你校英文报正在开展主题为"急救知识"的征文比赛。请你用英语写一篇短文向报社投稿，介绍自己所了解的急救知识
6	1.Art	人与社会	A brief history of western painting and chinese art; famous	*n.*: sculpture, sculptor, gallery, faith, aim, possession, technique, perspective, coincidence, masterpiece, attempt, impressionism,	Persuasive writing: a letter of advice 写作情境：你的朋友John来信说下周要来中

续 表

Book	Unit	Thematic Context	Topics	Word Bank	Writing
6	1.Art	人与社会	Artists and works of art	impressionist, post-impressionist, shadow, landscape, figure, clay, critic, bonze, marble, exhibition, scholar, flesh, geometry, bunch, avenue, preference, reputation, civilization, Egypt, district, committee, signature *v.*: adopt, possess, predict, carve, display, appeal *adj.*: realistic, abstract, faithful, conventional, typical, evident, humanistic, superb, ridiculous, controversial, specific, delicate, allergic, aggressive, fragile, circular, metropolitan, Egyptian, visual, fragrant, contemporary, permanent *adv.*: faithfully, consequently, effectively	国北京旅游，他对艺术品有浓厚的兴趣，希望你为他介绍去哪里参观，并为他介绍有什么值得看的艺术品。请根据如下内容写一篇短文： 故宫博物院 1. 世界闻名 2. 位于北京市中心，占地72万平方米 3. 艺术藏品种类繁多 4. 拥有绘画、雕塑、书法（如王羲之、颜真卿等人的作品）等艺术珍品 5. 门票不贵，通常游客众多 6. 值得一看
	2.Poems	人与社会	Different types of poems; reading, writing and listening to poetry	*n.*: poem, poetry, poet, rhyme, emotion, nursery, repetition, pattern, cottage, sparrow, kitten, minimum, translation, branch, sorrow, librarian, trunk, cement, section, diploma, exchange, sponsor, blank, compass, bride, bridegroom, championship, darkness, warmth, scholarship, pianist, violinist, load	Persuasive writing: a letter of advice 写作情境： 假设你是李华，正在教你的英国朋友Leslie学习汉语。请你发微信告知他下次上课的计划。内容包括：

续 表

Book	Unit	Thematic Context	Topics	Word Bank	Writing
6	2.Poems	人与社会	Different types of poems; reading, writing and listening to poetry	*v.*: tick, convey, hush, take it easy, run out of, be made up of, tease, dread, melt, await, transform, revolve, utter, try out, let out *adj.*: concrete, contradictory, flexible, salty, endless, bare, brimful, appropriate *adv.*: endlessly, eventually, forever	1.时间和地点 2.内容是学习唐诗 3.课前准备：简要了解唐朝的历史
	3.A healthy life	人与社会	Health problems: smoking, HIV/AIDS and drugs; attitudes towards HIV/AIDS	*n.*: cigarette, alcohol, abuse, fitness, stress, obesity, fluid, adolescent, adolescence, nicotine, withdrawal, effect, sex, lung, resolve, packet, relaxation, chemist, gum, pill, injection, comprehension, robbery, survival, needle, prejudice, judgement, abortion, cigar, embarrassment *v.*: ban, accustom, quit, strengthen, decide on, feel like doing, weaken, take risks, get into, inject, spill *adj.*: alcoholic, sexual, stressful, due, tough, addicted, accustomed, bad-tempered, automatic, mental, pregnant, abnormal, breathless, unfit, desperate, disappointed, male, female, ashamed, illegal, slippery, immune, embarrassed, awkward *adv.*: automatically, mentally, awkwardly	Persuasive writing: a letter of advice 写作情境： 假设你是李华，由于各种原因，你校很多同学养成了熬夜的习惯，这对健康造成了很大危害。请你以"The Harmful Effects of Staying up Late"为题，写一篇短文，给你校的英文内刊投稿，让熬夜的同学意识到熬夜的危害并改掉这一坏习惯

续 表

Book	Unit	Thematic Context	Topics	Word Bank	Writing
6	4.Global warming	人与自然	Global warming; pollution; the importance of protecting the earth	*n.*: greenhouse, graph, phenomenon, fossil, fuel, quantity, byproduct, measurement, data, trend, catastrophe, flood, drought, famine, environmentalist, consequence, range, tendency, existence, individual, commitment, pollution, growth, appliance, motor, can, circumstance, microwave, disagreement, agreement, educator, contribution, imperative, heading, slogan, presentation *v.*: consume, come about, subscribe, tend, go up, result in, oppose, be opposed to, state, keep on, glance, advocate, put up with, refresh *adj.*: renewable, random, opposed, mild, environmental, steady, widespread, economical, average, outer, electrical, casual, nuclear *adv.*: steadily	Persuasive writing: speech 写作情境: 假设你校将举办城市环保宣传活动。请你用英语写一篇演讲稿,内容包括: 1.垃圾现状 2.提出倡议
	5.The power of nature	人与自然	Volcanoes; crater lakes; cyclones; floods	*n.*: diagram, volcano, eruption, ash, crater, lava, hurricane, questionnaire, equipment, observatory, database, wave, spaceman, suit, helmet, boot, potential, geology, sample, candidate, threat, bungalow, tornado, typhoon, tsunami, novelist, thunderstorm, fog, document, rainbow, balcony, shot, sweat, anxiety, evaluation,	

续 表

Book	Unit	Thematic Context	Topics	Word Bank	Writing
6	5.The power of nature	人与自然	Volcanoes; crater lakes; cyclones; floods	appreciation, persuasion *v.*: erupt, appoint, burn to the ground, fountain, make one's way, threaten, shoot, tremble, panic, glance through, bathe, arouse, appreciate, guarantee *adj.*: volcanic, molten, absolute, actual, precious, anxious, uncomfortable, unconscious, spectacular *adv.*: alongside, absolutely, anxiously	
7	1.Living well	人与自我	Disability; life of disabled people	*n.*: disability, hearing, eyesight, syndrome, lap, ambition, dictation, entry, bench, microscope, absence, fellow, firm, annoyance, parrot, tank, tortoise, psychology, conduct, encouragement, mainstream, politics, abolition, slavery, literature, companion, assistance, congratulation, bowling, graduation, certificate, architect, access, wheelchair, row, basement, exit, approval, dignity, profit, community *v.*: bump, cut out, annoy, sit around, make fun of, abolish, resign, congratulate, impair, meet with, adapt to *adj.*: ambitious, noisy, suitable, beneficial, clumsy, fellow, outgoing, annoyed, firm, encouraging, fulfilling, adequate, accessible, handy *adv.*: psychologically, outwards	

续 表

Book	Unit	Thematic Context	Topics	Word Bank	Writing
7	2.Robots	人与社会	Robots; literary work about science	*n.*: fiction, desire, satisfaction, bonus, apron, sympathy, favor, pile, fingernail, haircut, makeup, cushion, bedding, necklace, clerk, counter, affair, armchair, cuisine, staff, mailbox, receiver, affection, biography, imagination, navy, transfusion, master's degree, biochemistry, talent, chapter, framework, thinking, divorce, assessment *v.*: desire, test out, alarm, scan, accompany, ring up, turn around, declare, envy, leave ... alone, set aside, be bound to, obey, disobey *adj.*: household, alarmed, overweight, elegant, absurd, awful, digital, grand, bound, holy, part-time, junior, talented, theoretical *adv.*: aside	
	3.Under the sea	人与自然	Nature: animals and plants under the sea; legends of the sea	*n.*: migration, witness, accommodation, shore, telescope, teamwork, depth, lip, shark, relationship, conservation, iceberg, seaside, net, target, tide, dimension, cell, seaweed, flashlight, boundary, pension, pensioner *v.*: yell, pause, dive, flee, drag, urge, abandon, help ... out, reflect, jog, be aware of, suck, scare, leap, refund	

续 表

Book	Unit	Thematic Context	Topics	Word Bank	Writing
7	3.Under the sea	人与自然	Nature: animals and plants under the sea; legends of the sea	*adj.*: annual, opposite, pure, aware, vivid, neat, narrow, sharp, tasty, giant, gray, shallow, steep, awesome *adv.*: annually, offshore, meantime, overboard	
	4.Sharing	人与社会	Helping others; voluntary work	*n.*: volunteer, share, gift, assistance, airmail, fortnight, roof, textbook, concept, bucket, weed, hut, rectangle, platform, broom, interpreter, grill, leftover, privilege, paperwork, comb, arrangement, astronaut, angle, catalogue, anniversary, seed, supplement, distribution, security *v.*: take part in, be dying to, make difference to, make contributions to, have an effect on, pay a visit to, be worth it if ..., do something out of the ordinary, donate, be in need, hear from, adjust, sniff, participate, dry out, dry up, toast, purchase, distribute, operate *adj.*: muddy, weekly, relevant, remote, rectangular, evil, voluntary, political, financial *adv.*: otherwise	
	5.Travelling abroad	人与社会	National consciousness and international	*n.*: motherland, visa, queue, cafeteria, lecture, idiom, qualification, preparation, shopkeeper, comfort,	

Book	Unit	Thematic Context	Topics	Word Bank	Writing
7	5.Travell-ing abroad	人与社会	Awareness; studying abroad; travelling abroad	substitute, requirement, essay, tutor, revision, draft, enterprise, cage, apology, seminar, videophone, bachelor, routine, minibus, battery, site, drill, agent, destination, inn, hike *v*.: adjust to, keep it up, fit in, recommend, comfort, bark, acknowledge, contradict, occupy, be occupied with, drill, govern, hike, settle in *adj*.: comfortable, academic, revise, numb, autonomous, optional, parallel, abundant *adv*.: comfortably, onwards	
8	1.A land of diversity	人与自然; 人与社会	History and geography of the USA; nationality and people; customs and culture	*n*.: distinction, immigrant, immigration, strait, means, majority, ministry, adventurer, hardship, rail, percentage, Italy, Denmark, boom, aircraft, crossing, vice, nephew, pole, applicant, customs, socialist, socialism, cattle, cable, tram, luggage, brake, conductor, bakery, ferry, justice, punishment, authority *v*.: illustrate, live on, make a life, elect, keep up, occur, immigrate, indicate, shave, slip, team up with, hire, mark out, take in, apply for, mourn, reform, grasp, insert	

续 表

Book	Unit	Thematic Context	Topics	Word Bank	Writing
8	1.A land of diversity	人与自然；人与社会	History and geography of the USA; nationality and people; customs and culture	*adj.*: distinct, prehistoric, federal, Italian, racial, apparent, fascinating, miserable, civil, thoughtful, thankful *adv.*: back to back, apparently, nowhere *prep.*: despite	
	2.Cloning	人与社会	Natural clones and man-made clones; the history of cloning; controversy about cloning	*n.*: cutting, twin, breakthrough, procedure, embryo, carrier, correction, objection, impact, medium, side road, fate, constitution, loaf, flour, assumption, feather, regulation, nonsense, popularity, drawback, decoration, opera, chorus *v.*: differ, undertake, pay off, cast, cast down, object, obtain, attain, forbid, accumulate, owe, retire, bother, be bound to, strike, strike into one's heart, bring back to life, resist, restore, adore, hatch *adj.*: exact, identical, commercial, straightforward, unable, complicated, arbitrary, moral, conservative, compulsory, reasonable, initial, vain *adv.*: altogether, shortly, from time to time, merely, fairly *prep.*: in favor of, in vain, in good/poor condition	

Book	Unit	Thematic Context	Topics	Word Bank	Writing
8	3.Inventors and Inventions	人与社会	Inventions; patent applications; great inventors	*n.*: patent, courtyard, walnut, product, powder, perfume, jelly, cube, caution, expectation, recognition, criterion, dot, rod, file, string, glue, greengrocer, identification, rainfall, directory, court, courtroom, lantern, jam, forehead, beaten track, wire, straw, current, helicopter, triangle, refrigerator, extension, version, competence, personnel *v.*: call up, distinguish, set about, seize, claim, dial, dive into, set out to do, tap, reproduce, associate, hang on, get through, ring back, ring off *adj.*: amphibious, merciful, stainless, cubic, abrupt, merry, passive, cautious, convenient, valid, ripe, freezing, innocent, dynamic, multiple, stable, invaluable, practical *adv.*: now and then, abruptly, merrily, occasionally *prep.*: out of order	
	4.Pygmalion	人与社会	Literary work; drama	*n.*: adaptation, caption, plot, professor, garment, wallet, output, thief, handkerchief, remark, gutter, ambassador, acquaintance, handful, amazement, fortune, status, stocking, believer, cookie, teapot, cream, nail, wax, disk, shilling, referee, laundry, bathtub, waist, vest, alphabet	

Book	Unit	Thematic Context	Topics	Word Bank	Writing
8	4.Pygmalion	人与社会	Literary work; drama	*v.*: whistle, hesitate, disguise, classify, betray, condemn, pass ... off as, make one's, disapprove, rob, show ... in, curtsy, compromise, sob, overlook, fade, fade out *adj.*: classic, fateful, woollen, uncomfortable, troublesome, mistaken, brilliant, upper, extraordinary, authentic, effective, superior, antique, musical, shabby, horrible, disgusting *adv.*: uncomfortably, properly, generally speaking, once more, heartily *prep.*: in disguise, in amazement, in terms of, in need of	
	5.Meeting your ancestors	人与社会	General knowledge of archaeology; anthropology as well as history	*n.*: archaeology, archaeologist, starvation, accuracy, quilt, excavation, mat, beast, centimeter, sharpener, scraper, bead, botany, analysis, seashell, category, significance, album, scratch, academy, receptionist, onion, skateboard, kindergarten, yogurt, radioactivity, division, wrinkle, vein, spear, eyebrow, cheekbone, arrowhead, axe, hammer, punctuation, craftsmanship *v.*: identify, interrupt, assume, sharpen, cut up, scrape, spit, ripen, delete, pulse, applaud,	

续 表

Book	Unit	Thematic Context	Topics	Word Bank	Writing
8	5.Meeting your ancestors	人与社会	General knowledge of archaeology; anthropology as well as history	look ahead, howl, accelerate, arrest, date back to, worship, be fed up with *adj.*: alternative, archaeological, acute, tentative, ample, primitive, botanical, significant, systematic, radioactive, dizzy, messy, gay, skilful *adv.*: regardless, somehow, gaily *prep.*: regardless of, at most	

第二节 基于教材单元主题与话题的
写作情境创设（新人教版）

（胡翠娥 郭秀云 谢晖 刘美艳）

Book	Unit	Thematic Context	Topics	Word Bank	Writing
1	Welcome Unit	人与自我	First impressions; student profiles	*v.*: explore, impress, experience, feel confident, concentrate on, made a deep impression on, make new friends, worry about, learn from, leave me alone, lie in, look forward to, come true, make plans for, exchange experience, take notes, look up, get along with, form the habit of, make up one's mind, be busy doing sth. *n.*: impression, experiment, hobby, personality, learning method *adj.*: senior, happy, anxious, excited,	A self profile 假定你是李华，将去新加坡参加一个中学生交流活动。请根据所给提示，用英语写一篇短文介绍自己。 内容包括： 1.个人基本情况； 2.自己的性格和爱好； 3.未来的打算。 注意：①词数100左右；②可以适当增加细节，以使行文连贯。 参考范文： My name is Li Hua, a 15-year-old girl studying in Senior 1 Xinhua Middle School now. I am outgoing and cheerful, so it is easy for me to get along well with others. I study many kinds of subjects at school, among which I like English best. Besides, I have formed the

续　表

Book	Unit	Thematic Context	Topics	Word Bank	Writing
	Welcome Unit	人与自我	First impressions; student profiles	annoyed, frightened, awkward, active, outgoing, kind, friendly, helpful, difficult, annoying, curious, cheerful *adv.*: newly	habit of reading books at the weekend. You'll never see me without an English novel or a Chinese science fiction. Not only do I like listening to music, but I also enjoy watching English movies in my spare time, which helps me to relax and learn more about western culture. I have made up my mind to study medicine when I am at college. I am looking forward to making my dream come true.
1	1.Teenage Life	人与自我	The freshmen challenge; a Letter of advice; the face-down generation	*v.*: volunteer, debate, enjoy, prefer, date, challenge, make all the difference, clean up, give directions to, be interested in, be fond of, be excited about, be crazy about, have a passion for, find great pleasure in, enjoy doing, make decisions, join the club, sign up for, make the team, keep up with, give a speech, intend to, take part in, attract the attention, call on, ask for advice, recommend that, play computer games, make it very difficult to, become addicted to, feel lonely	A letter of advice 假设你是李华，你的笔友John写信告知你，他因为不能适应新的高中学习生活而整日闷闷不乐。请你给他回一封信，内容如下： 1.告诉他这是正常现象； 2.给他提几点建议； 3.希望和祝愿。 参考范文： Dear John, You wrote that you have been upset all day since you went into your senior high school. I understand quite well that you are unhappy. I recommend that you ask your teachers and classmates for help if you are in trouble. They will try their best to help you. Actually, it is not

Book	Unit	Thematic Context	Topics	Word Bank	Writing
1	1.Teenage Life	人与自我	The freshmen challenge; a Letter of advice; the face-down generation	*n.*: teenage, teenager, volunteer, debate, hearing, challenge, solution, camp, expert, relationship, after-class activity, development, team-work *adj.*: simple, challenging, exciting, interesting, comfortable, ordinary, suitable, unhappy, uncomfortable, homesick, responsible, confusing, hopeful *adv.*: outdoors, obviously, completely, finally, strangely	unusual for a student of your age to feel uncomfortable in a new environment. I think you should not be so anxious. You can talk to your classmates, which can help you to be more social. Besides, it's better for you to discuss the problems you can't solve with them. Hope my suggestions are helpful to you. All the best. Yours, Li Hua
	2. Travelling Around	人与自我	A travel plan to Xi'an; be a good tourist; a travel plan	*v.*: apply, rent, pack, type, admire, contact, transport, hike, request, comment, recognize, unearth, apply for, take control of, make up, check in, check out, go on a trip *n.*: visa, rent, pack, arrangement, source, flat, site, flight, accommodation, path, destination, architecture, architect, brochure, package, civilization, transport,	A travel plan 假定你是李华，你的英国笔友Jack想来中国旅行。请根据以下要点提示，给他写一封电子邮件，建议他乘坐公共交通工具游玩，原因如下： 1.节省能源，减少污染； 2.缓解交通拥挤； 3.节省开支。 注意：①词数80左右；②邮件的开头和结尾已给出，不计入总词数。 参考词汇：减少 reduce；公共交通 public transport 参考范文： Dear Jack, I'm happy that you are coming

续 表

Book	Unit	Thematic Context	Topics	Word Bank	Writing
1	2. Travelling Around	人与自我	A travel plan to Xi'an; be a good tourist; a travel plan	hike, credit, view, sight, statue, tomb, places of interest, convenient transportation *adj.*: amazing, amazed, narrow, flat, official, unique, econ-omic, famous/well-known *adv.*: extremely	to visit our country. You know air pollution is becoming worse and worse, so I advise you to tour China by public transport, such as by bus, by train and by subway. There are many advantages of using public transport. Firstly, we can save lots of energy. In turn, we can reduce air pollution. Secondly, using public transport can make roads less crowded. Finally, it's much cheaper to travel by public transport. So you can save your money. I hope you will have a good time in China! Yours sincerely, Li Hua
	3.Sports and Fitness	人与社会	Living legends; going positive; cool cold sports;	*v.*: ski, host, track, work out, sweat, make it, master, set an example, injure, lose heart, give up, compete, make sense, pretend, pretend to do sth., cheat, make a difference, cut ... out, compare with/to, jog, stress *n.*: fitness, soccer, stadium, boxing, badminton, marathon, event, host, track, track and field, gym,	A page in a wellness book 假设你是李华，写一篇短文介绍一下自己过去和现在在健身方面的情况，注意以下要点： 过去： 1. 认为运动不重要，浪费时间，影响学习； 2. 不爱好运动，体重增加，容易生病，经常气喘吁吁。 现在： 1.定期锻炼，增强了体力； 2.体重减轻了，感觉比以前健康和强壮。 将来：虽然运动需要决心，我将继续坚持锻炼。

续　表

Book	Unit	Thematic Context	Topics	Word Bank	Writing
1	3.Sports and Fitness	人与社会	Living legends; going positive; cool cold sports;	gymnastics, sweat, legend, athlete, master, honor, glory, medal, championship, champion, determination, injury, captain, strength, failure, cheat, audience, diet, push-up, error *adj.*: injured, graceful, slim, fit, strong *adv.*: apart, rather	参考范文： In the past, I thought there was no sense in taking exercise. I believe it wasted a lot of time, which would affect my study. So I showed no interest in sports. Gradually I put on weight and fell ill easily. Sometimes, I felt breathless even when walking. I realize that it makes great sense for students to do more exercise. At present, I take exercise regularly. In my spare time, I often work out, building up my strength. To my delight, I have reduced my weight and fell healthier and stronger than before. 　Even if taking exercise needs more determination, I will stick to it and I will be sure to make it.
	4.Natural Disasters	人与自然	The night the earth didnt' sleep; the story of an eyewitness;	*v.*: slide, flood, rescue, damage, destroy, evacuate, affect, shelter, crack, ruin, shock, trap, bury, breathe, revive, unify, suffer, erupt, supply, survive, tap, whistle, calm, aid, crash, sweep, strike, wave, deliver *n.*: disaster, tornado, drought, landslide, tsunami, flood, magnitude, rescue,	A summary of a news report Follow the steps below to write a summary for the text on Page 50. Step 1: Read the text and write a list of the main details. Step 2: Write down the main idea of each paragraph. Step 3: Organize the ideas and draft the summary. For several days, strange things occurred in the countryside of northeastern Hebei. Then, on 28 July, 1976, an earthquake hit Tangshan City. The city was

续 表

Book	Unit	Thematic Context	Topics	Word Bank	Writing
1	4.Natural Disasters	人与自然	The night the earth didnt' sleep; the story of an eyewitness;	damage, helicopter, death, shelter, brick, metal, shock, electricity, trap, revival, effort, wisdom, context, volcano, supply, typhoon, hurricane, power, tap, pipe, whistle, emergency, aid, first aid kit, wave, strike, summary, effect, length *adj.*: percent, calm	greatly affected and nearly destroyed. Many people were killed or injured. The rescue work began soon after the quakes. Soldiers and medical workers arrived to find survivors and help the people who had lost everything. With strong support from the government and the tireless efforts of the people, a new Tangshan was built.
	5.Languages Around the World	人与社会	The chinese writing system: connecting the past and the present; learning English polyglots: what are they and who can be one?	*v.*: refer, carve, regard, appreciate, struggle, beg, demand, relate, refer to, date back to, play a greater role in, reach the goal, get high marks, bridge the gap *n.*: billion, attitude, reference, system, factor, base, bone, symbol, dynasty, variety, means, character, calligraphy, affair, petrol, subway, apartment, gap, vocabulary, description *adj.*: native, major, classic, global, specific, equal *adv.*: equally	A blog about English studay 写作任务: 假设你是李华，在某英语学习交流网站看到你的网友发帖，寻求提高英语写作能力的建议。请你写一篇回帖，提出一些你在这方面的建议 注意：词数100左右 参考范文： Knowing that you are asking for advice on how to improve your English writing, I'm more than glad to offer you some suggestions. A good way to improve your writing is to read some good articles, through which, not only can you broaden your horizons, but also enlarge your vocabulary. To keep a journal is another useful way to improve your writing. It is natural for beginners to make

Book	Unit	Thematic Context	Topics	Word Bank	Writing
1	5.Languages Around the World	人与社会	The chinese writing system: connecting the past and the present; learning English polyglots: what are they and who can be one?		mistakes in writing, but don't worry. Finding out the reason why you make these mistakes will help you avoid the same mistakes and enable you to write better. I hope that, my suggestions will be helpful to you.
2	1.Cultural Heritage	人与社会	From problems to solutions; promoting culture through digital images; new discoveries from the past	*v.*: preserve, promote, establish, limit, prevent, investigate, conduct, donate, disappear, attempt, download, identify, forgive, quote, take part in, give way to, keep balance, lead to, make a proposal, turn to, contrast, prevent ... from, donate ... to, make sure *n.*: temple, mount, clue, application, balance, proposal, protest, committee, issue, loss, contribution, department, fund, document, entrance, process, exit, mirror, roof, dragon, comparison, opinion, image, cave, tradition	A letter of appeal 写作任务：由于各种原因，越来越多的文化遗产遭到破坏，甚至消失。请你根据以下要点向同学们发出倡议：1.阐述保护文化遗产的意义；2.号召同学们立即行动起来保护文化遗产。注意：①词数100左右；②可以适当增加细节，以使行文连贯。参考范文：Dear schoolmates, As we all know, more and more cultural relics have been damaged. Some of them are facing the danger of disappearing, which should draw everyone's attention. First of all, cultural relics represent our historic cultures. Secondly, they can help us pass down our traditional cultures from generation to

续 表

Book	Unit	Thematic Context	Topics	Word Bank	Writing
2	1.Cultural Heritage	人与社会	From problems to solutions; promoting culture through digital images; new discoveries from the past	*adj.*: creative, former, likely, worthwhile, professional, digital *adv.*: within, overseas, further, forever	generation. What's more, cultural relics are of great value, so protecting them can help us enhance our cultural confidence. Since protecting cultural relics is so important, let's take action in no time and do our best to protect them.
	2.Wildlife Protection	人与社会	A day in the clouds; wildlife protection posters; the strange table of the milu dear	*v.*: hunt, alarm, endanger, concern, adapt, measure, remind, reserve, observe, shoot, attack, recover, stir, exist, reduce, remove, die out, be aware of, make progress, be concerned about, adapt to, make out, remind sb. of sth., watch over, *n.*: poster, hunter, species, shark, rate, rating, extinction, mass, habitat, average, prince, authority, whale, pressure, antelope, plain, herd, beauty, profit, fur, threat, harmony, goods, creature, deer, kangaroo, insect, net, neighbourhood, binoculars, dolphin, emotion, skin, Tibet *adj.*: illegal, alarming, extinct, aware, con-	A poster about an endangered animal 写作任务： 动物保护协会的官网正面向全世界中学生征集关于保护朱鹮的英语海报，请你根据所给提示用英语写一份海报应征。 现状：1981年只有不到10只，经保护目前有5000只左右，但在野外数量稀少。 面临的威胁：生存环境恶化、天敌威胁以及栖息地减少等。 注意：①词数100左右；②可以适当增加细节，以使行文连贯。 参考范文： Work Together to Give the Crested Ibis a Home There were only less than 10 crested ibises in 1981. Through years of efforts, the number has reached to about 5,000, but there are few in the wild. Now the crested ibis is still facing many threats, including

Book	Unit	Thematic Context	Topics	Word Bank	Writing
2	2.Wildlife Protection	人与社会	A day in the clouds; wildlife protection posters; the strange table of the milu dear	cerned, living, sacred, effective, due *adv.*: immediately, on earth, on average, under pressure,	environmental degradation, the threat of its natural enemies and habitat loss. Let's take action now to protect habitats of the crested ibis and give this rare creature a home.
	3. The Internet	人与自我	Stronger together: how we have been changed by the internet; online safety; my day online	*v.* : chat with, stream videos, update, download, keep sb. company, surf, benefit, inspire, go through, confirm, press the button, keep track of, click, keep in mind, give out, avoid, have access to, depend, look up *n.*: blog post, blogger, search engine, identity, cash, database, software, network, distance, charity, function, Wi-Fi, file, privacy, theft, target, troll, cyberbully, guideline, tip, comment, case, golden rules *adj.*: convenient, stuck, tough, rude, false, particular, embarrassing, upset, familiar, private *prep. & conj.*: plus	A blog post 最近，你在博客上发起一次英语征文活动，邀请读者围绕 " Online shopping safety tips" 这个话题，谈谈对于网络购物安全的建议 注意: 1.词数80左右 2.可以适当增加细节，以使行文连贯。 参考范文: Today, I want to blog about online shopping safety, which has caused a wide attention nowadays. Here are my tips. First of all, it is easy for us to be open-minded and try a new website, but for the sake of safety, shopping at a familiar website is a better choice. Secondly, some people shop online with public Wi-Fis, which can make them become the targets of hackers. So it's much safer to shop at home. Besides, remember to use a strong password. It's better to use a mix of numbers and

Book	Unit	Thematic Context	Topics	Word Bank	Writing
2	3. The Internet	人与自我	Stronger together: how we have been changed by the internet; online safety; my day online		letters. Then, you have a better chance of being safe while shopping online. Do you have some good advice to share with us? Post your comments below.
	4.History and Traditions	人与社会	What's in a name? beautiful ireland and Its traditions; hello from Cairo and Athens	*v.*: join ... to, belong to, break away from, add to, surround, keep your eyes for, charge, approach, ensure, roll, have a great influence on, excite, inspire, make up, experience, roar, date back to, explore, be referred to, record, introduce ... to, share ... with, greet ... with *n.*: Confucius, tradition, culture, custom, relic, philosophy, location, amount, gallery, landscape, ancestor, position, courtyard, poet, county, feast, sense, ocean, scent, crowd, mix, historic sites, quote, folk music, dancing, countryside *adj.*: national, peaceful, fascinating, generous, eager, dotted, nearby, well-known, striking,	An introduction of a place 假如你是李华，请你给某英文报社的"城市风采"栏目写一篇短文，介绍我们伟大祖国的首都——北京。要点如下： 基本概况：人口约2000万人，面积16 000多平方千米，位于华北平原北部。 历史与文化：有3000多年的历史，是我国的政治、文化中心，有很多大学，其中清华大学和北京大学是最著名的。 交通与旅游：交通便利，有天安门广场、故宫博物院、长城、鸟巢等很多旅游景点。 注意：①80词左右，可以适当增加细节，以使行文连贯；②开头和结尾已给出。 参考范文： Beijing, the capital of China, is a beautiful city, located in the north of China.. Beijing has a population of about 20 million and covers an area of more than 16,000 square kilometers.

续 表

Book	Unit	Thematic Context	Topics	Word Bank	Writing
2	4.History and Traditions	人与社会	What's in a name? beautiful ireland and Its traditions; hello from Cairo and Athens	friendly, present, ancient	Beijing has a history of over 3,000 years. Being, the political and cultural center of China, has many key universities, of which Peking University and Tsinghua University are the most famous. Beijing is also a fascinating place for holidays and it's convenient to travel there. There are many places of interest, such as Tian'anmen Square, the Palace Museum, the Great Wall as well as the Bird's Nest. Now, Beijing is playing a more and more important role in the world.
	5.Music	人与自我	The virtual choir; a speech about the impact of music; cat's in the cradle	v.: perform, enable sb. to do, prove, award, fall in love with, cure, try out, assume, ache, get through n.: hip-hop, techno, energy, soul, instrument, composition, virtual choir, performance, performer, composer, conductor, phenomenon, stage, relief, album, impact, talent, piano, rap, disease, treatment, satisfaction, equipment, reaction, band	A speech about how music can change a person's life 假如你是高三学生李华，你们学校举办了一次题目为"我与音乐"的演讲比赛，请结合自身感受写一篇演讲稿。 注意：①80词左右，可以适当增加细节，以使行文连贯。②开头和结尾已给出。 参考范文： Ladies and gentlemen, Good morning! I am Li Hua. It's an honour to be here and share my view on music. I am crazy about music, or I should say that music is an important

续 表

Book	Unit	Thematic Context	Topics	Word Bank	Writing
2	5.Music	人与自我	The virtual choir; a speech about the impact of music; cat's in the cradle	*adj.*: classical, ordinary, original, gradual, capable, absorbed, previous, romantic, unemployed, various *adv.*: altogether, thus, nowadays, moreover, in addition to, from then on	part in my life. Have you got a particular type of music that touches your heart? I guess the answer is yes. Actually, I like many kinds of music, so I'd like to talk about my favourite music here. Well, I like New Age music best. It is mixed with some modern melody, and it sounds very nice and pure, which can take me to dreamland. I feel completely relaxed, and forget all my trouble when immersed in the music world. In a word, music plays a very important role in my life. This is my story about music. If there is a chance, I hope you can share your story. Thank you!